PRENTICE HALL MATHEMATICS

ALGEBRA 1

Study Guide & Practice Workbook

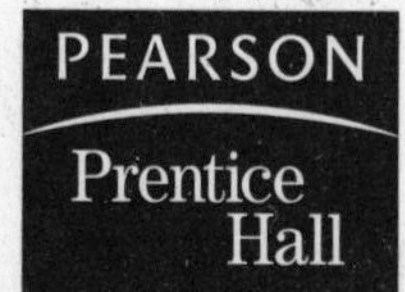

Boston, Massachusetts
Upper Saddle River, New Jersey

ISBN: 0-13-125450-2
12 08 07

Study Guide & Practice Workbook

Contents

Answers appear in the back of each Grab & Go File.

Chapter 1

Chapter 2

Chapter 3

Chapter 4

Chapter 5

Chapter 6

Chapter 7

Chapter 8

Contents (cont.)

Name ______________________ Class ____________ Date ____________

Reteaching 1-1

Using Variables

OBJECTIVE: Using variables as a shorthand way of expressing relationships

MATERIALS: None

You often hear word phrases such as *half as much* or *three times as deep*. These phrases describe mathematical relationships. You can translate word phrases like these into mathematical relationships called *expressions*.

Example

Translate the following word expressions into algebraic expressions.

the sum of x and 15	seven times x
$x + 15$	$7x$
Remember that "sum" means to add.	Remember that "times" mean to multiply.

Example

Translate the following word sentence into an algebraic equation.

The weight of the truck is two times the weight of the car.

The weight of the truck is two times the weight of the car. ← **Write an equal sign under the word *is*. Whatever is written to the left of *is* belongs on the left side of the =. Whatever is written to the right of *is* belongs on the right side of the =.**

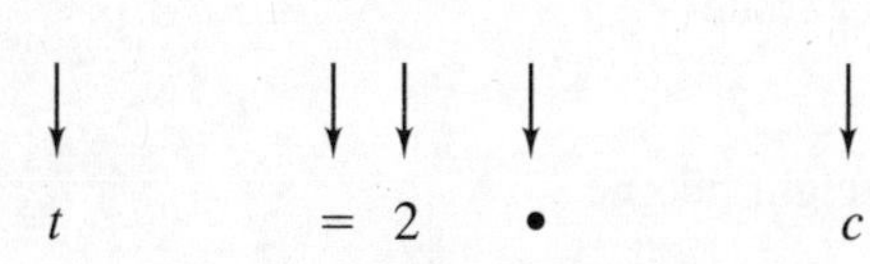

$t \quad = 2 \quad \bullet \quad c$ ← **Represent the unknown amounts with variables.**

$t = 2c$ ← **The translation is complete. Check to make sure you have translated all parts of the equation.**

Exercises

Translate the following word expressions and sentences into algebraic expressions or equations.

1. a number increased by 5

2. 8 subtracted from a number

3. a number divided by 9

4. 3 less than five times a number

5. A number multiplied by 12 is 84.

6. 7 less than n is 22.

7. 8 times a number x is 72.

8. A number divided by 3 is 18.

Name ______________________ Class ______________ Date ______________

Practice 1-1

Using Variables

Write an algebraic expression for each phrase.

1. 7 increased by x
2. p multiplied by 3
3. 10 decreased by m
4. n less than 7
5. the product of 2 and q
6. 3 more than m

Write a phrase for each algebraic expression.

7. $\frac{8}{a}$
8. $s - 10$
9. $x + 13$
10. $ab + 2$

Define a variable and write an algebraic expression for each phrase.

11. the difference of 8 and a number
12. the sum of 4 and a number
13. the product of 2 and a number
14. 3 increased by a number
15. 10 plus the quotient of a number and 15
16. 12 less than a number

Define a variable and write an algebraic equation to model each situation.

17. What is the total cost of buying several shirts at $24.95 each?
18. The number of gal of water used to water trees is 30 times the number of trees.
19. What is the amount of money in a bank containing only dimes?
20. What is the number of marbles left in a 48-marble bag after some marbles have been given away?
21. The total cost equals the price of the tickets multiplied by eight people.
22. What is the cost of buying several pairs of pants at $32.95 per pair?

Write an equation to model the relationship in each table.

23.

Number of Tickets	Total Cost
2	$7
4	$14
6	$21

24.

Number of Hours	Distance Traveled
1	55 mi
3	165 mi
5	275 mi

25.

Number of Hours	Total Pay
8	$40
12	$60
16	$80

26.

Total Cost	Change from $10
$10.00	$0
$9.00	$1.00
$7.50	$2.50

27.

Number of Days	Length
1	0.45 in.
4	1.80 in.
8	3.60 in.

28.

Miles Traveled	Miles Remaining
0	500
125	375
350	150

Name ______________________ Class ______________ Date ______________

Reteaching 1-2

Exponents and Order of Operations

OBJECTIVE: Using the order of operations

MATERIALS: Three index cards or small pieces of paper

Review the order of operations to help you with this activity.

Order of Operations

1. Perform any operations inside grouping symbols.
2. Simplify any term with exponents.
3. Multiply and divide in order from left to right.
4. Add and subtract in order from left to right.

Example

Write + on the first index card, − on the second card, and × on the third card. Shuffle the cards and place them face down on your desk. Randomly pick cards to fill in the blanks with operation signs. Once you have filled in the operation signs, simplify the expression.

6___(9___7)___8	←	**Pick cards to fill in the blanks with operation signs.**
$6 \times (9 - 7) + 8$	←	**Subtract 7 from 9 inside the grouping symbols.**
$6 \times 2 + 8$	←	**Do multiplication and division first. Multiply 6 by 2.**
$12 + 8$	←	**Do addition and subtraction last. Add 12 and 8 to get the answer.**
20	←	**The answer is 20.**

Exercises

Randomly pick cards to fill in the operation symbols of the following expressions. Simplify the expressions.

1. 7____5____1

2. (3____9)____4

3. 8____2____(5____10)

4. (3____7____6)____1

Simplify each expression by following the order of operations.

5. $(5 \cdot 3) - 18$

6. $5 \cdot (3 - 18)$

7. $2 \cdot (27 - 13 \cdot 2)$

8. $2 \cdot 27 - 13 \cdot 2$

9. $18 \div (9 - 15 \div 5)$

10. $18 \div 9 - 15 \div 5$

11. $2 \cdot 8 - 6^2$

12. $2 \cdot (8 - 6^2)$

Name ______________________ Class ______________ Date ____________

Practice 1-2

Exponents and Order of Operations

Simplify each expression.

1. $4 + 6(8)$
2. $\frac{4(8 - 2)}{3 + 9}$
3. $4 \times 3^2 + 2$
4. $40 \div 5(2)$
5. $2.7 + 3.6 \times 4.5$
6. $3[4(8 - 2) + 5]$
7. $4 + 3(15 - 2^3)$
8. $17 - [(3 + 2) \times 2]$
9. $6 \times (3 + 2) \div 15$

Evaluate each expression.

10. $\frac{a + 2b}{5}$ for $a = 1$ and $b = 2$
11. $\frac{5m + n}{5}$ for $m = 6$ and $n = 15$
12. $x + 3y^2$ for $x = 3.4$ and $y = 3$
13. $7a - 4(b + 2)$ for $a = 5$ and $b = 2$

Simplify each expression.

14. $\frac{100 - 15}{9 + 8}$
15. $\frac{2(3 + 4)}{7}$
16. $\frac{3(4 + 12)}{2(7 - 3)}$
17. $14 + 3 \times 4$
18. $8 + 3(4 + 3)$
19. $3 + 4[13 - 2(6 - 3)]$
20. $8(5 + 30 \div 5)$
21. $(3.4)(2.7) + 5$
22. $50 \div 2 + 15 \times 4$
23. $7(9 - 5)$
24. $2(3^2) - 3(2)$
25. $4 + 8 \div 2 + 6 \times 3$
26. $(7 + 8) \div (4 - 1)$
27. $5[2(8 + 5) - 15]$
28. $(6 + 8) \times (8 - 4)$
29. $12\left(\frac{6 + 30}{9 - 3}\right)$
30. $14 + 6 \times 2^3 - 8 \div 2^2$
31. $\frac{7(14) - 3(6)}{2}$
32. $14 \div [3(8 - 2) - 11]$
33. $3\left(\frac{9 + 13}{6}\right)$
34. $\frac{4(8 - 3)}{3 + 2}$
35. $5 + 4^2 \times 8 - 2^3 \div 2^2$
36. $4^2 + 5^2(8 - 3)$
37. $5(3^2 + 2) - 2(6^2 - 5^2)$

Evaluate each expression for $a = 2$ and $b = 6$.

38. $2(7a - b)$
39. $(a^3 + b^2) \div a$
40. $3b \div (2a - 1) + b$
41. $\frac{5a + 2}{b}$
42. $\frac{3(b - 2)}{4(a + 1)}$
43. $9b + a^4 \div 8$

Use the expression $r + 0.12m$ to calculate the cost of renting a car. The basic rate is r. The number of miles driven is m.

44. The basic rate is \$15.95. The car is driven 150 mi.
45. The basic rate is \$32.50. The car is driven 257 mi.

Evaluate each expression for $s = 3$ and $t = 9$.

46. $8(4s - t)$
47. $(2t - 3s) \div 4$
48. $t^2 - s^4$
49. $s(3t + 6)$
50. $\frac{5s^2}{t}$
51. $\frac{2t^2}{s^3}$

Name ______________________ Class ______________ Date ______________

Reteaching 1-3

Exploring Real Numbers

OBJECTIVE: Classifying numbers	**MATERIALS:** None

Review the following chart which shows the different classifications of real numbers.

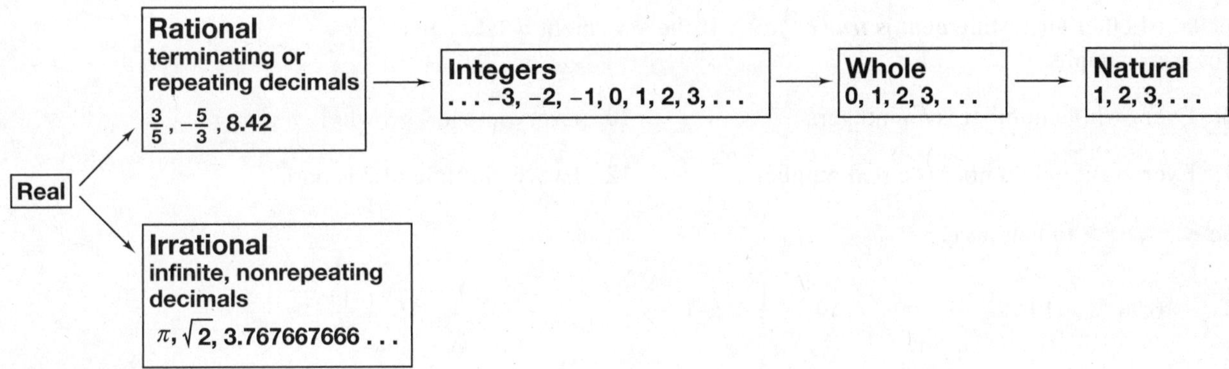

Example

Given the numbers $-4.4, \frac{14}{5}, 0, -9, 1\frac{1}{4}, -\pi$ and 32, tell which numbers belong to each set.

Natural:	32	numbers used to count
Whole:	0, 32	natural numbers and zero
Integers:	0, −9, 32	whole numbers and their opposites
Rational:	$-4.4, \frac{14}{5}, 0, -9, 1\frac{1}{4}, 32$	integers and terminating and repeating decimals
Irrational:	$-\pi$	infinite, nonrepeating decimals
Real:	$-4.4, \frac{14}{5}, 0, -9, 1\frac{1}{4}, -\pi, 32$	rational and irrational numbers

Exercises

Name the set(s) of numbers to which each number belongs.

1. $\frac{-5}{6}$ **2.** 35.99 **3.** 0 **4.** $4\frac{1}{8}$

5. $\sqrt{5}$ **6.** −80 **7.** $\frac{17}{5}$ **8.** $\frac{12}{3}$

9. $\sqrt{100}$ **10.** $-\sqrt{4}$ **11.** 3.24 **12.** 3π

Give an example of each kind of number.

13. irrational number

14. whole number

15. negative integer

16. fractional rational number

17. rational decimal

18. natural number

Name ______________________ Class ______________ Date ______________

Practice 1-3

Exploring Real Numbers

Name the set(s) of numbers to which each number belongs.

1. -0.002 **2.** $12\frac{1}{2}$ **3.** 8 **4.** 5π

5. $\sqrt{7}$ **6.** -22 **7.** -3.4 **8.** $\sqrt{36}$

Decide whether each statement is *true* or *false.* If the statement is false, give a counterexample.

9. Every whole number is an integer.

10. Every integer is a whole number.

11. Every rational number is a real number.

12. Every multiple of 7 is odd.

Use <, =, or > to compare.

13. -10.98 ■ -10.99 **14.** $-\frac{1}{3}$ ■ -0.3 **15.** $-\frac{11}{5}$ ■ $-\frac{4}{5}$

16. $-\frac{1}{2}$ ■ $-\frac{5}{10}$ **17.** $-\frac{3}{8}$ ■ $-\frac{7}{16}$ **18.** $\frac{3}{4}$ ■ $\frac{13}{16}$

Write in order from least to greatest.

19. $-\frac{8}{9}, -\frac{7}{8}, -\frac{22}{25}$ **20.** $-3\frac{4}{9}, -3.45, -3\frac{12}{25}$ **21.** $-\frac{1}{4}, -\frac{1}{5}, -\frac{1}{3}$

22. $-1.7, -1\frac{3}{4}, -1\frac{7}{9}$ **23.** $-\frac{3}{4}, -\frac{7}{8}, -\frac{2}{3}$ **24.** $2\frac{3}{4}, 2\frac{5}{8}, 2.7$

Determine which set of numbers is most reasonable for each situation.

25. the number of dolphins in the ocean

26. the height of a basketball player

27. the number of pets you have

28. the circumference of a compact disk

Find each absolute value.

29. $\left|\frac{3}{10}\right|$ **30.** $|-327|$ **31.** $|-3.46|$ **32.** $\left|-\frac{1}{2}\right|$

33. Name the sets(s) of numbers to which each number in the table belongs. Choose among: whole numbers, integers, rational numbers, irrational numbers, and real numbers.

Type of Account	Principal	Rate	Time (years)	Interest
Checking	\$154.23	0.0375	$\frac{30}{365}$	\$.48
Savings	\$8000	0.055	$3\frac{1}{2}$	\$1540

Name ______________________ Class ____________ Date ____________

Reteaching 1-4

Adding Real Numbers

OBJECTIVE: Adding integers and decimals	**MATERIALS:** None

Review the following addition rules.

- To add two numbers with the same sign, *add* their absolute values. The sum has the same sign as the numbers.
- To add two numbers with different signs, find the *difference* of their absolute values. The sum has the same sign as the number with the greater absolute value.

Example

The following example shows you step by step how to add two numbers with different signs.

$-6 + 2$

$6 - 2$ ⟵ **Find the difference of their absolute values.**

4 ⟵ **Subtract.**

-4 ⟵ **Since -6 has the greater absolute value, the answer takes the negative sign.**

Exercises

Simplify. Be sure to check the sign of your answer.

1. $-3 + (-4)$ **2.** $12 + 5$ **3.** $-5 + 8$ **4.** $-8 + (-2)$

5. $-2 + (-3)$ **6.** $9 + (-12)$ **7.** $-3 + 5$ **8.** $-4 + 3$

9. $-2.3 + (-1.5)$ **10.** $4.5 + 3.1$ **11.** $-5.1 + 2.8$ **12.** $13.9 + 7.3$

13. $1.3 + (-1.1)$ **14.** $-3.6 + (-6.7)$ **15.** $1.4 + (-21.4)$ **16.** $-9.8 + 3.5$

Evaluate each expression for $a = 5$ and $b = -4$.

17. $-a + (-b)$ **18.** $-a + b$ **19.** $a + b$ **20.** $a + (-b)$

Evaluate each expression for $h = 3.4$.

21. $2.5 + h$ **22.** $-2.5 + h$ **23.** $2.5 + (-h)$ **24.** $-2.5 + (-h)$

25. $h + 7.1$ **26.** $-h + 7.1$ **27.** $h + (-7.1)$ **28.** $-h + (-7.1)$

Name ______________________ Class ______________ Date ______________

Practice 1-4

Adding Real Numbers

Simplify each expression.

1. $6 + (-4)$
2. $-2 + (-13)$
3. $-18 + 4$
4. $15 + (-32)$
5. $-27 + (-14)$
6. $8 + (-3)$
7. $-12.2 + 31.9$
8. $-2.3 + (-13.9)$
9. $19.8 + (-27.4)$
10. $\frac{1}{4} + \left(-\frac{3}{4}\right)$
11. $\frac{2}{3} + \left(-\frac{1}{3}\right)$
12. $-\frac{7}{12} + \frac{1}{6}$
13. $2\frac{2}{3} + (-1)$
14. $-3\frac{3}{4} + 1\frac{1}{2}$
15. $2\frac{1}{3} + \left(-4\frac{2}{3}\right)$
16. $-6.3 + 8.2$
17. $-3.82 + 2.83$
18. $-7.8 + 9$
19. $|-12| + |-21|$
20. $|-13 + 6|$
21. $-14 + |-7|$

Evaluate each expression for $m = 2.5$.

22. $-m + 1.6$
23. $-3.2 + m$
24. $-2.5 + (-m)$

Simplify.

25. $-3 + (-6) + 14$
26. $4 + (-8) + (-14)$
27. $2.7 + (-3.2) + 1.5$
28. $-2.5 + (-1.2) + (-2.3)$
29. $\frac{1}{2} + \left(-\frac{1}{3}\right) + \frac{1}{4}$
30. $-\frac{2}{3} + \left(-\frac{1}{3}\right) + \left(-1\frac{1}{3}\right)$

Simplify.

31. $\begin{bmatrix} 4 & -1 \\ 2 & 5 \end{bmatrix} + \begin{bmatrix} -1 & 2 \\ -2 & -3 \end{bmatrix}$
32. $\begin{bmatrix} -4.7 \\ 2.3 \\ -1.5 \end{bmatrix} + \begin{bmatrix} 5.1 \\ -2.7 \\ 2.6 \end{bmatrix}$

33. The temperature at 5:00 A.M. is −38°F. The temperature rises 20° by 11:00 A.M. What is the temperature at 11:00 A.M.?

34. A football team has possession of the ball on their own 15-yd line. The next two plays result in a loss of 7 yd and a gain of 3 yd, respectively. On what yard line is the ball after the two plays?

35. Suppose your opening checking account balance is $124.53. After you write a check for $57.49 and make a deposit of $103.49, what is your new balance?

36. During an emergency exercise, a submarine dives 37 ft, rises 16 ft, and then dives 18 ft. What is the net change in the submarine's position after the second dive?

Name ______________________ Class ______________ Date ______________

Reteaching 1-5

Subtracting Real Numbers

OBJECTIVE: Subtracting integers and decimals **MATERIALS:** None

Review the following subtraction rules.

- To subtract a number, rewrite the problem to add the opposite of the number.
- Follow the rules for addition of numbers.

Example

The following example shows you step by step how to subtract two numbers.

$5 - 11$

$5 + (-11)$ ⟵ **Rewrite the problem to add the opposite of the number.**

$11 - 5$ ⟵ **Find the difference of their absolute values.**

6 ⟵ **Subtract.**

-6 ⟵ **Since −11 has the greater absolute value, the answer takes the negative sign.**

Exercises

Simplify. Be sure to check the sign of your answer.

1. $7 - 12$ **2.** $6 - 9$ **3.** $4 - (-5)$ **4.** $7 - (-3)$

5. $-6 - 4$ **6.** $-7 - 2$ **7.** $-5 - (-4)$ **8.** $-3 - (-10)$

9. $-3.1 - (-5.4)$ **10.** $8.3 - 5.1$ **11.** $-7.8 - 6.6$ **12.** $-4.8 - 2.5$

13. $8.7 - 2.5$ **14.** $-4.6 - (-3)$ **15.** $-9.3 - (-8.1)$ **16.** $-9.9 - 3.8$

Evaluate each expression for $a = -4$ and $b = 3$.

17. $a - b$ **18.** $-a - b$ **19.** $a - (-b)$ **20.** $-a - (-b)$

21. $3b - a$ **22.** $-|b|$ **23.** $|a - b|$ **24.** $|a| - 3|b|$

Subtract. (Hint: Subtract corresponding elements.)

25. $\begin{bmatrix} -3 & -2 \\ 0 & 1 \end{bmatrix} - \begin{bmatrix} 3 & 1 \\ 2 & 4 \end{bmatrix}$ **26.** $\begin{bmatrix} \frac{1}{2} \\ -1 \end{bmatrix} - \begin{bmatrix} \frac{2}{3} \\ -3 \end{bmatrix}$

Name ______________________ Class ______________ Date ______________

Practice 1-5

Subtracting Real Numbers

Simplify.

1. $13 - 6$
2. $19 - 35$
3. $-4 - 8$
4. $-14 - (-6)$
5. $18 - (-25)$
6. $-32 - 17$
7. $-6.8 - 14.6$
8. $-9.3 - (-23.9)$
9. $-8.2 - 0.8$
10. $18.3 - (-8.1)$
11. $-3 - (-15)$
12. $6.4 - 17$
13. $\frac{3}{4} - 1\frac{1}{4}$
14. $-\frac{1}{3} - \frac{2}{3}$
15. $-\frac{1}{4} - \left(-\frac{3}{4}\right)$
16. $|-11| - |-29|$
17. $|-4 - 8|$
18. $|9.8| - |-15.7|$
19. $|-8 - (-32)|$
20. $|3.7 - (-6.8)|$
21. $2.83 - 3.82$

Evaluate each expression for $c = -3$ and $d = -6$.

22. $c - d$
23. $-c - d$
24. $-c - (-d)$
25. $|c + d|$
26. $-c + d$
27. $3c - 2d$

Simplify.

28. $8 - (-4) - (-5)$
29. $6 - 10 - 4$
30. $10 - 14 - 15$
31. $-6 - 3 - (-2)$
32. $-5 + 7 - 9$
33. $-2 - 2 - 4$

Subtract.

34. $\begin{bmatrix} -3 & -1 \\ 2 & 4 \end{bmatrix} - \begin{bmatrix} 5 & -2 \\ -3 & 8 \end{bmatrix}$
35. $\begin{bmatrix} 6.1 & -4 \\ -3.7 & -2.1 \end{bmatrix} - \begin{bmatrix} 7.0 & -2.3 \\ -1.6 & 4.2 \end{bmatrix}$

36. The temperature in the evening was 68°F. The following morning, the temperature was 39°F. What is the difference between the two temperatures?
37. What is the difference in altitude between Mt. Everest, which is about 29,028 ft above sea level, and Death Valley, which is about 282 ft below sea level?
38. Suppose the balance in your checking account was $234.15 when you wrote a check for $439.87. (This is known as overdrawing your account.) Describe the account's new balance.
39. After three plays in which a football team lost 7 yd, gained 3 yd, and lost 1 yd, respectively, the ball was placed on the team's own 30-yd line. Where was the ball before the three plays?

Name ______________________ Class ______________ Date ______________

Reteaching 1-6

Multiplying and Dividing Real Numbers

OBJECTIVE: Multiplying and dividing integers and decimals

MATERIALS: A number cube

Review the following multiplication and division rules.

- The product or quotient of two positive numbers is always positive.
- The product or quotient of two negative numbers is always positive.
- The product or quotient of a positive and a negative number is always negative.

Example

Roll the number cube to determine the signs of the numbers in the following example. If you roll an even number (2, 4, or 6), write + in the blank to make the number positive. If you roll an odd number (1, 3, or 5), write a − in the blank to make the number negative. Decide what sign the answer will have before you calculate the answer.

____ 56 ÷ ____ 7 ⟵ **Roll the number cube to fill in the blanks.**

$-56 \div (+7)$ ⟵ **Suppose your first roll was a 3, so 56 is negative. Suppose your second roll was 6, so 7 is positive. Now that you have the signs of the numbers, decide what the sign of the answer will be. Dividing a negative number by a positive number results in a negative number.**

-8 ⟵ **The answer is −8.**

Exercises

Roll the number cube to determine the signs of the numbers in the following exercises. Remember to decide what sign the answer will have before you calculate the answer.

1. ____ 20 · ____ 8
2. ____ 3.2 · ____ 10
3. ____ 27 ÷ ____ 3
4. ____ 14 · ____ 4
5. ____ 120 ÷ ____ 12
6. ____ 45 ÷ ____ 9
7. ____ 1.4 · ____ 3
8. ____ 96 ÷ ____ 8

Simplify each expression.

9. $4(-2)$
10. $-6(12)$
11. $-2(-5)$
12. $-8(11)$
13. $(-7)^2$
14. $-10(-5)$

Name ______________________ Class ______________ Date ______________

Practice 1-6

Multiplying and Dividing Real Numbers

Simplify each expression.

1. $(-2)(8)$
2. $(-6)(-9)$
3. $(-3)^4$
4. -2^5
5. $(6)(-8)$
6. $(-14)^2$
7. $2(-4)(-6)$
8. $-30 \div (-5)$
9. $\frac{-52}{-13}$
10. $(-8)(5)(-3)$
11. -7^2
12. -3^5
13. $\frac{-68}{17}$
14. $\frac{(-4)(-13)}{-26}$
15. $\frac{225}{(-3)(-5)}$

Evaluate each expression.

16. x^3 for $x = -5$
17. $s^2t \div 10$ for $s = -2$ and $t = 10$
18. $-2m + 4n^2$ for $m = -6$ and $n = -5$
19. $\frac{v}{w}$ for $v = \frac{2}{5}$ and $w = -\frac{1}{2}$
20. $-cd^2$ for $c = 2$ and $d = -4$
21. $(x + 4)^2$ for $x = -11$
22. $\left(\frac{a}{b}\right)^2 + b^3$ for $a = 24$ and $b = -6$
23. $4p^2 + 7q^3$ for $p = -3$ and $q = -2$
24. $(e + f)^4$ for $e = -3$ and $f = 7$
25. $5f^2 - z^2$ for $f = -1$ and $z = -4$

Simplify each expression.

26. $2^4 - 3^2 + 5^2$
27. $(-8)^2 - 4^3$
28. $32 \div (-7 + 5)^3$
29. $\frac{3}{4} \div \left(-\frac{3}{7}\right)$
30. $18 + 4^2 \div (-8)$
31. $26 \div [4 - (-9)]$
32. $4^3 - (2 - 5)^3$
33. $-(-4)^3$
34. $(-8)(-5)(-3)$
35. $(-3)^2 - 4^2$
36. $\frac{-45}{-15}$
37. $(-2)^6$
38. $\frac{-90}{6}$
39. $\frac{-15}{(7 - 4)}$
40. $\frac{195}{-13}$

Evaluate each expression.

41. $(a + b)^2$ for $a = 6$ and $b = -8$
42. $d^3 \div e$ for $d = -6$ and $e = -3$
43. $(m + 5n)^3$ for $m = 2$ and $n = -1$
44. $j^5 - 5k$ for $j = -4$ and $k = -1$
45. $xy + z$ for $x = -4$, $y = 3$, and $z = -3$
46. $4s \div (-3t)$ for $s = -6$ and $t = -2$
47. $\frac{r^3}{s}$ for $r = -6$ and $s = -2$
48. $\frac{-h^5}{-4}$ for $h = 4$

Name ______________________ Class ______________ Date ______________

Reteaching 1-7

The Distributive Property

OBJECTIVE: Using the Distributive Property	**MATERIALS:** None

You can compare the Distributive Property to distributing paper to the class. Just as you distribute a piece of paper to each person in the class, you distribute the number immediately outside the parentheses to each term inside the parentheses by multiplying.

Example

Simplify $3(2x + 3)$ by using the Distributive Property.

$3(2x + 3)$ ⟵ **Draw arrows to show that 3 is distributed to the 2*x* and to the 3.**

$3(2x) + 3(3)$ ⟵ **Use the Distributive Property.**

$6x + 9$ ⟵ **Simplify.**

Example

Simplify $-(4x + 7)$ by using the Distributive Property.

$-1(4x + 7)$ ⟵ **Rewrite using the Multiplication Property of −1.**

$-1(4x + 7)$ ⟵ **Draw arrows to show that −1 is distributed to the 4*x* and to the 7.**

$-1(4x) + (-1)(7)$ ⟵ **Use the Distributive Property.**

$-4x - 7$ ⟵ **Simplify.**

Exercises

Draw arrows to show the Distributive Property. Then simplify each expression.

1. $2(5x + 4)$
2. $\frac{1}{4}(12x - 8)$
3. $4(7x - 3)$
4. $5(4 + 2x)$
5. $6(5 - 3x)$
6. $0.1(30x - 50)$
7. $(2x - 4)3$
8. $(3x + 4)7$
9. $8(x + y)$
10. $-(4x + 3)$
11. $-(-2x + 1)$
12. $-(-6x - 3)$
13. $-(14x - 3)$
14. $-(-7x - 1)$
15. $-(3x + 4)$

Name ______________________ Class ______________ Date ______________

Practice 1-7

The Distributive Property

Simplify each expression.

1. $2(x + 6)$
2. $-5(8 - b)$
3. $4(-x + 7)$
4. $(5c - 7)(-3)$
5. $-2.5(3a + 5)$
6. $-(3k - 12)$
7. $-\frac{3}{4}(12 - 16d)$
8. $\frac{2}{3}(6h - 1)$
9. $(-3.2x + 2.1)(-6)$
10. $3.5(3x - 8)$
11. $4(x + 7)$
12. $-2.5(2a - 4)$
13. $\frac{2}{3}(12 - 15d)$
14. $-2(k - 11)$
15. $-\frac{1}{3}(6h + 15)$
16. $(2c - 8)(-4)$
17. $-(4 - 2b)$
18. $2(3x - 9)$
19. $4(2r + 8)$
20. $-5(b - 5)$
21. $3(f + 2)$
22. $6h + 5(h - 5)$
23. $-5d + 3(2d - 7)$
24. $7 + 2(4x - 3)$
25. $2(3h + 2) - 4h$
26. $2(4 + y)$
27. $\frac{1}{2}(2n - 4) - 2n$
28. $-w + 4(w + 3)$
29. $0.4(3d - 5)$
30. $-4d + 2(3 + d)$
31. $2x + \frac{3}{4}(4x + 16)$
32. $2(3a + 2)$
33. $5(t - 3) - 2t$
34. $5(b + 4) - 6b$
35. $\frac{2}{5}(5k + 35) - 8$
36. $0.4(2s + 4)$
37. $\frac{2}{3}(9b - 27)$
38. $\frac{1}{2}(12n - 8)$
39. $0.5(2x - 4)$
40. $2(a - 4) + 15$
41. $13 + 2(5c - 2)$
42. $7 + 2(\frac{1}{5}a - 3)$
43. $5(3x + 12)$
44. $2(m + 1)$
45. $4(2a + 2) - 17$
46. $-4x + 3(2x - 5)$
47. $3(t - 12)$
48. $-6 - 3(2k + 4)$

Write an expression for each phrase.

49. 5 times the quantity x plus 6
50. twice the quantity y minus 8
51. the product of -15 and the quantity x minus 5
52. 32 divided by the quantity y plus 12
53. -8 times the quantity 4 decreased by w
54. the quantity x plus 9 times the quantity 7 minus x

Name ______________________ Class ______________ Date ______________

Reteaching 1-8

Properties of Real Numbers

OBJECTIVE: Recognizing properties **MATERIALS:** None

The properties of real numbers allow you to write equivalent expressions.

The Commutative Properties of Addition and Multiplication allow you to add or to multiply two numbers in any order.

$a + b = b + a$ $\quad\quad$ $a \cdot b = b \cdot a$

$3 + 6 = 6 + 3$ $\quad\quad$ $12 \cdot 4 = 4 \cdot 12$

The Associative Properties of Addition and Multiplication allow you to regroup numbers.

$(a + b) + c = a + (b + c)$ $\quad\quad$ $(a \cdot b) \cdot c = a \cdot (b \cdot c)$

$(1 + 3) + 6 = 1 + (3 + 6)$ $\quad\quad$ $(1 \cdot 3) \cdot 6 = 1 \cdot (3 \cdot 6)$

The Distributive Property distributes multiplication over addition and subtraction.

$a(b + c) = ab + ac$ $\quad\quad$ $a(b - c) = ab - ac$

$3(4 + 6) = (3 \cdot 4) + (3 \cdot 6)$ $\quad\quad$ $5(9 - 3) = (5 \cdot 9) - (5 \cdot 3)$

Example

Name the property that each equation illustrates.

$72 + 56 = 56 + 72$ ← **Commutative Property of Addition: The order of the addends is changed.**

$4(5 - 9) = (4 \cdot 5) - (4 \cdot 9)$ ← **Distributive Property: The 4 is distributed.**

$30 \cdot (14 \cdot 5) = (30 \cdot 14) \cdot 5$ ← **Associative Property of Multiplication: The numbers are regrouped.**

Exercises

Name the property that each equation illustrates.

1. $(17 + 4) + 9 = 17 + (4 + 9)$

2. $7(3 + 4) = (7 \cdot 3) + (7 \cdot 4)$

3. $84 \cdot 26 = 26 \cdot 84$

4. $(3 \cdot 6) \cdot 7 = 3 \cdot (6 \cdot 7)$

5. $8(6 - 3) = (8 \cdot 6) - (8 \cdot 3)$

6. $4.2 + 3.4 = 3.4 + 4.2$

Write the number that makes each statement true.

7. $27 + \_\_\_\_ = 12 + 27$

8. $(8 + 20) + 9 = \_\_\_\_ + (20 + 9)$

9. $9(8 - 5) = (\_\_\_\_ \cdot 8) - (\_\_\_\_ \cdot 5)$

10. $8 \cdot 10 = 10 \cdot \_\_\_\_$

11. $3 \cdot (9 \cdot 6) = (3 \cdot 9) \cdot \_\_\_\_$

12. $7(6 + 4) = (\_\_\_\_ \cdot 6) + (\_\_\_\_ \cdot 4)$

Name ______________________ Class ______________ Date ______________

Practice 1-8

Properties of Real Numbers

Name the property that each equation illustrates.

1. $83 + 6 = 6 + 83$
2. $8 + x = x + 8$
3. $1 \cdot 4y = 4y$
4. $15x + 15y = 15(x + y)$
5. $(8 \cdot 7) \cdot 6 = 8 \cdot (7 \cdot 6)$
6. $\frac{2}{3}\left(\frac{3}{2}\right) = 1$
7. $3(a + 2b) = 3a + 6b$
8. $7x + 2y = 2y + 7x$
9. $7 + (8 + 15) = (7 + 8) + 15$
10. $x + (-x) = 0$
11. $x + y = y + x$
12. $6 \cdot (x \cdot y) = (6 \cdot x) \cdot y$
13. $16 + 0 = 16$
14. $3w + 5y = 5y + 3w$
15. $7(3 + 4y) = 21 + 28y$
16. $0 = 30 \cdot 0$
17. $4a + (5b + 6c) = (4a + 5b) + 6c$
18. $ab + c = ba + c$
19. $wr = rw$
20. $20(a + b) = 20(b + a)$

Give a reason to justify each step.

21. a. $4c + 3(2 + c) = 4c + 6 + 3c$
 b. $= 4c + 3c + 6$
 c. $= (4c + 3c) + 6$
 d. $= (4 + 3)c + 6$
 e. $= 7c + 6$

22. a. $8w - 4(7 - w) = 8w - 28 + 4w$
 b. $= 8w + (-28) + 4w$
 c. $= 8w + 4w + (-28)$
 d. $= (8 + 4)w + (-28)$
 e. $= 12w + (-28)$
 f. $= 12w - 28$

23. a. $5(x + y) + 2(x + y) = 5x + 5y + 2x + 2y$
 b. $= 5x + 2x + 5y + 2y$
 c. $= (5 + 2)x + (5 + 2)y$
 d. $= 7x + 7y$

Use mental math to simplify each expression.

24. $48 + 27 + 2 + 3$
25. $10 \cdot 72 \cdot 5 \cdot 2$
26. $10 \cdot 8 \cdot 3 \cdot 10$
27. $8\frac{1}{2} + 4\frac{1}{3} + 2\frac{1}{2} + 2\frac{2}{3}$
28. Henry bought an apple for \$0.75, some apricots for \$1.50, some cherries for \$3.25, and three bananas for \$1.50. Find the total cost of the fruit.
29. Suppose you buy some camping supplies. You purchase waterproof matches for \$3.95, a compass for \$18.25, flashlight batteries for \$3.75, and a map for \$2.05. Find the total cost of the supplies.
30. You go to the video store and rent some DVDs for \$8.50 and a video game for \$3.69. While there, you buy a box of popcorn for \$2.31 and a candy bar for \$1.50. Find the total cost of the items.

Name ______________________ Class ______________ Date ______________

Reteaching 1-9

Graphing Data on the Coordinate Plane

OBJECTIVE: Identifying coordinates on the coordinate plane

MATERIALS: Graph paper

Coordinates give the location of a point. To locate a point (x, y) on a graph, start at the origin, $(0, 0)$. Move x units to the right or to the left along the x-axis and y units up or down along the y-axis.

Example

Give the coordinates of points A, B, C, and D.

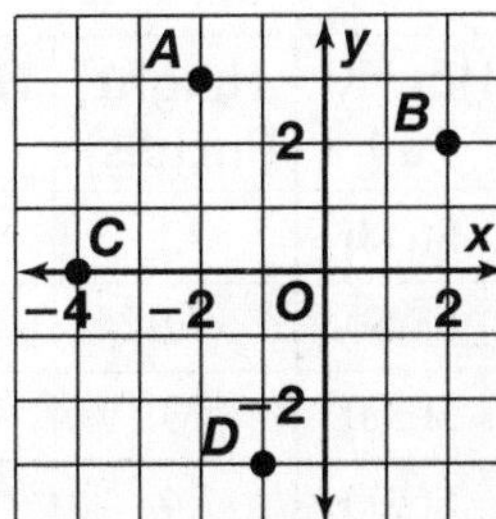

Point A is 2 units to the left of the origin and 3 units up. The coordinates of A are $(-2, 3)$.

Point B is 2 units to the right of the origin and 2 units up. The coordinates of B are $(2, 2)$.

Point C is 4 units to the left of the origin and 0 units up. The coordinates of C are $(-4, 0)$.

Point D is 1 unit to the left of the origin and 3 units down. The coordinates of D are $(-1, -3)$.

Exercises

Name the coordinates of each point.

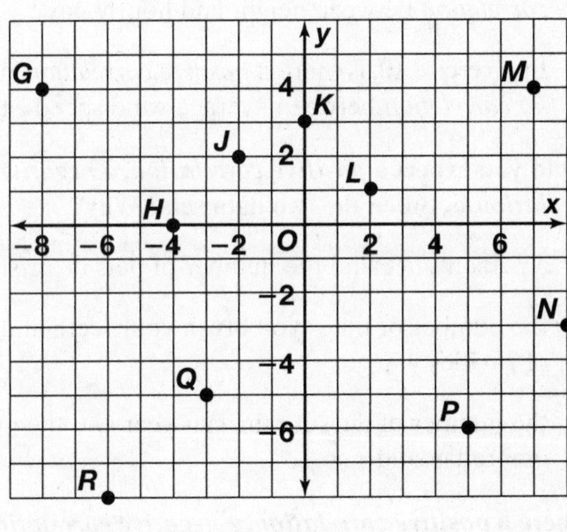

1. G 2. H
3. J 4. K
5. L 6. M
7. N 8. P
9. Q 10. R

Graph the points on the same coordinate plane.

11. $S(3, -5)$ 12. $T(0, 0)$
13. $U(-1, -2)$ 14. $V(4, 5)$
15. $W(0, 3)$ 16. $Z(-5, 0)$

Name ____________________ Class ____________ Date ____________

Practice 1-9

Graphing Data on the Coordinate Plane

Name the coordinates of each point on the graph at the right.

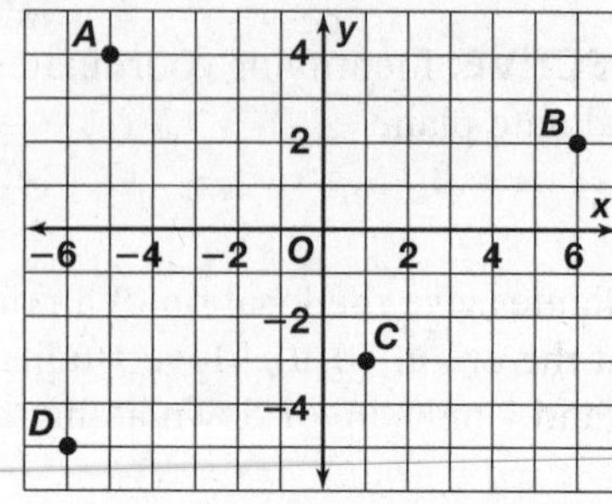

1. A
2. B
3. C
4. D

In which quadrant would you find each point?

5. (−3, 4)
6. (−6, −6)
7. (1, 5)
8. (8, −9)

Use the data in each table to draw a scatter plot.

9. **Height and Hourly Pay of Ten People**

Height (inches)	Hourly Pay	Height (inches)	Hourly Pay
62	$6.00	72	$8.00
65	$8.50	72	$6.00
68	$6.50	73	$7.50
70	$6.00	74	$6.25
70	$7.50	74	$8.00

10. **Speed of Winds in Some U.S. Cities**

Station	Average Speed (mi/h)	Highest Speed (mi/h)
Atlanta, GA	9.1	60
Casper, WY	12.9	81
Dallas, TX	10.7	73
Mobile, AL	9.0	63
St. Louis, MO	9.7	60

Source: National Climatic Data Center

11. In Exercise 9, is there a *positive correlation*, a *negative correlation*, or *no correlation* between height and hourly pay?

12. In Exercise 10, is there a *positive correlation*, a *negative correlation*, or *no correlation* between average wind speed and highest wind speed?

Would you expect a *positive correlation*, a *negative correlation*, or *no correlation* between the two data sets? Why?

13. a person's age and the number of pets he or she has

14. the number of times you brush your teeth and the number of cavities you get

15. the number of days it rains per year and the number of umbrellas sold

Is there a *positive correlation*, a *negative correlation*, or *no correlation* between the two data sets in each scatter plot?

16. 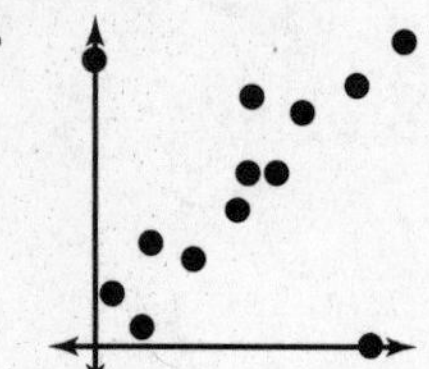

17. 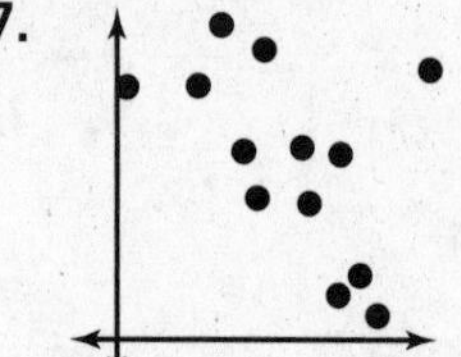

18. 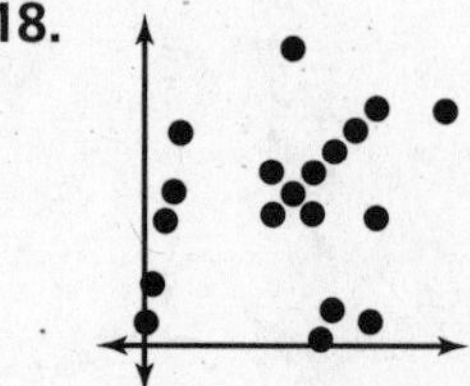

Name ______________________ Class ______________ Date ______________

Reteaching 2-1

Solving One-Step Equations

OBJECTIVE: Solving one-step equations

MATERIALS: Tiles

As you model an equation with tiles, ask yourself what operation has been performed on the variable. With the tiles, perform the inverse operation on each side of the equation. Simplify by removing zero pairs.

Examples

Model each equation with tiles and solve.

1. $x + 4 = 6$

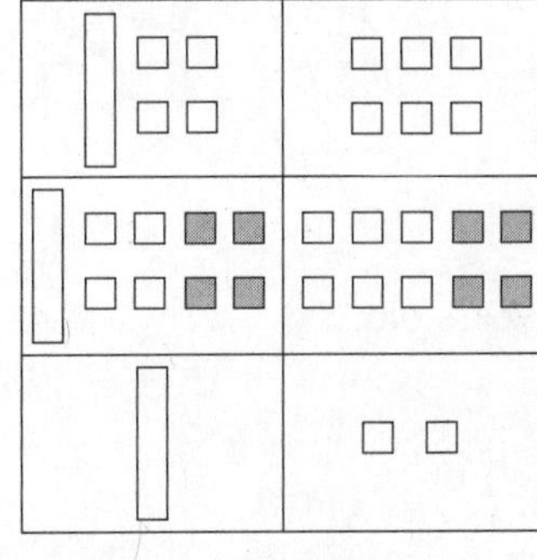

← **Model the equation with tiles.**

← **Subtract 4 from each side of the equation.**

← **Simplify by removing zero pairs.**

$x = 2$

2. $3x = 9$

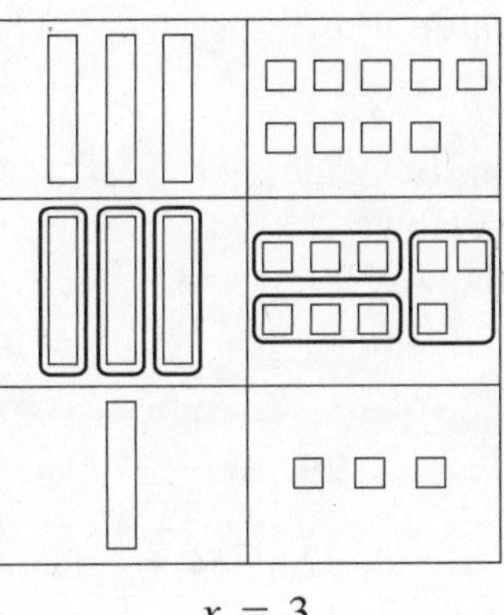

← **Model the equation with tiles.**

← **Divide each side into three identical groups.**

← **Solve for x.**

$x = 3$

Exercises

Model each equation with tiles and solve.

1. $x + 3 = 10$
2. $y - 4 = 2$
3. $-6 = 3y$
4. $2x = 6$
5. $y + 1 = 4$
6. $5y = 10$
7. $x - 5 = 4$
8. $12 = 4x$
9. $x + 4 = 2$

Solve.

10. $17 = -8 + x$
11. $-0.5 = \frac{d}{4}$
12. $0.8 = \frac{a}{5}$
13. $5.2 + h = 0.3$
14. $14 = x + 7$
15. $6x = 15$

Name ______________________ Class ______________ Date ______________

Practice 2-1

Solving One-Step Equations

Solve each equation. Check your answer.

1. $g - 6 = 2$
2. $15 + b = 4$
3. $8 = h + 24$
4. $63 = 7x$
5. $x + 7 = 17$
6. $-2n = -46$
7. $\frac{c}{14} = -3$
8. $\frac{x}{2} = 13$
9. $\frac{a}{5} = 3$
10. $r - 63 = -37$
11. $5 + d = 27$
12. $2b = -16$
13. $4y = 48$
14. $c - 25 = 19$
15. $a + 4 = 9.6$
16. $x + 29 = 13$
17. $-3d = -63$
18. $3f = -21.6$
19. $-\frac{x}{8} = 12$
20. $a - \frac{1}{3} = \frac{2}{3}$
21. $n - 3 = -3$

Write an equation to model each situation. Then solve.

22. A stack of 12 bricks is 27 in. high. What is the height of each brick?
23. The sum of Juanita's age and Sara's age is 33 yr. If Sara is 15 years old, how old is Juanita?
24. The tallest player on the basketball team is $77\frac{3}{4}$ in. tall. This is $9\frac{1}{2}$ in. taller than the shortest player. How tall is the shortest player?
25. The equatorial diameter of Jupiter is about 89,000 mi. This is about 11.23 times the equatorial diameter of Earth. What is the equatorial diameter of Earth? Round to the nearest integer.
26. The distance from Baltimore to New York is about 171 mi. This is about 189 mi less than the distance from Baltimore to Boston. How far is Baltimore from Boston if you stop in New York along the way?

Solve each equation. Check your answer.

27. $y - 8 = -15$
28. $a + 27.7 = -36.6$
29. $3x = 27$
30. $a + 5 = -19$
31. $m - 9.5 = -27.4$
32. $-54 = -6s$
33. $x + \frac{1}{3} = \frac{5}{6}$
34. $-\frac{s}{3} = 7$
35. $\frac{m}{12} = -4.2$
36. $\frac{a}{3} = -11$
37. $-\frac{z}{8} = -3.7$
38. $-\frac{y}{11} = -6.1$
39. $-17.5 = 2.5d$
40. $b - 48 = -29$
41. $96 = -3h$
42. $-4.2x = 15.96$
43. $x + 87.8 = 38.1$
44. $-5x = 85$
45. $-\frac{x}{5} = 4.8$
46. $d + \frac{2}{3} = -\frac{1}{2}$
47. $-\frac{t}{2} = -9$
48. $45.6 = 6x$
49. $19.5 = -39.5 + f$
50. $m - 21 = -43$

Name ______________________ Class ______________ Date ____________

Reteaching 2-2

Solving Two-Step Equations

OBJECTIVE: Solving two-step equations **MATERIALS:** None

The order of operations tells you to do multiplication and division before you do addition and subtraction. However, when solving two-step equations, you must first do any addition or subtraction necessary to isolate the variable on one side of the equation. Start by asking yourself, "Has any adding or subtracting been done to the variable?" If the answer is yes, perform the inverse operation. Then repeat this step for multiplication and division.

Example

Write the steps and solve the equation.

$3x + 4 = 10$ ← **Think: Is any adding or subtracting being done to the variable? 4 is being added. What is the inverse of adding 4?**

$3x + 4 - 4 = 10 - 4$ ← **Subtract 4 from each side.**

$3x = 6$ ← **Simplify.**

$3x = 6$ ← **Think: Is any multiplying or dividing being done to the variable? It is being multiplied by 3. What is the inverse of multiplying by 3?**

$\frac{3x}{3} = \frac{6}{3}$ ← **Divide each side by 3.**

$x = 2$ ← **Simplify.**

Exercises

Fill in the blanks to complete the steps and solve the equation.

1. $\frac{s}{6} - 5 = -8$ ← **Think: Is any adding or subtracting being done to the variable? ________ is being ________ . What is the ________ of subtracting 5?**

$\frac{s}{6} - 5 + 5 = -8 + 5$ ← **________ 5 to ________ side.**

$\frac{s}{6} = -3$ ← **Simplify.**

$\frac{s}{6} = -3$ ← **Think: Is any multiplying or dividing being done to the variable? It is being ________ by 6. What is the inverse of ________ by 6?**

$6\left(\frac{s}{6}\right) = 6(-3)$ ← **Multiply each ________ by ________ .**

$s =$ ________ ← **Simplify.**

Solve each equation.

2. $3x - 4 = 8$

3. $\frac{x}{4} + 3 = 10$

4. $4y + 5 = -7$

Name ______________________ Class ______________ Date ______________

Practice 2-2

Solving Two-Step Equations

Solve each equation. Check your answer.

1. $5a + 2 = 7$
2. $2x + 3 = 7$
3. $3b + 6 = 12$
4. $9 = 5 + 4t$
5. $4a + 1 = 13$
6. $-t + 2 = 12$

Write an equation to model each situation. Then solve.

7. You want to buy a bouquet of yellow roses and baby's breath for \$16. The baby's breath costs \$3.50 per bunch, and the roses cost \$2.50 each. You want one bunch of baby's breath and some roses for your bouquet. How many roses can you buy?

8. Suppose you walk at the rate of 210 ft/min. You need to walk 10,000 ft. How many more minutes will it take you to finish if you have already walked 550 ft?

9. Suppose you have shelled 6.5 lb of pecans, and you can shell pecans at a rate of 1.5 lb per hour. How many more hours will it take you to shell a total of 11 lb of pecans?

10. To mail a first class letter, the U.S. Postal Service charges \$.34 for the first ounce and \$.21 for each additional ounce. It costs \$1.18 to mail your letter. How many ounces does your letter weigh?

11. Suppose you want to buy one pair of pants and several pairs of socks. The pants cost \$24.95, and the socks are \$5.95 per pair. How many pairs of socks can you buy if you have \$50.00 to spend?

Solve each equation. Check your answer.

12. $5.8n + 3.7 = 29.8$
13. $67 = -3y + 16$
14. $-d + 7 = 3$
15. $\frac{m}{9} + 7 = 3$
16. $6.78 + 5.2x = -36.9$
17. $5z + 9 = -21$
18. $3x - 7 = 35$
19. $36.9 = 3.7b - 14.9$
20. $4s - 13 = 51$
21. $9f + 16 = 70$
22. $11.6 + 3a = -16.9$
23. $-9 = -\frac{h}{12} + 5$
24. $-c + 2 = 5$
25. $-67 = -8n + 5$
26. $22 = 7 - 3a$
27. $\frac{k}{3} - 19 = -26$
28. $-21 = \frac{n}{3} + 2$
29. $3x + 5.7 = 15$
30. $\frac{a}{5} - 2 = -13$
31. $2x + 23 = 49$
32. $\frac{x}{2} + 8 = -3$

Justify each step.

33. $24 - x = -16$
   a. $24 - x - 24 = -16 - 24$
   b. $-x = -40$
   c. $-1(-x) = -1(-40)$
   d. $x = 40$

34. $\frac{x}{7} + 4 = 15$
   a. $\frac{x}{7} + 4 - 4 = 15 - 4$
   b. $\frac{x}{7} = 11$
   c. $7(\frac{x}{7}) = 7(11)$
   d. $x = 77$

35. $-8 = 2x - 5$
   a. $-8 + 5 = 2x - 5 + 5$
   b. $-3 = 2x$
   c. $-\frac{3}{2} = \frac{2x}{2}$
   d. $-\frac{3}{2} = x$

Name ______________________ Class ______________ Date ______________

Reteaching 2-3

Solving Multi-Step Equations

OBJECTIVE: Combining like terms	**MATERIALS:** None

Example

Simplify $3a - 6x + 4 - 2a + 5x$ by combining like terms.

Ring each term that has the variable a. Draw a rectangle around each term that has the variable x, and a triangle around each constant term.

$3a$ 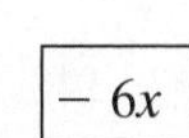 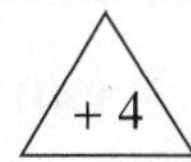 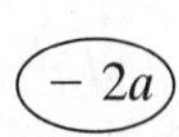

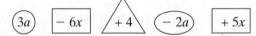

Group the like terms by reordering the terms so that all matching shapes are together.

 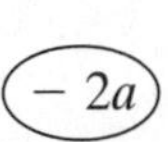 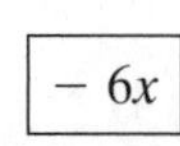 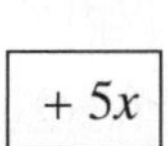 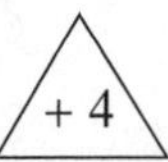

Combine like terms by adding coefficients.

$a - x + 4$

Exercises

Draw circles, rectangles, and triangles to help you combine like terms and simplify each expression.

1. $3a + 5 - x + 7x - 2a$

2. $2x - 5 + 3a - 5x + 10a$

3. $7b - b - x + 5 - 2x - 7b$

4. $-6m + 3t + 4 - 4m - 2t$

5. $2r + 3s - 5r$

6. $4 - p - 2x + 3p - 7x$

7. $3k - 2x + 6k + 5$

8. $3 + 2a - 7x + 2.5 + 5x$

9. $4a + 3 - 2y - 5a - 7 + 4y$

10. $c - 3 + 2x - 6c + 4x$

Simplify each expression.

11. $2b + 2 - x + 4$

12. $-5 - c - 4 + 3c$

13. $\frac{1}{2}a - 5 - \frac{1}{2}a$

14. $1.5y - 1.5 + 0.5y + 0.5z + 1$

15. $6a + 3b - 2a + 4$

16. $\frac{2}{3}a + 5 - \frac{1}{3}a - 7$

17. $-8 + x - 2 + 3x$

18. $x + y - z + 4x - 5y + 2z$

19. $\frac{7}{8}x + 5 - \frac{3}{8}x - 4$

20. $10y - 3x + 5 - 8 - 2y$

Name ______________________ Class ______________ Date ______________

Practice 2-3

Solving Multi-Step Equations

Solve each equation. Check your answer.

1. $2n + 3n + 7 = -41$
2. $2x - 5x + 6.3 = -14.4$
3. $2z + 9.75 - 7z = -5.15$
4. $3h - 5h + 11 = 17$
5. $2t + 8 - t = -3$
6. $6a - 2a = -36$
7. $3c - 8c + 7 = -18$
8. $7g + 14 - 5g = -8$
9. $2b - 6 + 3b = 14$
10. $2(a - 4) + 15 = 13$
11. $7 + 2(a - 3) = -9$
12. $13 + 2(5c - 2) = 29$
13. $5(3x + 12) = -15$
14. $4(2a + 2) - 17 = 15$
15. $2(m + 1) = 16$
16. $-4x + 3(2x - 5) = 31$
17. $-6 - 3(2k + 4) = 18$
18. $3(t - 12) = 27$
19. $-w + 4(w + 3) = -12$
20. $4 = 0.4(3d - 5)$
21. $-4d + 2(3 + d) = -14$
22. $2x + \frac{3}{4}(4x + 16) = 7$
23. $2(3a + 2) = -8$
24. $5(t - 3) - 2t = -30$
25. $5(b + 4) - 6b = -24$
26. $\frac{2}{5}(5k + 35) - 8 = 12$
27. $0.4(2s + 4) = 4.8$
28. $\frac{2}{3}(9b - 27) = 36$
29. $\frac{1}{2}(12n - 8) = 26$
30. $0.5(2x - 4) = -17$
31. $18 = \frac{c + 5}{2}$
32. $\frac{2}{9}s = -6$
33. $\frac{1}{3}x = \frac{1}{2}$
34. $\frac{2}{3}g + \frac{1}{2}g = 14$
35. $\frac{3x + 7}{2} = 8$
36. $\frac{2x - 6}{4} = -7$
37. $\frac{2}{3}k + \frac{1}{4}k = 22$
38. $-\frac{4}{7}h = -28$
39. $-8 = \frac{4}{5}k$
40. $\frac{3}{4} - \frac{1}{3}z = \frac{1}{4}$
41. $-9 = \frac{3}{4}m$
42. $\frac{5}{6}c - \frac{2}{3}c = \frac{1}{3}$
43. $\frac{4}{5} = -\frac{4}{7}g$
44. $\frac{9x + 6 - 4x}{2} = 8$
45. $-\frac{1}{6}d = -4$

Write an equation to model each situation. Then solve.

46. The attendance at a baseball game was 400 people. Student tickets cost \$2 and adult tickets cost \$3. Total ticket sales were \$1050. How many tickets of each type were sold?

47. The perimeter of a pool table is 30 ft. The table is twice as long as it is wide. What is the length of the pool table?

48. Lopez spent $\frac{1}{3}$ of his vacation money for travel and $\frac{2}{5}$ of his vacation money for lodging. He spent \$1100 for travel and lodging. What is the total amount of money he spent on his vacation?

49. Victoria weighs $\frac{5}{7}$ as much as Mario. Victoria weighs 125 lb. How much does Mario weigh?

50. Denise's cell phone plan is \$29.95 per month plus \$.10 per minute for each minute over 300 minutes of call time. Denise's cell phone bill is \$99.95. For how many minutes was she billed?

Name ______________________ Class ______________ Date ____________

Reteaching 2-4

Equations with Variables on Both Sides

OBJECTIVE: Solving equations with variables on both sides

MATERIALS: None

To solve equations with variables on both sides, use these strategies:

- Rewrite the equation until all terms with variables are combined on one side and all constant terms are combined on the other side. As you rewrite the equation, use inverse operations and the equality properties.
- When you perform an operation on one side, you must do the same on the other.

Example

Solve $5a - 12 = 3a + 7$.

$\boxed{\bigcirc 5a} - 12 = \bigcirc 3a + 7$ ← **Circle all the terms with variables.**

$5a \boxed{-12} = 3a \boxed{+7}$ ← **Put rectangles around all constant terms. Plan steps to collect variable terms on one side and constant terms on the other.**

$5a - 12 - 3a = 3a + 7 - 3a$ ← **To get variables on the same side, subtract 3*a* from each side.**

$2a - 12 = 7$ ← **Combine like terms.**

$2a - 12 + 12 = 7 + 12$ ← **To get constants on the other side, add 12 to each side.**

$2a = 19$ ← **Combine like terms.**

$a = 9.5$ ← **To undo multiplication by 2, divide each side by 2.**

Check $5(9.5) - 12 \stackrel{?}{=} 3(9.5) + 7$

$47.5 - 12 \stackrel{?}{=} 28.5 + 7$

$35.5 = 35.5$ ✓

In what other ways could you solve for *a*? You could add 12 to each side, then subtract 3*a* from each side. Or, you could subtract 5*a* from each side, then subtract 7 from each side.

Exercises

Fill in the blanks to show a plan to solve each equation.

1. $9x + 4 = 6x - 11$ __________ 6*x* __________ each side; subtract __________ from each side.
2. $4b - 13 = 7b - 28$ Subtract __________ from each side; __________ 28 __________ each side.

Use circles and rectangles to mark the variables and constant terms. Write a plan that tells the steps you would use and then solve each equation.

3. $7c - 4 = 9c - 11$
4. $3 - 4d = 6d - 17$
5. $5e + 13 = 7e - 21$

Solve and check each equation.

6. $8f - 12 = 5f + 12$
7. $3k + 5 = 2(k + 1)$
8. $9 - x = 3x + 1$

Name ______ Class ______ Date ______

Practice 2-4

Equations with Variables on Both Sides

Solve each equation. Check your answer. If appropriate, write *identity* or *no solution.*

1. $7 - 2n = n - 14$
2. $2(4 - 2r) = -2(r + 5)$
3. $3d + 8 = 2d - 7$
4. $6t = 3(t + 4) - t$
5. $8z - 7 = 3z - 7 + 5z$
6. $7x - 8 = 3x + 12$
7. $3(n - 1) = 5n + 3 - 2n$
8. $2(6 - 4d) = 25 - 9d$
9. $4s - 12 = -5s + 51$
10. $8(2f - 3) = 4(4f - 8)$
11. $6k - 25 = 7 - 2k$
12. $3v - 9 = 7 + 2v - v$
13. $4(b - 1) = -4 + 4b$
14. $\frac{1}{4}x + \frac{1}{2} = \frac{1}{4}x - \frac{1}{2}$
15. $6 - 4d = 16 - 9d$
16. $\frac{2}{3}a - \frac{3}{4} = \frac{3}{4}a$
17. $2s - 12 + 2s = 4s - 12$
18. $3.6y = 5.4 + 3.3y$
19. $4.3v - 6 = 8 + 2.3v$
20. $4b - 1 = -4 + 4b + 3$
21. $\frac{2}{3}(6x + 3) = 4x + 2$
22. $6y + 9 = 3(2y + 3)$
23. $4g + 7 = 5g - 1 - g$
24. $2(n + 2) = 5n - 5$
25. $6 - 3d = 5(2 - d)$
26. $6.1h = 9.3 - 3.2h$
27. $-4.4s - 2 = -5.5s - 4.2$
28. $3(2f + 4) = 2(3f - 6)$
29. $\frac{3}{4}t - \frac{5}{6} = \frac{2}{3}t$
30. $3v + 8 = 8 + 2v + v$
31. $\frac{1}{2}d - \frac{3}{4} = \frac{3}{5}d$
32. $5(r + 3) = 2r + 6$
33. $8 - 3(p - 4) = 2p$

Write an equation to model each situation. Then solve. Check your answer.

34. Hans needs to rent a moving truck. Suppose Company A charges a rate of \$40 per day and Company B charges a \$60 fee plus \$20 per day. For what number of days is the cost the same?

35. Suppose a video store charges nonmembers \$4 to rent each video. A store membership costs \$21 and members pay only \$2.50 to rent each video. For what number of videos is the cost the same?

36. Suppose your club is selling candles to raise money. It costs \$100 to rent a booth from which to sell the candles. If the candles cost your club \$1 each and are sold for \$5 each, how many candles must be sold to equal your expenses?

Find the value of *x*.

37.

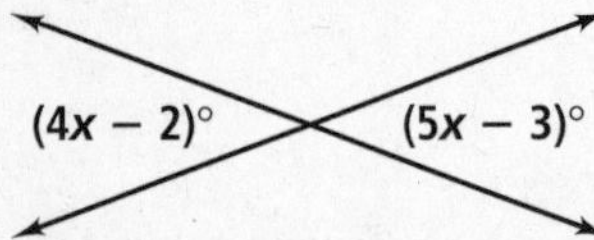

38.

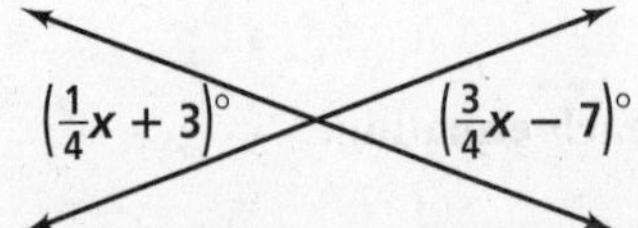

39.

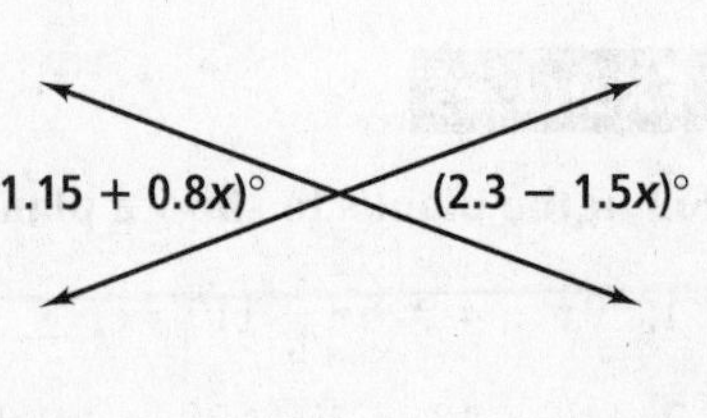

Name ______________________ Class ______________ Date ______________

Reteaching 2-5

Equations and Problem Solving

OBJECTIVE: Solving real-world problems involving equations with variables on both sides

MATERIALS: None

A table is useful in organizing information from a real-world problem. Below are examples of tables for several types of application problems.

	Rate	× Time	= Distance
Object 1			
Object 2			

	Length	× Width	= Area
Rectangle 1			
Rectangle 2			

Example

An airplane takes off from an airport at 7:00 A.M. traveling at a rate of 350 mi/h. Two hours later, a jet takes off from the same airport following the same flight path at 490 mi/h. In how many hours will the jet catch up with the airplane?

Define: Let $t =$ the time the airplane travels.
Let $t - 2 =$ the time the jet travels.

Set up table:

	Rate	× Time	= Distance
Airplane	350	t	$350t$
Jet	490	$t - 2$	$490(t - 2)$

Relate: distance traveled by airplane = distance traveled by jet

Write:

$350t = 490(t - 2)$

$350t = 490t - 980$ ← **Use the distributive property.**

$350t - 490t = 490t - 980 - 490t$ ← **Subtract 490*t* from each side.**

$-140t = -980$ ← **Combine like terms.**

$\frac{-140t}{-140} = \frac{-980}{-140}$ ← **Divide each side by −140.**

$t = 7$ ← **Simplify.**

Final answer: The jet will catch up with the airplane in 5 hours.

Exercises

Solve each problem.

1. Mary leaves her house at noon, traveling in her car at 45 mi/h. Later, Mary's brother Joe leaves their house and travels in the same direction at 60 mi/h. If Joe leaves at 2:00 P.M., at what time will he catch up with Mary?

2. Mike leaves school on his bike at 1:00 P.M., traveling at 12 mi/h. Janis leaves the same school one quarter of an hour later, traveling at 16 mi/h in the same direction. At what time will Janis catch up with Mike?

Name ____________________ Class ____________________ Date ____________________

Practice 2-5

Equations and Problem Solving

Write and solve an equation for each situation.

1. A passenger train's speed is 60 mi/h, and a freight train's speed is 40 mi/h. The passenger train travels the same distance in 1.5 h less time than the freight train. How long does each train take to make the trip?

2. Lois rode her bike to visit a friend. She traveled at 10 mi/h. While she was there, it began to rain. Her friend drove her home in a car traveling at 25 mi/h. Lois took 1.5 h longer to go to her friend's than to return home. How many hours did it take Lois to ride to her friend's house?

3. May rides her bike the same distance that Leah walks. May rides her bike 10 km/h faster than Leah walks. If it takes May 1 h and Leah 3 h to travel that distance, how fast does each travel?

4. The length of a rectangle is 4 in. greater than the width. The perimeter of the rectangle is 24 in. Find the dimensions of the rectangle.

5. The length of a rectangle is twice the width. The perimeter is 48 in. Find the dimensions of the rectangle.

6. At 10:00 A.M., a car leaves a house at a rate of 60 mi/h. At the same time, another car leaves the same house at a rate of 50 mi/h in the opposite direction. At what time will the cars be 330 miles apart?

7. Marla begins walking at 3 mi/h toward the library. Her friend meets her at the halfway point and drives her the rest of the way to the library. The distance to the library is 4 miles. How many hours did Marla walk?

8. Fred begins walking toward John's house at 3 mi/h. John leaves his house at the same time and walks toward Fred's house on the same path at a rate of 2 mi/h. How long will it be before they meet if the distance between the houses is 4 miles?

9. A train leaves the station at 6:00 P.M. traveling west at 80 mi/h. On a parallel track, a second train leaves the station 3 hours later traveling west at 100 mi/h. At what time will the second train catch up with the first?

10. It takes 1 hour longer to fly to St. Paul at 200 mi/h than it does to return at 250 mi/h. How far away is St. Paul?

11. Find three consecutive integers whose sum is 126.

12. The sum of four consecutive odd integers is 216. Find the four integers.

13. A rectangular picture frame is to be 8 in. longer than it is wide. Dennis uses 84 in. of oak to frame the picture. What is the width of the frame?

14. Each of two congruent sides of an isosceles triangle is 8 in. less than twice the base. The perimeter of the triangle is 74 in. What is the length of the base?

Name ______________________ Class ______________ Date ______________

Reteaching 2-6

Formulas

OBJECTIVE: Solving a literal equation for one of its variables	**MATERIALS:** None

Variables are symbols used to represent numbers. Any symbol can be used. Notice how these literal equations have been rewritten using geometric symbols.

$a = b + c$ ○ = ▲ + □

$xy = pq$ ○ · ● = ▲ · □

$\frac{s}{t} = \frac{r}{q}$ $\frac{○}{●} = \frac{□}{▲}$

Example

Solve ○ · ● = ▲ · □ for ▲ and then for □.

Solving for ▲: ○ · ● = ▲ · □

$\frac{○●}{□} = \frac{▲□}{□}$ ⟵ **Divide each side by □, □ ≠ 0.**

$\frac{○●}{□} = ▲$ ⟵ **Simplify.**

Solving for □: ○ · ● = ▲ · □

$\frac{○●}{▲} = \frac{▲□}{▲}$ ⟵ **Divide each side by ▲, ▲ ≠ 0.**

$\frac{○●}{▲} = □$ ⟵ **Simplify.**

Exercises

Solve each literal equation for ○. Show your steps.

1. ○ + □ = ▲

2. $\frac{○}{●} = \frac{□}{▲}$

3. Choose your own symbols (such as ❀, ✈, ★, ❤) and use them to write a literal equation. Solve for one of the symbols. Show each step.

Solve each equation for the given variable.

4. $5x + a = y; a$

5. $m = 6(p + q); q$

6. $2x + 3y = 8; x$

7. $xy = 3z; z$

8. $w = 3(x + y + z); y$

9. $2w - 8y = z; y$

Name ______________________ Class ______________ Date ______________

Practice 2-6

Formulas

Solve each formula in terms of the given variable.

1. $ad = f$; a
2. $n + 3 = q$; n
3. $2(j + k) = m$; k
4. $2s + t = r$; t
5. $m + 2n = p$; n
6. $\frac{2}{w} = \frac{x}{5}$; w
7. $5a - b = 7$; a
8. $h = \frac{p}{n}$; p
9. $5d - 2g = 9$; g
10. $x + 3y = z$; x
11. $y = mx + b$; x
12. $V = \ell wh$; ℓ

The formula $A = 2h(\ell + w)$ gives the lateral area A of a rectangular solid with length ℓ, width w, and height h.

13. Solve this formula for h.
14. Find h if $A = 144\text{ cm}^2$, $\ell = 7$ cm, and $w = 5$ cm.
15. Solve this formula for ℓ.
16. Find ℓ if $A = 729.8\text{ in.}^2$, $h = 17.8$ in., and $w = 6.4$ in.
17. Find h if $A = 37.4\text{ ft}^2$, $\ell = 4.3$ ft, and $w = 6.7$ ft.
18. Find ℓ if $A = 9338\text{ m}^2$, $h = 29$ m, and $w = 52$ m.

The formula $P = \frac{F}{A}$ gives the pressure P for a force F and an area A.

19. Solve this formula for A.
20. Find A if $P = 14.8\text{ lb/in.}^2$ and $F = 2960$ lb.
21. Solve this formula for F.
22. Find F if $P = 240\text{ lb/in.}^2$ and $A = 20\text{ in.}^2$.
23. Find A if $P = 46.8\text{ lb/in.}^2$ and $F = 2340$ lb.
24. Find F if $P = 24.5\text{ lb/in.}^2$ and $A = 33.8\text{ in.}^2$.

Solve each formula in terms of the given variable.

25. $3n - t = s$; t
26. $\frac{b + 3}{e} = \frac{f}{2}$; e
27. $w = 2xyz$; y
28. $k = 3mh + 3$; h
29. $ab = 6 + cd$; a
30. $2a + 4b = d$; b
31. $4xy + 3 = 5z$; y
32. $-2(3a - b) = c$; b

The formula $V = \frac{1}{3}\ell wh$ gives the volume V of a rectangular pyramid with length ℓ, width w, and height h.

33. Solve this formula for w.
34. Find w if $V = 64\text{ m}^3$, $\ell = 6$ m, and $h = 4$ m.
35. Solve this formula for h.
36. Find h if $V = 30.45\text{ ft}^3$, $\ell = 6.3$ ft, and $w = 2.5$ ft.
37. Find w if $V = 2346\text{ in.}^3$, $\ell = 17$ in., and $h = 18$ in.
38. Find h if $V = 7\text{ ft}^3$, $\ell = \frac{7}{4}$ ft, and $w = \frac{3}{4}$ ft.

Solve each formula in terms of the given variable.

39. $2m - 3p = 1$; p
40. $a = b + cd$; b
41. $a + b = 2xz$; z
42. $x = 2y + 3z$; y
43. $\frac{a}{b} = \frac{c}{d}$; d
44. $2ab + 4 = d$; a
45. $\frac{5}{2} = \frac{1}{2}(b - c)$; b
46. $d(a - b) = c$; a

Name ______________________ Class ______________ Date ______________

Reteaching 2-7

Using Measures of Central Tendency

OBJECTIVE: Finding measures of central tendency **MATERIALS:** None

In working with statistical data, it is often useful to determine a single quantity that best describes the set of data. The best quantity to choose is usually one of the most popular measures of central tendency: the mean, the median, or the mode.

	Definitions
Mean	The **mean** is the sum of the data items in a set divided by the number of data items in the set.
Median	The **median** is the middle value in a set of data when the numbers are arranged in numerical order. If the set has an even number of data items, the median is the mean of the two middle data values.
Mode	The **mode** is the data item that occurs most often in a data set.

Example

Find the mean, median, and mode of the set of data: 34 46 31 40 33 40.

Mean: $\frac{34 + 46 + 31 + 40 + 33 + 40}{6} = \frac{224}{6} = 37.\overline{3}$ ⟵ **Add the data items and divide by the number of data items in the set.**

Median: 31 33 34 40 40 46 ⟵ **Arrange the data items in increasing order.**

$\frac{34 + 40}{2} = 37$ ⟵ **Since there is an even number of data values, find the mean of the two middle data values.**

Mode: The mode is 40 since it occurs most often.

Exercises

Find the mean, median, and mode of each set of data.

1. daily sales of a store: \$834 \$1099 \$775 \$900 \$970
2. number of points scored in 8 soccer games: 0 10 4 11 7 6 3 2
3. number of days above 50°F in the last five months: 6 8 15 22 9
4. heights of players on a basketball team in inches: 72 74 70 77 76 72
5. resting heart rates in beats per minute: 76 70 64 70 72 68

Name ______________________ Class ______________ Date ____________

Practice 2-7

Using Measures of Central Tendency

Find the mean, median, mode, and range.

1. number of cars sold in the past 10 days
   1 5 3 2 1 0 4 2 6 1

2. utility bills for the past 6 months
   \$90 \$120 \$140 \$135 \$112 \$126

3. prices of a sweater in 5 different stores
   \$31.25 \$27.50 \$28.00 \$36.95 \$32.10

4. scores on a 10-point quiz
   7 9 10 8 4 2 6 10 8

5. hourly wages
   \$7.25 \$6.75 \$8.10 \$9.56 \$7.10 \$7.75

6. ages of students on the quiz team
   15 15 14 16 17 16 16 15

Write and solve an equation to find the value of x.

7. 4.8, 1.6, 5.2, x; mean 3.7

8. 40, 98, 94, 102, 21, x; mean 88

9. 100, 172, 85, 92, x; mean 115

10. 25.6, 19.3, 19, x, mean 24

11. In his eight games against Boston, a baseball pitcher threw the following number of strikeouts: 1, 2, 4, 2, 1, 3, 3, and 0. In his five games against St. Louis, he recorded strikeouts as follows: 3, 1, 2, 3, and 2. Did the pitcher average more strikeouts against Boston or against St. Louis?

12. Randy had grades of 85, 92, 96, and 89 on his last four math tests. What grade does he need on his next test to have an average of 92?

13. To test the exhaust fumes of a car, an inspector took six samples. The exhaust samples contained the following amounts of gas in parts per million (ppm): 8, 5, 7, 6, 9, and 5. If the maximum allowable mean is 6 ppm, did the car pass the test? Explain.

14. A coffee machine is considered reliable if the range of amounts of coffee that it dispenses is less than 2 fluid ounces (fl oz). In eight tries, a particular machine dispensed the following amounts: 7.1, 6.8, 7.6, 7.1, 7.4, 6.8, 7, and 6.7 fl oz. Is the machine reliable? Explain.

15. According to its producer, an off-Broadway show would make a profit if an average of at least 1100 tickets were sold per show. For the past 12 shows, the number of tickets sold was as follows: 1000, 800, 1600, 900, 1200, 900, 800, 1700, 900, 1200, 1000, and 1200. Using the mean as the average, did the show make a profit for these 12 shows?

16. **a.** A bakery collected the following data about the number of loaves of fresh bread sold on each of 24 business days. Make a stem-and-leaf plot for the data.

43	39	17	38	50	42	34	28	37	42	40	33
72	36	45	21	29	44	41	37	40	35	51	54

   b. Find the mean, median, mode, and range of the data.

17. **a.** The following numbers of calls were made to the police department in the last 24 days. Make a stem-and-leaf plot for the data.

32	42	35	52	58	52	46	61	52	63	81	61
63	39	41	48	62	61	58	34	49	47	49	31

   b. Find the mean, median, mode, and range of the data.

Name ______________________ Class ______________ Date ______________

Reteaching 3-1

Inequalities and Their Graphs

OBJECTIVE: Identifying solutions of inequalities	**MATERIALS:** None

A sentence that contains the symbol $>$, $<$, $\geq$, or $\leq$ is called an **inequality.** An inequality expresses the relative order of two mathematical expressions. The sentence can be either numerical or variable.

Symbol	Description
$>$	is greater than
$<$	is less than
$\leq$	is less than or equal to
$\geq$	is greater than or equal to

Example

One way to determine whether a number is a solution of an inequality is to plot the number on a number line.

Is each number a solution of $x > -2.5$?

a. 3

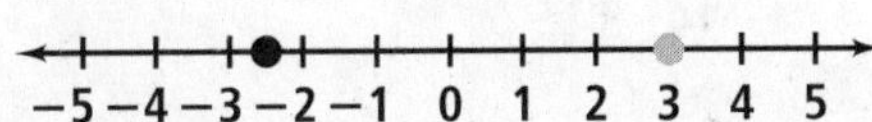

Since 3 is to the right of -2.5, it is greater than -2.5, so it is a solution. $3 > -2.5$

b. -5

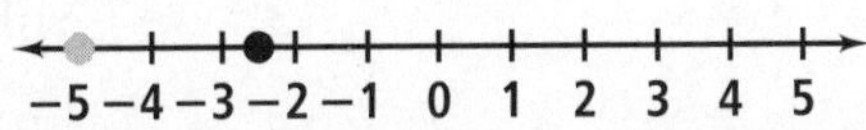

Since -5 is to the left of -2.5, it is less than -2.5, so it is not a solution. $-5 \ngtr -2.5$

c. -2

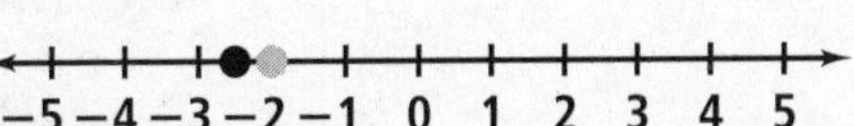

Since -2 is to the right of -2.5, it is greater than -2.5, so it is a solution. $-2 > -2.5$

d. -2.5

This is a special case: -2.5 is not greater than itself. Therefore, it is not a solution. $-2.5 \ngtr -2.5$

Exercises

Is each number a solution of $x \leq 8$?

1. -2 **2.** 7 **3.** -7 **4.** 8

Is each number a solution of $x \leq -9$?

5. 9 **6.** -14 **7.** -8.5 **8.** -6

Name ______________________ Class ______________ Date ______________

Practice 3-1

Inequalities and Their Graphs

Determine whether each number is a solution of the given inequality.

1. $x \leq -8$ a. -10 b. 6 c. -8
2. $-1 > x$ a. 0 b. -3 c. -6
3. $w < \frac{18}{7}$ a. 5 b. -2 c. $3\frac{1}{2}$
4. $0.65 \geq y$ a. 0.43 b. -0.65 c. 0.56
5. $2y + 1 > -5$ a. -4 b. -2 c. 4
6. $7x - 14 \leq 6x - 16$ a. 0 b. -4 c. 2
7. $n(n - 6) \geq -4$ a. 3 b. -2 c. 5

Write an inequality for each graph.

8. 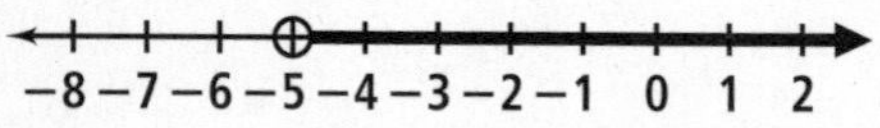 −8 −7 −6 −5 −4 −3 −2 −1 0 1 2

9. 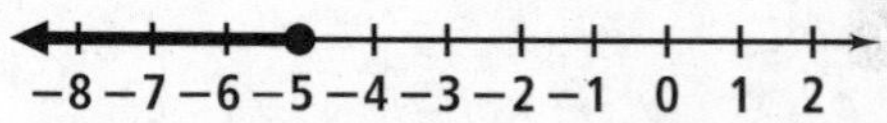 −8 −7 −6 −5 −4 −3 −2 −1 0 1 2

10. 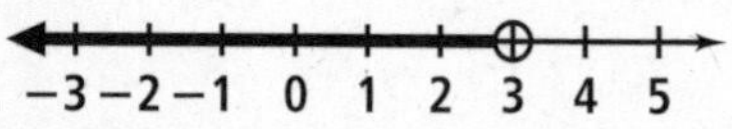 −3 −2 −1 0 1 2 3 4 5

11. 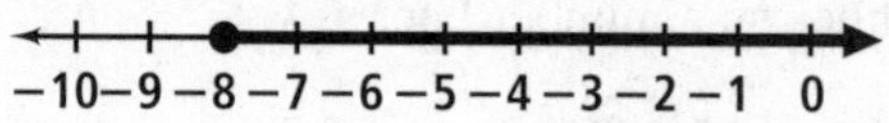 −10 −9 −8 −7 −6 −5 −4 −3 −2 −1 0

Write each inequality in words and then graph.

12. $x > 6$
13. $y \leq -10$
14. $8 \geq b$
15. $-4 < w$
16. $x < -7$
17. $x \geq 12$

Define a variable and write an inequality to model each situation.

18. The temperature in a refrigerated truck must be kept at or below 38°F.
19. The maximum weight on an elevator is 2000 pounds.
20. A least 20 students were sick with the flu.
21. The maximum occupancy in an auditorium is 250 people.
22. The maximum speed on the highway is 55 mi/h.
23. A student must have at least 450 out of 500 points to earn an A.
24. The circumference of an official major league baseball is at least 9.00 inches.

Match the inequality with its graph.

25. $6 < x$
26. $-6 \geq x$
27. $4 > x$
28. $x \leq -4$

A. 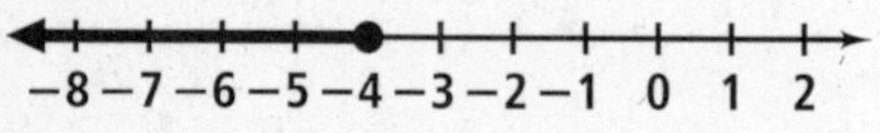 −8 −7 −6 −5 −4 −3 −2 −1 0 1 2

B. 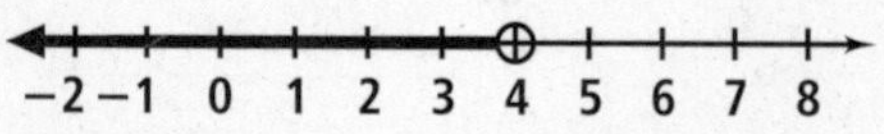 −2 −1 0 1 2 3 4 5 6 7 8

C. 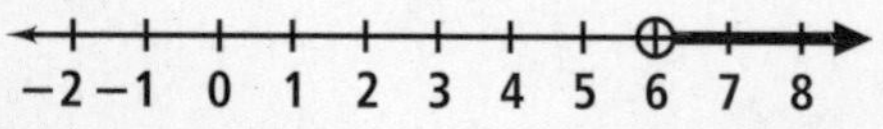 −2 −1 0 1 2 3 4 5 6 7 8

D. 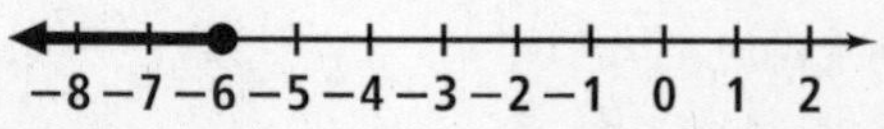 −8 −7 −6 −5 −4 −3 −2 −1 0 1 2

Name ______________________ Class ____________ Date ____________

Reteaching 3-2

Solving Inequalities Using Addition and Subtraction

OBJECTIVE: Using addition and subtraction to solve one-step inequalities

MATERIALS: Tiles

- To solve one-step inequalities, use the same strategies you use to solve equations. Apply the Addition and Subtraction Properties of Inequality.
- When you add or subtract the same quantity from each side of an inequality, the direction of the inequality symbol stays the same.

Example

Using tiles, solve the inequality $x - 3 < 4$.

a. Model the inequality with tiles.

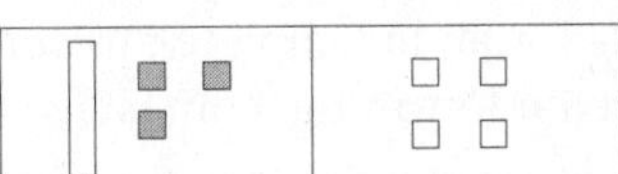

$x - 3 < 4$

b. Add or subtract the same quantity on each side to get the variable alone on one side of the inequality symbol.

For this example, add 3 to each side.

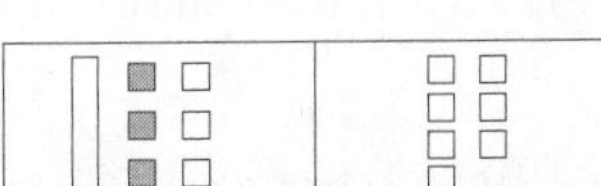

$x - 3 + 3 < 4 + 3$

c. Simplify by removing zero pairs.

d. Write the solution to the inequality.

$x < 7$

Note that even though you are adding the same quantity to each side of the inequality, the direction of the inequality symbol stays the same.

Exercises

Use tiles and steps a–d to model and solve each inequality.

1. $y - 2 < 4$

2. $x - 4 < 1$

3. $7 < w + 2$

4. $x - 6 > 10$

5. $10 \leq y + 8$

6. $a - 1 > 3$

7. $4 + h \leq 7$

8. $s - 3 > 2$

9. $b + 3 < 8$

Solve.

10. $x - 9 < 6$

11. $a - 7 > 5$

12. $b - 4 < 10$

13. $c + 5 > 7$

14. $6 + d < 11$

15. $f - 4 > 15$

16. The band must earn at least \$75 for a trip. Band members already earned \$35. Write and solve an inequality to find how much money they still need to earn.

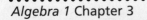

Name ______________________ Class ______________ Date ______________

Practice 3-2

Solving Inequalities Using Addition and Subtraction

Solve each inequality. Graph and check the solution.

1. $n - 7 \geq 2$	**2.** $10 + y > 12$	**3.** $3.2 < r + 4.7$	**4.** $7 + b > 13$
5. $n + \frac{3}{4} > \frac{1}{2}$	**6.** $-\frac{5}{7} \geq c + \frac{2}{7}$	**7.** $g + 4.6 < 5.9$	**8.** $0 > d - 2.7$
9. $f + 4 \geq 14$	**10.** $x + 1 \leq -3$	**11.** $d - 13 \leq -8$	**12.** $m - 7 \geq -8$
13. $12 + v < 19$	**14.** $-4 \leq t + 9$	**15.** $6 < y - 3$	**16.** $a + 15 > 19$
17. $8 + d < 9$	**18.** $s + 3 \leq 3$	**19.** $9 + h \leq 5$	**20.** $7.6 \geq t - 2.4$

Write and solve an inequality that models each situation.

21. It will take at least 360 points for Kiko's team to win the math contest. The scores for Kiko's teammates were 94, 82, and 87, but one of Kiko's teammates lost 2 of those points for an incomplete answer. How many points must Kiko earn for her team to win the contest?

22. This season, Nora has 125 at-bats in softball. By the end of the season she wants to have at least 140 at-bats. How many more at-bats does Nora need to reach her goal?

23. The average wind speed increased 19 mi/h from 8 A.M. to noon. The average wind speed decreased 5 mi/h from noon to 4 P.M. At 4 P.M., the average wind speed was at least 32 mi/h. What is the minimum value of the average wind speed at 8 A.M.?

24. Suppose it takes no more than 25 min for you to get to school. If you have traveled for 13.5 min already, how much longer, at most, might you take to get to school?

25. Joan has started a physical fitness program. One of her goals is to be able to run at least 5 mi without stopping. She can now run 3.5 mi without stopping. How many more miles must she run non-stop to achieve her goal?

26. Suppose you can get a higher interest rate on your savings if you maintain a balance of at least $1000 in your savings account. The balance in your savings account is now $1058. You deposit $44.50 into your account. What is the greatest amount that you can withdraw and still get the higher interest rate?

Solve each inequality. Graph and check the solution.

27. $\frac{3}{4} + z \geq -\frac{3}{4}$	**28.** $12 + d + 3 \leq 10$	**29.** $v - \frac{3}{4} > 1\frac{1}{4}$	**30.** $8 + m > 4$
31. $2 + f > -3$	**32.** $-27 \geq w - 24$	**33.** $b + \frac{1}{2} > \frac{3}{4}$	**34.** $12 + t < 4 - 15$
35. $-14 > -16 + u$	**36.** $-7 \leq -11 + z$	**37.** $38 \geq 33 + b$	**38.** $k - 27 < -29$
39. $a + 8 \leq 10$	**40.** $b + 6 > 17$	**41.** $13 < 8 + k - 6$	**42.** $j + 1.3 > 2.8$

Name ______________________________ Class ______________ Date ______________

Reteaching 3-3

Solving Inequalities Using Multiplication and Division

OBJECTIVE: Using multiplication and division to solve one-step inequalities	**MATERIALS:** Tiles, an index card or piece of paper with $<$ written on it

Example

Use tiles and the card to compare quantities as shown in these steps.

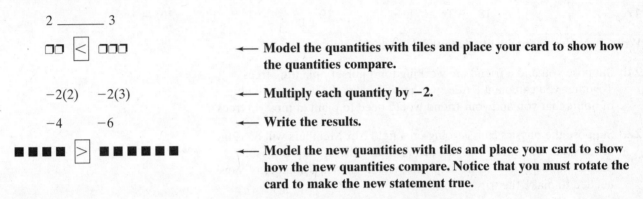

2 ______ 3

□□ $<$ □□□ ⟵ **Model the quantities with tiles and place your card to show how the quantities compare.**

$-2(2)$ $\quad -2(3)$ ⟵ **Multiply each quantity by -2.**

-4 $\quad -6$ ⟵ **Write the results.**

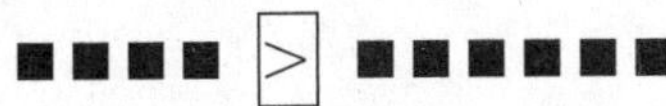

⟵ **Model the new quantities with tiles and place your card to show how the new quantities compare. Notice that you must rotate the card to make the new statement true.**

What happens to the direction of the inequality symbol when you multiply or divide an inequality by a negative number? The direction of the inequality symbol reverses.

Exercises

Model both lines of each exercise with tiles. Use your card to compare the quantities. Then fill in the blanks by writing $<$ or $>$.

1. 2 ______ 4

$-2(2)$ ______ $-2(4)$

2. -3 ______ -2

$-3(-3)$ ______ $-3(-2)$

3. 4 ______ -3

$\frac{4}{-2}$ ______ $\frac{-3}{-2}$

4. 3 ______ -1

$-1(3)$ ______ $-1(-1)$

5. -2 ______ 2

$\frac{-2}{-4}$ ______ $\frac{2}{-4}$

6. -1 ______ -3

$-3(-1)$ ______ $-3(-3)$

Solve and check.

7. $2.5a < 15$

8. $-3b > 21$

9. $6c < 24$

10. $\frac{x}{7} < -2$

11. $-\frac{y}{6} < \frac{2}{3}$

12. $8f > 56$

13. $-4.2d \geq 10.5$

14. $-\frac{2}{3}m \leq 10$

15. $-1.7x > -34$

16. $\frac{n}{8} \leq -2.5$

17. $-1.5k < 2.4$

18. $\frac{3}{5}p \geq -9$

19. $4t > -14$

20. $\frac{z}{15} > -\frac{2}{3}$

21. $-\frac{1}{2}w \leq -3.6$

Name ______________________ Class ______________ Date ____________

Practice 3-3

Solving Inequalities Using Multiplication and Division

Solve each inequality. Graph and check the solution.

1. $\frac{15}{8} \le \frac{5}{2}s$
2. $60 \le 12b$
3. $-\frac{4}{5}r < 8$
4. $\frac{5}{2} < \frac{n}{8}$
5. $-9n \ge -36$
6. $\frac{n}{7} \ge -6$
7. $-7c < 28$
8. $16d > -64$
9. $-\frac{t}{3} < -5$
10. $54 < -6k$
11. $\frac{w}{7} > 0$
12. $2.6v > 6.5$
13. $-4 < -\frac{2}{5}m$
14. $17 < \frac{p}{2}$
15. $0.9 \le -1.8v$
16. $-5 \le -\frac{x}{9}$
17. $-1 \ge \frac{d}{7}$
18. $-3x \ge 21$
19. $\frac{c}{12} < \frac{3}{4}$
20. $\frac{a}{4} \le -1$

Write and solve an inequality that models each situation.

21. Suppose you and a friend are working for a nursery planting trees. Together you can plant 8 trees per hour. What is the greatest number of hours that you and your friend would need to plant at most 40 trees?

22. Suppose the physics club is going on a field trip. Members will be riding in vans that will hold 7 people each including the driver. At least 28 people will be going on the field trip. What is the least number of vans needed to make the trip?

23. You need to buy stamps to mail some letters. The stamps cost \$.34 each. What is the maximum number of stamps that you can buy with \$3.84?

24. The Garcias are putting a brick border along one edge of their flower garden. The flower garden is no more than 31 ft long. If each brick is 6 in. long, what is the greatest number of bricks needed?

25. Janet needs to travel 275 mi for a conference. She needs to be at the conference in no more than 5.5 h. What is the slowest average speed that she can drive and still arrive at the conference on time?

Solve each inequality. Graph and check the solution.

26. $\frac{1}{4}h < 4.9$
27. $\frac{7}{3}x < 21$
28. $-\frac{1}{9}a > 9$
29. $\frac{b}{6} \le 2.5$
30. $-\frac{3}{5}q > 15$
31. $84 \le 21b$
32. $\frac{c}{12} > -\frac{5}{6}$
33. $80.6 \le -6.5b$
34. $-\frac{1}{9}p > \frac{1}{3}$
35. $-9z > 45$
36. $\frac{1}{7}y \le 6$
37. $-\frac{5}{7} > -\frac{k}{14}$
38. $6.8 > \frac{y}{5}$
39. $75 \le 15b$
40. $39 < -13k$
41. $2d < 8.8$
42. $8.5v > 61.2$
43. $-11n \ge -55$
44. $\frac{1}{4}y < 17$
45. $92 < -23k$

Name ______________________ Class ______________ Date ______________

Reteaching 3-4

OBJECTIVE: Solving multi-step inequalities and graphing the solutions on a number line

MATERIALS: None

As you solve multi-step inequalities, keep these strategies in mind.

- Circle all the terms with variables. Then decide on which side of the inequality you are going to collect the variable terms. You may want to select the side that has the variable term with the greatest coefficient.
- Rewrite the inequality by using inverse operations in the same way you solve equations. If you multiply or divide both sides by a negative number, reverse the direction of the inequality symbol.
- Check three values on your graph: the number where the arrow starts, a number to the right of the starting value, and another to the left.

Example

Solve $3x + 2 < 5 + 2x$. Graph and check the solution.

$\bigcirc\!\!\!\!\!3x + 2 < 5 \bigcirc\!\!\!\!\!\!+ 2x$ ← **Circle all the terms with variables.**

$3x \boxed{+2} < \boxed{5} + 2x$ ← **Box all constant terms. Plan your steps to collect variable terms on one side and constant terms on the other.**

$3x + 2 - 2x < 5 + 2x - 2x$ ← **To get variables on the left side, subtract 2x from each side.**

$x + 2 < 5$ ← **Simplify.**

$x + 2 - 2 < 5 - 2$ ← **To get constants on the right side, subtract 2 from each side.**

$x < 3$ ← **Simplify.**

−2 −1 0 1 2 3 4 ← **Graph your solution on a number line. Since 3 is not a solution, use an open circle.**

Check three values for the variable: 0, 3 (where the arrow starts), and 4.

$3(0) + 2 \overset{?}{<} 5 + 2(0)$	$3(3) + 2 \overset{?}{<} 5 + 2(3)$	$3(4) + 2 \overset{?}{<} 5 + 2(4)$
$2 < 5$ ✔	$11 \not< 11$ ✔	$14 \not< 13$ ✔

Exercises

Use circles and boxes to identify the variable and constant terms. Then solve, graph, and check your solution for each inequality.

1. $4x + 3 < 11$

2. $3x + 2 < 2x + 5$

3. $5x + 4 < 14$

4. $4x - 3 < 3x - 1$

5. $3x + 4 > 2x + 3$

6. $2x + 5 > -1$

Name ____________________ Class ____________ Date ____________

Practice 3-4

Solving Multi-Step Inequalities

Solve each inequality. Graph and check the solution.

1. $2z + 7 < z + 10$
2. $4(k - 1) > 4$
3. $1.5 + 2.1y < 1.1y + 4.5$
4. $h + 2(3h + 4) \geq 1$
5. $r + 4 > 13 - 2r$
6. $6u - 18 - 4u < 22$
7. $2(3 + 3g) \geq 2g + 14$
8. $2h - 13 < -3$
9. $-4p + 28 > 8$
10. $8m - 8 \geq 12 + 4m$
11. $5 + 6a > -1$
12. $\frac{1}{2}(2t + 8) \geq 4 + 6t$
13. $-5x + 12 < -18$
14. $2(3f + 2) > 4f + 12$
15. $13t - 8t > -45$
16. $2(c - 4) \leq 10 - c$
17. $\frac{1}{2}t - \frac{1}{3}t > -1$
18. $3.4 + 1.6v < 5.9 - 0.9v$

Write and solve an inequality that models each situation.

19. Ernest works in the shipping department loading shipping crates with boxes. Each empty crate weighs 150 lb. How many boxes, each weighing 35 lb, can Ernest put in the crate if the total weight is to be no more than 850 lb?

20. Beatriz is in charge of setting up a banquet hall. She has five tables that will seat six people each. If no more than 62 people will attend, how many tables seating four people each will she need?

21. Suppose it costs \$5 to enter a carnival. Each ride costs \$1.25. You have \$15 to spend at the carnival. What is the greatest number of rides that you can go on?

22. The cost to rent a car is \$19.50 plus \$.25 per mile. If you have \$44 to rent a car, what is the greatest number of miles that you can drive?

23. The student council is sponsoring a concert as a fund raiser. Tickets are \$3 for students and \$5 for adults. The student council wants to raise at least \$1000. If 200 students attend, how many adults must attend?

Solve each inequality. Check the solution.

24. $-18 < 2(12 - 3b)$
25. $5n + 3 - 4n < -5 - 3n$
26. $36 > 4(2d + 10)$
27. $2(5t - 25) + 5t < -80$
28. $3j + 2 - 2j < -10$
29. $\frac{2}{5}(5x - 15) \geq 4$
30. $7(2z + 3) > 35$
31. $2(3b - 2) < 4b + 8$
32. $\frac{1}{2}y + \frac{1}{4}y \geq -6$
33. $8(3f - 6) < -24$
34. $\frac{3}{4}k < \frac{3}{4} - \frac{1}{4}k$
35. $3(4g - 6) \geq 6(g + 2)$
36. $\frac{1}{2}(2g + 4) > -7$
37. $4(1.25y + 4.2) < 16.8$
38. $38 + 7t > -3(t + 4)$
39. $4(2d + 1) > 28$
40. $4(n - 3) < 2 - 3n$
41. $\frac{3}{4}d - \frac{1}{2} \leq 2\frac{1}{2}$

Reteaching 3-5

Compound Inequalities

OBJECTIVE: Solving compound inequalities and graphing the solutions on a number line	**MATERIALS:** Two highlighting markers in colors that combine to make a third color, for example, blue and yellow or pink and yellow

Before you graph, practice making overlapping lines with your two markers. Notice, for example, that marks from a yellow marker and a blue one overlap to make a green line. A pink line and a yellow line combine to make an orange line. (If you have trouble seeing some colors, ask a partner to help you.)

Example

Solve and graph $-3 < x + 5 \leq 2$.

$-3 < x + 5$ and $x + 5 \leq 2$ ← **Rewrite the compound inequality as two inequalities joined by *and*.**

$-3 - 5 < x + 5 - 5$ and $x + 5 - 5 \leq 2 - 5$

$-8 < x$ and $x \leq -3$ ← **Solve each inequality.**

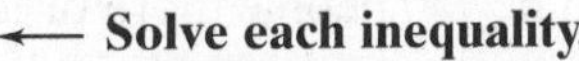

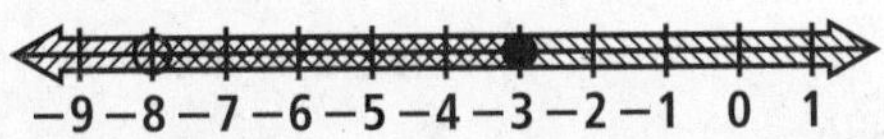

← **Graph the solutions separately on the same number line. Use a blue marker for one arrow ( ) and a yellow marker ( ) for the other. Notice that −8 is colored in only one of the graphs.**

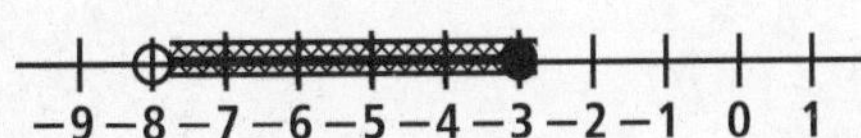

← **Graph the solution set of all the green points ( ). Think: *The green points are blue AND yellow.* This graph shows the solution set for the compound inequality.**

$-8 < x \leq -3$ ← **Write the solution set.**

Exercises

Solve each inequality and graph the solution. Hint: The solution set for *or* statements is all points that are blue or yellow or green.

1. $-3 \leq x - 5$ or $x + 5 \leq 2$
2. $x + 5 \leq 4$ or $-2x < -6$
3. $x - 2 \geq -6$ and $5 + x < 7$
4. $x - 2 \leq -6$ or $5 + x > 7$
5. $-3 \leq x + 1 < 3$
6. $3 \geq \frac{1}{2}x > -2$
7. $-5 \leq 2x - 1 < 7$
8. $3x < -6$ or $4x - 3 \geq 9$
9. $-5x < 15$ or $x \leq -5$
10. $-1 \leq \frac{1}{2}x + 1 < 0$
11. $1 - 2x \leq -5$ or $2x < -10$
12. $-9 < x - 7 \leq 1$

Name ______________________ Class ______________ Date ______________

Practice 3-5

Compound Inequalities

Solve each compound inequality and graph the solution.

1. $-5 < s + 5 < 5$
2. $1 < 3x + 4 < 10$
3. $k - 3 > 1$ or $k - 3 < -1$
4. $b - 2 > 18$ or $3b < 54$
5. $-4d > 8$ and $2d > -6$
6. $-4 < t + 2 < 4$
7. $-3 < 3 + s < 7$
8. $3j \geq 6$ or $3j \leq -6$
9. $-1 < \frac{1}{2}x < 1$
10. $g + 2 > -1$ or $g - 6 < -9$
11. $-6 < 9 + 3y < 6$
12. $3f > 15$ or $2f < -4$
13. $d - 3 > 4$ or $d - 3 < -4$
14. $1 > 2h + 3 > -1$
15. $7 + 2a > 9$ or $-4a > 8$
16. $2z > 2.1$ or $3z < -5.85$
17. $c - 1 \geq 2$ or $c - 1 \leq -2$
18. $h + 2.8 < 1.8$ or $h + 2.8 > 4.8$

Write and solve a compound inequality that represents each situation. Graph your solution.

19. The crowd that heard the President speak was estimated to be 10,000 people. The actual crowd could be 750 people more or less than this. What are the possible values for the actual crowd size?
20. Susie has designed an exercise program for herself. One part of the program requires her to walk between 25 and 30 miles each week. She plans to walk the same distance each day five days a week. What is the range of miles that she should walk each day?
21. A box of cereal must weigh more than 629.4 g and less than 630.6 g to pass inspection. The box in which the cereal is packaged weighs 5.5 g. What are the possible weights for the cereal?
22. Carmen works in a sporting goods store. Her goal is to sell between \$500 and \$600 worth of sporting equipment every week. So far this week, she has sold \$395 worth of equipment. During the rest of the week, what dollar amount must Carmen sell in order to reach her goal?

Solve each compound inequality and graph the solution.

23. $2n - 1 \geq 1$ or $2n - 1 \leq -1$
24. $2k - 3 > 3$ or $2k - 3 < -3$
25. $-1 < h - 2 < 1$
26. $2.2 + p > 1$ and $1.5p < -0.3$
27. $9 < x + 2 < 11$
28. $5m + 8 < 23$ or $6m > 48$
29. $-3 \leq \frac{3}{2}x + 6 \leq 3$
30. $7 > 5 - x > 6$
31. $\frac{1}{2}x + 1 > 1$ or $\frac{1}{2}x + 1 < -1$
32. $-2 \leq s - 4 \leq 2$
33. $w - 3 > 4$ or $w - 3 < -4$
34. $6 > 4x - 2 > -6$
35. $t + 5 < 2$ or $3t + 1 > 10$
36. $2g > 12$ and $3g < 24$
37. $6x - 3 \geq 3$ or $6x - 3 \leq -3$
38. $2y - 3 > -1$ or $5 - y > 4$

Name ______________________ Class ______________ Date ______________

Reteaching 3-6

Absolute Value Equations and Inequalities

OBJECTIVE: Solving absolute value inequalities **MATERIALS:** None

The absolute value of a real number x, written $|x|$, is the distance of x from 0 on the real number line.

An inequality such as $|x| < k$, where k is a positive real number, is true for values of x that are less than k units from 0 on the number line. These are the numbers between $-k$ and k on the number line. Thus, x is a solution of $|x| < k$ whenever $-k < x < k$.

An inequality such as $|x| > k$, where k is a positive real number, is true for values of x that are more than k units from 0 on the number line. These are the numbers to the left of $-k$ and to the right of k on the number line. Thus, x is a solution of $|x| > k$ whenever $x < -k$ or $x > k$.

Example

Solve each inequality and graph the solution.

a. $|t + 3| < 4$ ← **The inequality is in the form $|x| < k$.**

$-4 < t + 3 < 4$ ← **Replace the form $|x| < k$ with the form $-k < x < k$. Here the expression $t + 3$ is in the place of x and $k = 4$.**

$-7 < t < 1$ ← **Subtract 3 from each part of the inequality.**

−8 −7 −6 −5 −4 −3 −2 −1 0 1 2

b. $|2y + 1| \geq 3$ ← **The inequality is in the form $|x| \geq k$.**

$2y + 1 \leq -3$ or $2y + 1 \geq 3$ ← **Replace the form $|x| \geq k$ with the form $x \leq -k$ or $x \geq k$. Here the expression $2y + 1$ is in the place of x and $k = 3$.**

$2y \leq -4$ or $2y \geq 2$ ← **Subtract 1 from each side of each inequality.**

$y \leq -2$ or $y \geq 1$ ← **Divide each side of each inequality by 2.**

−5 −4 −3 −2 −1 0 1 2 3 4 5

Exercises

Solve each inequality and graph the solution.

1. $|c| < 5$

2. $|u| \geq 1$

3. $|a + 1| \leq 2$

4. $|3m - 2| > 1$

5. $\left|\frac{1}{2}y - 3\right| \geq \frac{1}{2}$

6. $|2n + 1| < 7$

7. $|4 - 2u| \leq 8$

8. $|2g + 5| > 3$

9. $|1 - 2y| \geq 9$

Name ____________________ Class ____________ Date ____________

Practice 3-6

Absolute Value Equations and Inequalities

Solve each inequality. Graph the solution.

1. $|d| > 2$
2. $|h| > 6$
3. $|2k| > 8$
4. $|s + 4| > 2$
5. $|3c - 6| \geq 3$
6. $|2n + 3| \leq 5$
7. $|3.5z| > |7|$
8. $\left|\frac{2}{3}x\right| \leq 4$
9. $9 > |6 + 3t|$
10. $|j| - 2 \geq 6$
11. $5 > |v + 2| + 3$
12. $|4y + 11| < 7$
13. $|2n - 1| \geq 1$
14. $\left|\frac{1}{2}x + 1\right| > 1$
15. $-2|h - 2| > -2$
16. $3|2x| \leq 12$
17. $3|s - 4| + 21 \leq 27$
18. $-6|w - 3| < -24$
19. $-\frac{1}{2}|6x - 3| \leq -\frac{3}{2}$
20. $-2|3j| - 8 \leq -20$

Solve each equation. If there is no solution, write *no solution.*

21. $|a| = 9.5$
22. $|b| = -2$
23. $|d| - 25 = -13$
24. $|6z| + 3 = 21$
25. $|3c| - 45 = -18$
26. $-2 = -\frac{|z|}{7}$
27. $|x| = -0.8$
28. $-4|7 + d| = -44$

Write and solve an absolute value equation or inequality that represents each situation.

29. The average number of cucumber seeds in a package is 25. The number of seeds in the package can vary by three. Find the range of acceptable numbers of seeds in each package.

30. The mean distance of the earth from the sun is 93 million miles. The distance varies by 1.6 million miles. Find the range of distances of the earth from the sun.

31. Leona was in a golf tournament last week. All four of her rounds of golf were within 2 strokes of par. If par was 72, find the range of scores that Leona could have shot for each round of the golf tournament.

32. Victor's goal is to earn $75 per week at his after-school job. Last month he was within $6.50 of his goal. Find the range of amounts that Victor might have earned last month.

33. Members of the track team can run 400 m in an average time of 58.2 s. The fastest and slowest times vary from the average by 6.4 s. Find the range of times for the track team.

34. The ideal length of a particular metal rod is 25.5 cm. The measured length may vary from the ideal length by at most 0.025 cm. Find the range of acceptable lengths for the rod.

35. When measured on a particular scale, the weight of an object may vary from its actual weight by at most 0.4 lb. If the reading on the scale is 125.2 lb, find the range of actual weights of the object.

36. One poll reported that the approval rating of the job performance of the President of the United States was 63%. The poll was said to be accurate to within 3.8%. What is the range of actual approval ratings?

Name ______________________ Class ______________ Date ______________

Reteaching 4-1

Ratio and Proportion

OBJECTIVE: Solving proportions **MATERIALS:** None

An equation that states that two ratios are equal is called a proportion. In a proportion, the cross products are equal.

Example

Use cross products to find out if the proportion $\frac{2}{7} = \frac{10}{40}$ is true.

$\frac{2}{7} = \frac{10}{40}$

$2 \cdot 40 = 7 \cdot 10$ ⟵ **Write cross products.**

$80 = 70$ ⟵ **Simplify.**

$80 \neq 70$ ⟵ **Proportion is not true since 80 does not equal 70.**

Use cross products to write and solve equations involving proportions.

Solve: $\frac{5}{6} = \frac{25}{x}$

$\frac{5}{6} = \frac{25}{x}$ ⟵ **The cross products are $5x$ and $6 \cdot 25$ or 150.**

$5x = 6 \cdot 25$ ⟵ **Set cross products equal to each other.**

$5x = 150$ ⟵ **Simplify.**

$\frac{5x}{5} = \frac{150}{5}$ ⟵ **Use the Division Property of Equality.**

$x = 30$ ⟵ **Simplify.**

Exercises

Determine if the proportions are true. (Hint: the cross products should be equal.)

1. $\frac{6}{10} = \frac{12}{20}$
2. $\frac{4}{5} = \frac{7}{8}$
3. $\frac{33}{22} = \frac{24}{16}$

Solve each proportion.

4. $\frac{x}{5} = \frac{2}{10}$
5. $\frac{9}{180} = \frac{n}{60}$
6. $\frac{2}{x} = \frac{8}{36}$
7. $\frac{2}{6} = \frac{4}{x}$
8. $\frac{30}{125} = \frac{n}{100}$
9. $\frac{3}{18} = \frac{t}{6}$
10. $\frac{t}{5} = \frac{3}{5}$
11. $\frac{28}{8} = \frac{7}{x}$
12. $\frac{9}{n} = \frac{18}{2}$

Name ______________________ Class ______________ Date ______________

Practice 4-1

Ratio and Proportion

Find each unit rate.

1. \$60 for 8 h
2. $\frac{\$3}{4 \text{ lb}}$
3. $\frac{861 \text{ bagels}}{3 \text{ d}}$
4. $\frac{850 \text{ cal}}{1.25 \text{ h}}$
5. An 8-ounce bottle of lotion costs \$4.50. What is the cost per ounce?
6. A pound of coffee costs \$14.99. What is the cost per ounce?

Which pairs of ratios could form a proportion? Justify your answer.

7. $\frac{10}{24}, \frac{7}{18}$
8. $\frac{6}{9}, \frac{10}{15}$
9. $\frac{3}{4}, \frac{18}{24}$
10. $\frac{16}{2}, \frac{8}{1}$
11. $-\frac{4.8}{4}, -\frac{6.4}{5}$

Solve each proportion.

12. $\frac{g}{5} = \frac{6}{10}$
13. $\frac{z}{4} = \frac{7}{8}$
14. $\frac{13.2}{6} = \frac{m}{12}$
15. $-\frac{m}{5} = -\frac{2}{5}$
16. $\frac{5.5}{11} = \frac{x}{5}$
17. $-\frac{2}{3} = -\frac{10}{t}$
18. $\frac{4}{6} = \frac{x}{24}$
19. $\frac{s}{3} = \frac{7}{10}$
20. $\frac{4}{9} = \frac{10}{r}$
21. $\frac{x}{4.8} = \frac{6}{3.2}$
22. $\frac{5}{4} = \frac{c}{12}$
23. $-\frac{32}{h} = -\frac{1}{3}$
24. $\frac{2}{6} = \frac{p}{9}$
25. $\frac{f}{6} = \frac{3}{4}$
26. $\frac{15}{a} = \frac{3}{8}$
27. $\frac{3}{4} = \frac{k}{24}$
28. $\frac{a}{6} = \frac{3}{9}$
29. $\frac{4}{5} = \frac{k}{9}$
30. $\frac{3}{y} = \frac{5}{8}$
31. $\frac{t}{7} = \frac{9}{21}$
32. $\frac{2}{9} = \frac{10}{x}$
33. $\frac{x}{15} = \frac{3}{4}$
34. $\frac{18}{11} = \frac{49.5}{x}$
35. $\frac{2}{1.2} = \frac{5}{x}$
36. $-\frac{x-1}{4} = \frac{2}{3}$
37. $\frac{3}{6} = \frac{x-3}{8}$
38. $\frac{2x-2}{14} = \frac{2x-4}{6}$
39. $\frac{x+2}{x-2} = \frac{4}{8}$
40. $\frac{x+2}{6} = \frac{x-1}{12}$
41. $-\frac{x+8}{10} = -\frac{x-3}{2}$
42. You are riding your bicycle. It takes you 28 min to go 8 mi. If you continue traveling at the same rate, how long will it take you to go 15 mi?
43. Suppose you traveled 84 mi in 1.5 h. Moving at the same speed, how many mi would you cover in $3\frac{1}{4}$ h?
44. A canary's heart beats 130 times in 12 s. Use a proportion to find how many times its heart beats in 50 s.
45. Your car averages 18 mi per gal on the highway. If gas costs \$1.85 per gal, how much does it cost in dollars per mi to drive your car on the highway?

Name ______________________ Class ______________ Date ______________

Reteaching 4-2

Proportions and Similar Figures

OBJECTIVE: Finding missing measures of similar figures

MATERIALS: None

Setting up a proportion can help determine the missing lengths from similar figures. Remember the following:

- Always compare corresponding sides when writing the ratios.
- Be consistent by keeping sides of the same figure either in the denominators or numerators.

Example

$\triangle ABC \sim \triangle DEF$
Find the length of x.

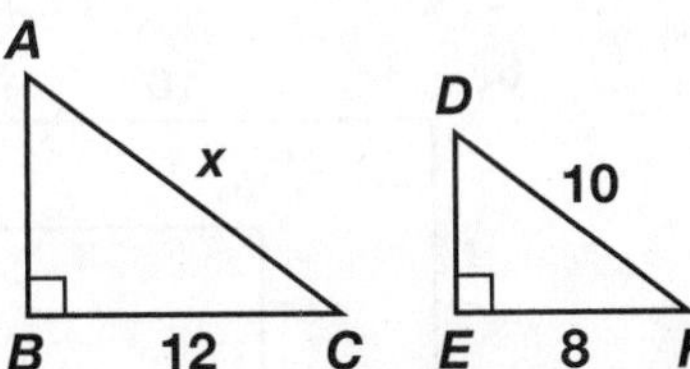

BC corresponds to EF
AC corresponds to DF

$\frac{AC}{DF} = \frac{BC}{EF}$ ⟵ **Notice the numerators, AC and BC, are sides of the same triangle.**

$\frac{x}{10} = \frac{12}{8}$ ⟵ **Substitute appropriate values.**

$8x = 10 \cdot 12$ ⟵ **Write the cross products.**

$\frac{8x}{8} = \frac{120}{8}$ ⟵ **Divide each side by 8.**

$x = 15$ ⟵ **Simplify.**

Exercises

Find the length of x.

1. $\triangle TUV \sim \triangle QUP$

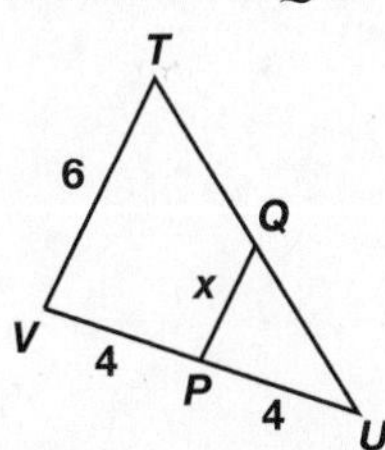

2. $\triangle KLM \sim \triangle KHJ$

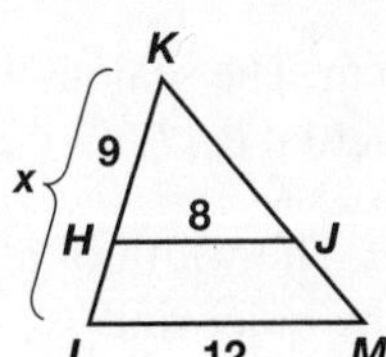

3. $\triangle PQR \sim \triangle MNP$

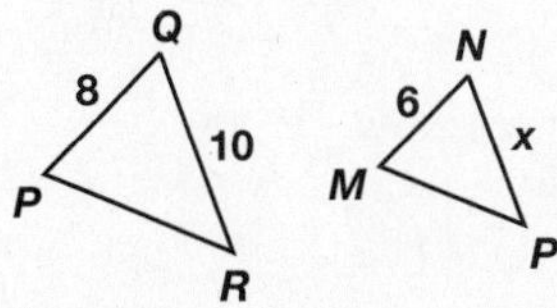

4. $\triangle ABC \sim \triangle DEF$

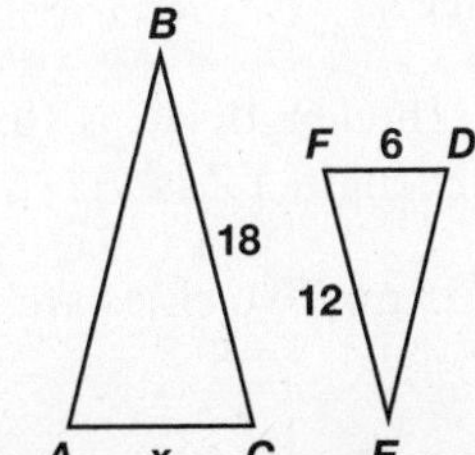

Name ______________________ Class ______________ Date ______________

Practice 4-2

Proportions and Similar Figures

Each pair of figures is similar. Find the length of *x*.

1. 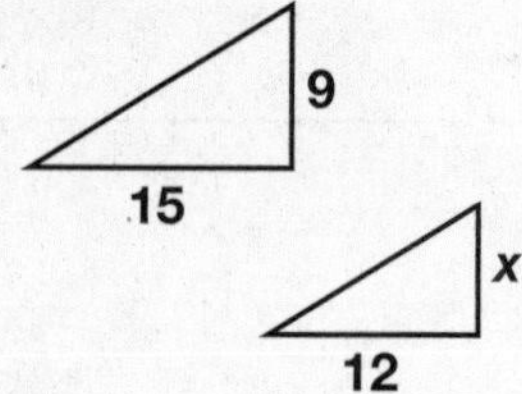

2. 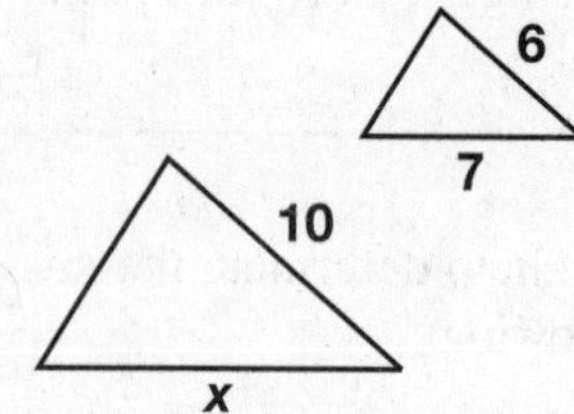

3. 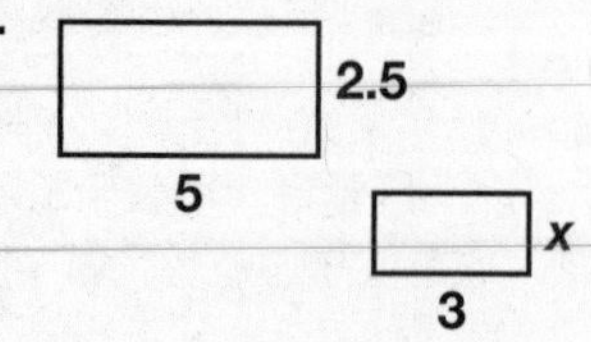

4. 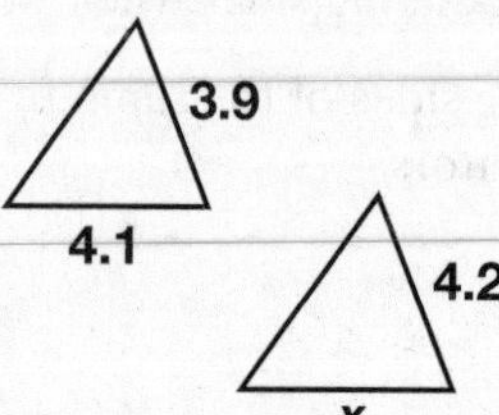

5. 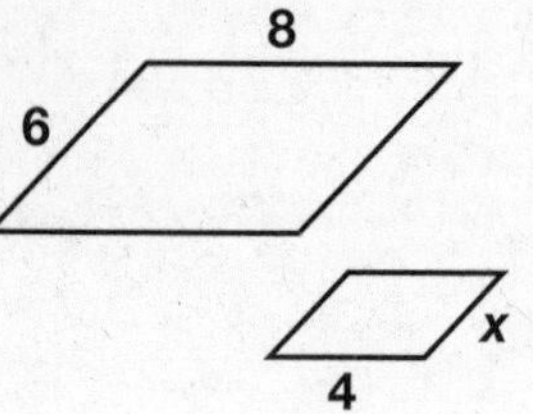

6. 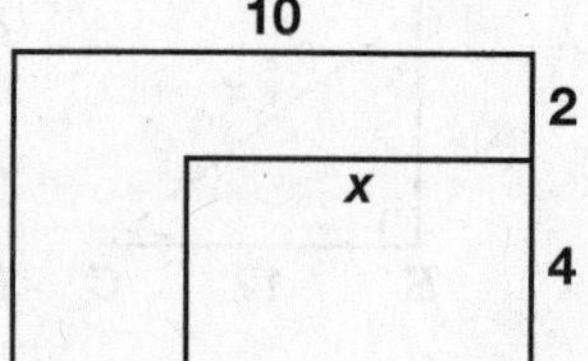

7. 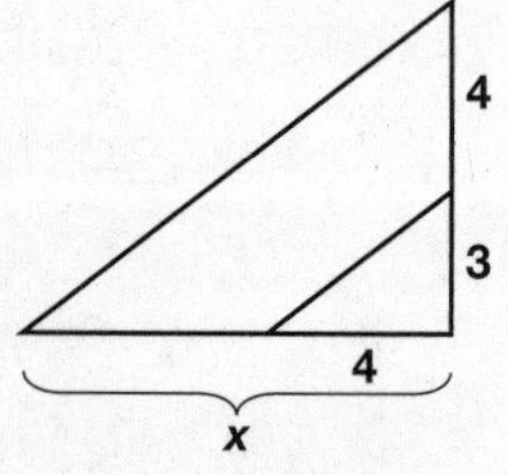

8. 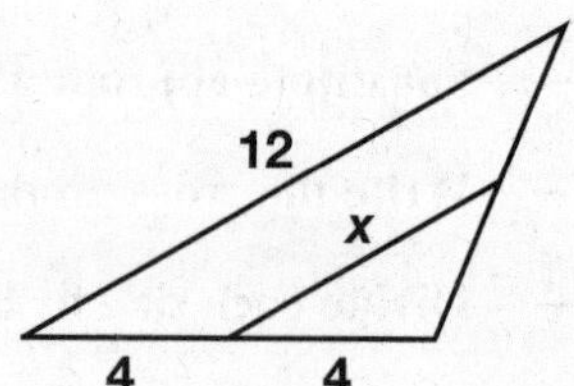

Use a proportion to solve.

9. $\triangle ABC$ is similar to $\triangle XYZ$. The length AB is 10. The length BC is 7. Find the length XY if the length YZ is 14.

10. Marty has a scale model of a car. The scale is 1 in. : 32 in. If the model is 6.75 in. long, how long is the actual car?

11. A blueprint scale is 1 in. : 12 ft. The width of a building is 48 ft. What is the width of the building on the blueprint?

12. Angie is using similar triangles to find the height of a tree. A stick that is 5 ft tall casts a shadow that is 4 ft long. The tree casts a shadow that is 22 ft long. How tall is the tree?

13. $\triangle ABC$ is similar to $\triangle XYZ$. The length AC is 10. The length BC is 16. What is the length XZ if the length YZ is 12?

14. A map has a scale of 1 in. : 25 mi. Two cities are 175 mi apart. How far apart are they on the map?

Name ______________ Class ______________ Date ______________

Reteaching 4-3

Proportions and Percent Equations

OBJECTIVE: Using equations to solve problems involving percents

MATERIALS: None

To solve percent problems, you can often represent words with math symbols. This table shows some words and the symbols you can use to represent them.

word	what	is	of
symbol	n (or another variable)	=	×

Example

What is 30% of 20?

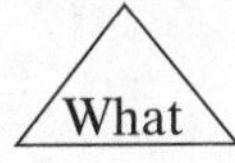

What [is] 30% (of) 20? ← **Draw a triangle around the word that represents the variable. Draw a rectangle around the word that represents =. Circle the word that represents ×.**

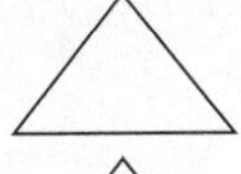

[ ] 30% ( ) 20? ← **Copy just the shapes and numbers, including percent.**

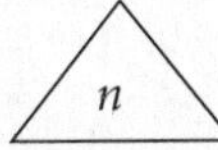

n [=] 0.30 (×) 20 ← **Inside each shape, represent the word with the correct symbol. Rewrite percents as decimals.**

$n = 0.30 \times 20$ ← **Write the equation.**

$n = 6$ ← **Solve the equation.**

30% of 20 is 6. ← **Answer the question.**

Exercises

Use rectangles, circles, and triangles to rewrite and answer each question.

1. What is 10% of 50?

2. 8 is 40% of what?

3. 25 is what percent of 100?

4. 7 is what percent of 35?

5. What is 30% of 50?

6. 3 is 25% of what?

7. 0.4 is what percent of 0.8?

8. What is 25% of 25?

9. What is 25% of $\frac{4}{7}$?

10. Kamala is 15 years old and her brother is 20. Kamala's age is what percent of her brother's?

11. Luis worked 12 h at the school library. That represents 25% of the total hours he has voluteered to work. How many hours has he volunteered to work?

12. The sales tax rate is 6%. What is the sales tax on $55?

Name ______________________ Class ______________________ Date ______________________

Practice 4-3

Proportions and Percent Equations

Solve each problem.

1. 25% of what is 28?
2. What percent of 72 is 18?
3. 60% of what is 45?
4. What percent of 12 is 6?
5. What is 60% of 12?
6. 75% of what is 48?
7. What is 20% of 650?
8. What percent of 150 is 90?
9. What percent of 90 is 63?
10. What is 38% of 60?
11. 22.5% of what is 42?
12. 45% of what is 99?
13. What percent of 210 is 10.5?
14. 160% of what is 124?
15. What is 39% of 1500?
16. What is 250% of 14?
17. What percent of 20 is 36?
18. What is 8.25% of 160?

Write an equation to model each question and solve.

19. Pablo has a goal to lose 25 lb. He has lost 16 lb. What percent of his goal has he reached?
20. You spent 16% of your vacation money on food. If you spent $48 on food, how much money did you spend on your vacation?
21. A writer earns $3400 a month. Last month she spent $204 on food. What percent of her income was spent on food?
22. Kiko spends 30% of her monthly income on rent. If she pays $810 for rent each month, what is her monthly income?
23. Suppose that 62.5% of freshmen entering a college graduate from it. If there are 2680 freshmen, how many will graduate from that college?

The formula for determining simple interest is $I = prt$. Using this formula, solve the following problems.

24. You invest $1500 for three years. Find the amount of simple interest you earn at an annual rate of 8.25%.
25. Suppose you invested $1200 for four years. You earned $312 in simple interest. What is the interest rate?
26. Suppose you invested some money at 8% simple interest for five years. If you received $500 in interest, how much money did you invest?

Write an equation to model each question and solve.

27. What is 7% of 480?
28. What percent of 80 is 48?
29. 90% of what is 27?
30. What is 150% of 26?
31. 125% of what is 175?
32. What is 10.25% of 280?
33. What is 35% of 360?
34. What percent of 36 is 9?
35. 75% of what is 90?
36. 45% of what is 36?
37. What is 80% of 120?
38. What percent of 20 is 8?
39. 25% of what is 92?
40. What percent of 30 is 90?
41. What is 39% of 800?

Name ______________________ Class ______________ Date ____________

Reteaching 4-4

Percent of Change

OBJECTIVE: Finding percent of change	**MATERIALS:** About 35 counters such as beans or paper clips

Use this ratio to find the percent of change from an original amount to a new amount:

$$\text{percent of change} = \frac{\text{amount of change}}{\text{original amount}}$$

Example

Jana's pay changed from $6/h to $7/h. Find the percent of change in her pay and whether it is a percent of increase or of decrease.

original amount **new amount** ← **Divide your paper into two areas, labeled "original amount" on the left and "new amount" on the right.**

← **Place 6 counters to represent $6 under the original amount and 7 counters under the new amount.**

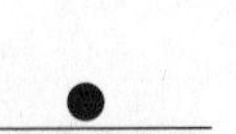

← **Find the difference between the amount of counters on the left and on the right.**

← **Put the counters representing the difference (amount of change) over the counters representing the original amount.**

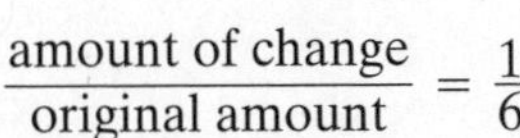

$\frac{\text{amount of change}}{\text{original amount}} = \frac{1}{6}$ ← **Write the ratio represented by the counters.**

The percent of increase is 16.67%. ← **Write the ratio as a percent.**

More counters under the original amount represents a percent of decrease.
More counters under the new amount represents a percent of increase.

Exercises

Use counters to find each percent of change. Describe the percent as an increase or decrease. Round percents to the nearest integer.

1. 8 in. to 12 in. **2.** 7 min to 5 min **3.** $3 to $4 **4.** 2 lb to 4 lb

Find each percent of change. Describe the percent as an increase or decrease. Round percents to the nearest integer.

5. Today eight students leave your classroom.

6. You put 5 pencils in a box that already has 12 pencils.

7. The length of a shadow changes from 75 feet to 65 feet.

Name ______________________ Class ______________ Date ____________

Practice 4-4

Percent of Change

Find each percent of change. Describe the percent of change as an increase or decrease. Round to the nearest whole number.

1. 36 g to 27 g
2. 40 cm to 100 cm
3. 90 in. to 45 in.
4. 500 lb to 1500 lb
5. \$90 to \$84.50
6. \$100 to \$140
7. \$15 to \$5.50
8. 100 mi to 175 mi
9. 280 m to 320 m
10. 58 to 76
11. 60 to 150
12. 600 mi to 480 mi
13. 18 to 27
14. 290 yd to 261 yd
15. 26.2 to 22.8
16. \$8.50 to \$12.75
17. $36\frac{1}{2}$ to $29\frac{1}{4}$
18. $74\frac{3}{4}$ to $66\frac{1}{2}$
19. $6\frac{3}{4}$ to $8\frac{1}{4}$
20. $15\frac{1}{2}$ to $18\frac{1}{4}$

Find each percent of change. Describe the percent of change as an increase or decrease. Round to the nearest whole number.

21. In 1985, the average price for gasoline was \$1.20/gal. In 2000, the average price for gasoline was \$1.56. Find the percent of change.
22. In 1980, Texas had 27 U.S. Representatives. That number increased to 30 in 2000. Find the percent of change.
23. In 1980, the average annual tuition charge for a four-year public university was \$840. The average annual tuition charge in 2000 was \$3356. What is the percent of change?
24. The United States imported 6,909,000 barrels of oil per day in 1980. In 2000, the United States imported 11,459,000 barrels of oil per day. What is the percent of change?
25. In 1977, the average number of households with cable television was 16.6%. In 2000, the average number of households with cable television was 68%. What is the percent of change?
26. In 1989, there were 38,000 licensed drivers under the age of 16. In 1999, the total number of licensed drivers under 16 was 33,248. Find the percent of change.
27. In 1990, Atlanta, GA, failed to meet air quality standards on 42 days. In 1999, Atlanta failed to meet air quality standards on 61 days. What is the percent of change?

Find the greatest possible error and the percent error for each measurement.

28. 3 cm
29. 0.5 cm
30. 6 cm
31. 16 in.
32. 36.85 g
33. 0.9 cm

Find the minimum and maximum possible areas for rectangles with the following measurements.

34. 8 cm × 10 cm
35. 3 in. × 5 in.
36. 8 m × 12 m

Find the minimum and maximum possible volume for a rectangular solid with the following measurements.

37. 16 in. × 22 in. × 18 in.
38. 13 cm × 15 cm × 18 cm
39. 3 m × 4 m × 5 m

Name ______________________ Class ______________ Date ____________

Reteaching 4-5

Applying Ratios to Probability

OBJECTIVE: Finding probability **MATERIALS:** None

The possible results of an experiment are **outcomes**. If you want to find the theoretical probability of a particular event, or a **favorable outcome**, you use this formula.

$$P(\text{event}) = \frac{\text{number of favorable outcomes}}{\text{number of possible outcomes}}$$

Example

Twenty-four students in your homeroom placed lunch orders today. The list sent to the cafeteria is shown at the right. If a student is randomly selected from your class, what is the probability that the student ordered pizza or a hamburger?

Pizza	9
Taco	3
Hot dog	4
Hamburger	6
Tuna sandwich	2

$$P(\text{pizza or hambuger}) = \frac{\text{number of favorable outcomes}}{\text{number of possible outcomes}}$$

$$= \frac{9 \text{ (number of pizza orders)} + 6 \text{ (number of hamburger orders)}}{24 \text{ (total number of orders)}}$$

$$= \frac{15}{24}$$

$$= \frac{5}{8}$$

Exercises

You are fishing in a pond stocked with fish. The table at the right shows a recent fish count. Find each probability.

Sunfish	90
Crappie	33
Smallmouth bass	15
Largemouth bass	12
Total	150

1. P(sunfish)
2. P(smallmouth bass)
3. P(largemouth bass)
4. P(sunfish or crappie)
5. P(catfish)
6. P(not a sunfish)
7. P(not a crappie or not a sunfish)
8. P(sunfish or smallmouth bass)
9. P(catfish or largemouth bass)
10. P(smallmouth or largemouth bass)

Name ______________________ Class ______________ Date ____________

Practice 4-5

Applying Ratios to Probability

A driver collected data on how long it takes to drive to work.

Time in minutes	20	25	30
Number of trips	4	8	2

1. Find P(the trip will take 25 min).
2. Find P(the trip will take 20 min).
3. Find P(the trip will take at least 25 min).

Use the data in the line plot to find each probability.

Student Birth Months

JAN	FEB	MAR	APR	MAY	JUN	JUL	AUG	SEP	OCT	NOV	DEC
					X						X
X		X			X				X		X
X		X			X	X		X	X		X
X	X	X	X		X	X	X	X	X	X	X

4. P(June)
5. P(October)
6. P(first six months of year)
7. P(May)
8. P(not December)
9. P(last three months of year)

A cereal manufacturer selects 100 boxes of cereal at random. Ninety-nine of the boxes are the correct weight. Find each probability.

10. P(the cereal box is the correct weight)
11. P(the cereal box is not the correct weight)
12. There are 24,000 boxes of cereal. Predict how many of the boxes are the correct weight.
13. One letter is chosen at random from the word *ALGEBRA*. Find each probability.
    - **a.** P(the letter is A)
    - **b.** P(the letter is a vowel)
14. Patrice has a 40% chance of making a free throw. What is the probability that she will miss the free throw?
15. A box of animal crackers contains five hippos, two lions, three zebras, and four elephants. Find the probability if one animal cracker is chosen at random.
    - **a.** P(a hippo)
    - **b.** P(not an elephant)
    - **c.** P(an elephant or a lion)
16. Anthony is making a collage for his art class by picking shapes randomly. He has five squares, two triangles, two ovals, and four circles. Find each probability.
    - **a.** P(circle is chosen first)
    - **b.** P(a square is not chosen first)
    - **c.** P(a triangle or a square is chosen first)

Name ______________________ Class ______________ Date ______________

Reteaching 4-6

Probability of Compound Events

OBJECTIVE: Finding the probability of independent and dependent events

MATERIALS: Colored counters and a small bag

To find the probability of two events that are **independent** (the probability of the first **does not** affect the second), multiply the probabilities of the events.

$$P(A \text{ and } B) = P(A) \cdot P(B)$$

To find the probability of two events that are **dependent** (the probability of the first **does** affect the second), multiply the probability of the first by the probability of the second happening after the first.

$$P(A \text{ then } B) = P(A) \cdot P(B \text{ after } A)$$

Examples

A bag contains 6 white counters, 5 red counters, and 19 counters of other colors.

A. Find the probability of choosing a white and then a red counter if you **replace** the first counter before choosing the second counter.

$P(A) = P(\text{white}) = \text{total number} \ldots\ldots = \frac{6}{30} \text{ or } \frac{1}{5}$

$P(B) = P(\text{red}) = \text{total number} \ldots\ldots = \frac{5}{30} \text{ or } \frac{1}{6}$

$P(A \text{ and } B) = \frac{1}{5} \cdot \frac{1}{6} = \frac{1}{30}$

The probability of choosing a white and then a red counter (with replacing the first counter) is $\frac{1}{30}$.

B. Find the probability of choosing a white and then a red counter if you **do not replace** the first counter before choosing the second counter.

$P(A) = P(\text{white}) = \text{total number} \ldots\ldots = \frac{6}{30} \text{ or } \frac{1}{5}$

$P(B) = P(\text{red}) = \text{total number} \ldots\ldots = \frac{5}{29}$

$P(A \text{ and } B) = \frac{1}{5} \cdot \frac{5}{29} = \frac{1}{29}$

The probability of choosing a white and then a red counter (without replacing the first counter) is $\frac{1}{29}$.

Exercises

Choose counters of two colors, *A* and *B*. Write down the number of each, and put them in a bag.

1. Find the probability of choosing a counter of color *A* and then a counter of color *B* if you replace the first before you pick the second.

2. Find the probability of choosing a counter of color *A* and then a counter of color *B* if you do not replace the first pick.

Name ____________________ Class ____________ Date ____________

Practice 4-6

Probability of Compound Events

1. Suppose you have a dark closet containing seven blue shirts, five yellow shirts, and eight white shirts. You pick two shirts from the closet. Find each probability.
   - a. P(blue then yellow) with replacing
   - b. P(blue then yellow) without replacing
   - c. P(yellow then yellow) with replacing
   - d. P(yellow then yellow) without replacing
   - e. P(yellow then white) with replacing
   - f. P(yellow then white) without replacing
   - g. P(blue then blue) with replacing
   - h. P(blue then blue) without replacing

A and B are independent events. Find the missing probability.

2. $P(A) = \frac{3}{7}$, $P(A \text{ and } B) = \frac{1}{3}$. Find $P(B)$.
3. $P(B) = \frac{1}{5}$, $P(A \text{ and } B) = \frac{2}{13}$. Find $P(A)$.
4. $P(B) = \frac{15}{16}$, $P(A \text{ and } B) = \frac{3}{4}$. Find $P(A)$.
5. $P(A) = \frac{8}{15}$, $P(B) = \frac{3}{4}$. Find $P(A \text{ and } B)$.
6. Suppose you draw two tennis balls from a bag containing seven pink, four white, three yellow, and two striped balls. Find each probability.
   - a. P(yellow then pink) with replacing
   - b. P(yellow then pink) without replacing
   - c. P(pink then pink) with replacing
   - d. P(pink then pink) without replacing
   - e. P(striped then striped) with replacing
   - f. P(striped then striped) without replacing
   - g. P(pink then white) with replacing
   - h. P(pink then white) without replacing

A and B are independent events. Find the missing probability.

7. $P(A) = \frac{3}{4}$, $P(A \text{ and } B) = \frac{1}{2}$. Find $P(B)$.
8. $P(A) = \frac{3}{7}$, $P(B) = \frac{1}{6}$. Find $P(A \text{ and } B)$.
9. $P(B) = \frac{9}{10}$, $P(A \text{ and } B) = \frac{3}{5}$. Find $P(A)$.
10. $P(B) = \frac{1}{4}$, $P(A \text{ and } B) = \frac{3}{20}$. Find $P(A)$.

Use an equation to solve each problem.

11. A bag contains green and yellow color tiles. You pick two tiles without replacing the first one. The probability that the first tile is yellow is $\frac{3}{5}$. The probability of drawing two yellow tiles is $\frac{12}{35}$. Find the probability that the second tile you pick is yellow.
12. A bag contains red and blue marbles. You pick two marbles without replacing the first one. The probability of drawing a blue and then a red is $\frac{4}{15}$. The probability that your second marble is red if your first marble is blue is $\frac{2}{3}$. Find the probability that the first marble is blue.

Name ______________________ Class ______________ Date ______________

Reteaching 5-1

Relating Graphs to Events

OBJECTIVE: Interpreting and sketching graphs from stories

MATERIALS: None

When you draw a graph without actual data, the graph is called a sketch. A sketch gives you an idea of what the graph will look like. Use the description and the sketch to answer the questions.

Example

Kira rides her bike to the park to meet a friend. When she arrives at the park, Kira and her friend sit on the bench and talk for a while. Kira then rides her bike home at a slower pace.

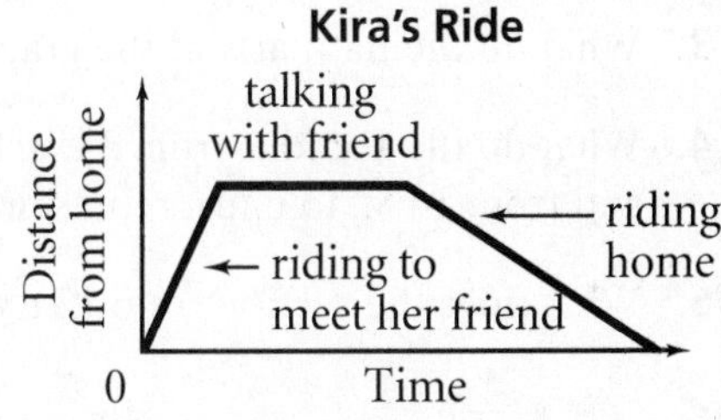

1. What does the vertical scale show?
   It shows distance from home.

2. What does the horizontal scale show?
   It shows time.

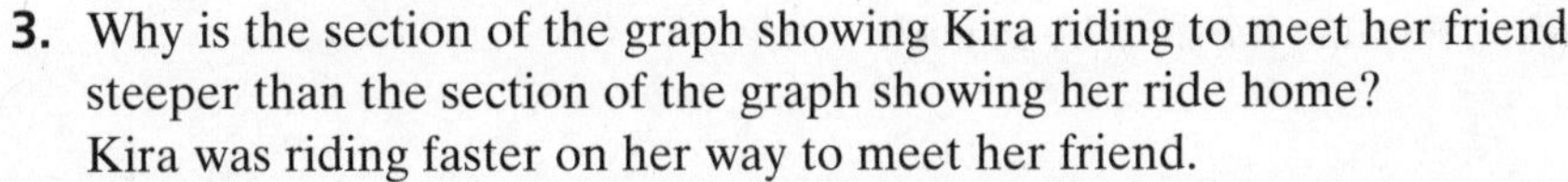

3. Why is the section of the graph showing Kira riding to meet her friend steeper than the section of the graph showing her ride home?
   Kira was riding faster on her way to meet her friend.

4. Why is the section of the graph flat when Kira is talking to her friend?
   Kira's distance from home is not changing, but time is still passing.

Exercises

To take photographs of the area where you live for a school project, you ride your bike to the top of Lookout Knoll. The road leading to the top is steep. When you arrive at the top, you rest and take some photographs. On the way back down the same road, you stop to take photographs from another location.

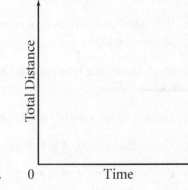

Total Distance

0 Time

1. What does the vertical scale show?

2. What does the horizontal scale show?

3. Draw a sketch of the trip comparing the distance you traveled to time. Label the sections.

4. Which parts of the graph represent your taking photographs? Explain.

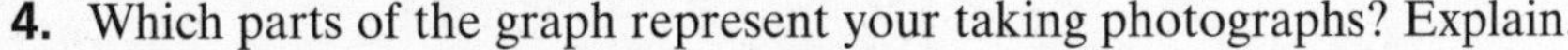

5. Which part of the graph is steeper, your ride to the top of Lookout Knoll or your ride down? Explain.

6. Suppose the vertical axis represents distance from the base of Lookout Knoll. With all other information remaining the same, draw a sketch of the trip comparing distance from the base of Lookout Knoll to time. Label the sections.

Name ______________________ Class ______________ Date ______________

Practice 5-1

Relating Graphs to Events

The graph shows the speed a student traveled on the way to school.

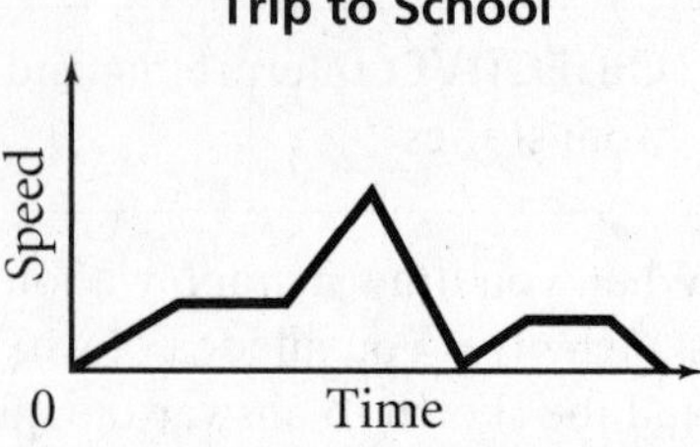

1. What do the flat parts of the graph represent?

2. Circle the sections of the graph that show the speed decreasing.

The graph shows the relationship between time and distance from home.

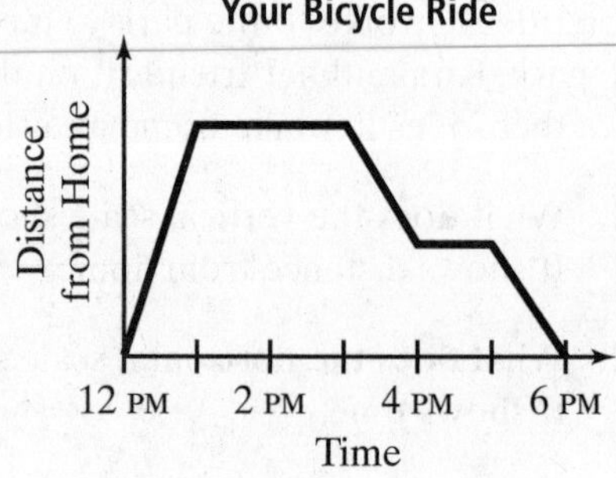

3. What do the flat parts of the graph represent?

4. What do the sections from 3 P.M. to 4 P.M. and from 5 P.M. to 6 P.M. represent?

5. What does the section from 12 P.M. to 1 P.M. represent?

Sketch a graph to describe the following. Explain the activity in each section of the graph.

6. your elevation above sea level as you hike in the mountains

7. your speed as you travel from home to school

8. the height of an airplane above the ground flying from Dallas, Texas to Atlanta, Georgia

9. the speed of a person driving to the store and having to stop at two stoplights

The graph shows the relationship between time and speed for an airplane.

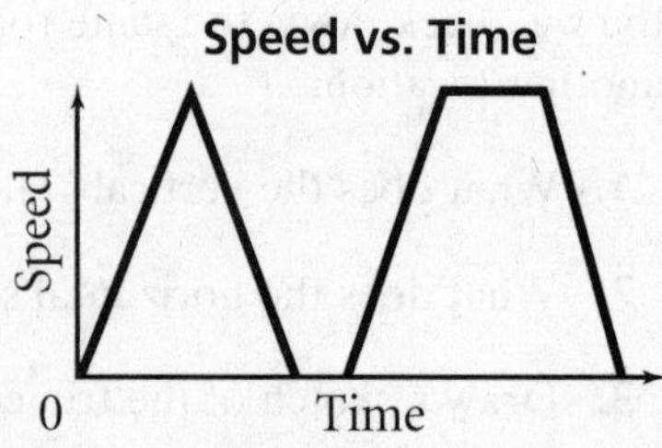

10. Circle the sections of the graph that show the speed increasing.

11. Circle the section of the graph that shows the plane not moving.

12. Circle the section of the graph that shows the plane moving at a constant speed.

Reteaching 5-2

Relations and Functions

OBJECTIVE: Evaluating functions	**MATERIALS:** None

A function is a relation that assigns exactly one value in the range to each value in the domain. A function rule may be given as an equation. The function $f(x) = 3x + 5$ will take a value x and change it into $3x + 5$. The function is read "f of x equals three x plus five," not "f times x." Evaluating a function means finding a value in the range for a given value from the domain.

Example

Evaluate $f(x) = 4x - 2$ for $x = 0, 1,$ and 2.

$f(x) = 4x - 2$

$f(0) = 4(0) - 2$ $\quad f(1) = 4(1) - 2$ $\quad f(2) = 4(2) - 2$ ← **Substitute each value for *x*.**

$f(0) = 0 - 2$ $\quad f(1) = 4 - 2$ $\quad f(2) = 8 - 2$ ← **Simplify.**

$f(0) = -2$ $\quad f(1) = 2$ $\quad f(2) = 6$

Exercises

Find the domain and range of each relation.

1. $\{(-4, 3), (-2, -1), (0, 0), (1, 4), (2, 6)\}$
2. $\{(-6, -4), (-3, -1), (1, 2), (2, 4), (3, 7)\}$

Determine whether each relation is a function.

3. $\{(-1, 2), (0, 3), (4, 3), (0, 5)\}$
4.

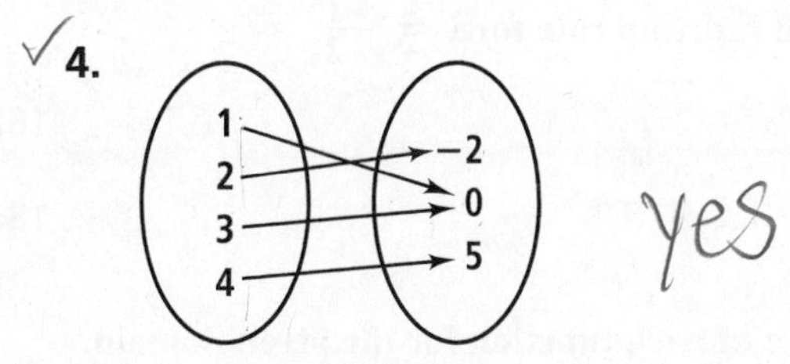

Evaluate each function rule for $x = -2$.

5. $f(x) = 4x$
6. $f(x) = -3x$
7. $f(x) = x - 2$
8. $f(x) = -2x + 1$
9. $f(x) = \frac{1}{2}x + 2$
10. $f(x) = -\frac{3}{2}x + 2$

Find the range of each function, given the domain.

11. $g(m) = m^2; \{-2, 0, 2\}$
12. $h(x) = -\frac{1}{3}x - 1; \{-3, 0, 6\}$
13. $h(n) = 3n^2 - 2n + 2; \{-1, 0, 1\}$
14. $g(n) = n^2 + n - 2; \{-2, 0, 2\}$
15. $g(x) = |x| + 2; \{-4, -2, 4\}$
16. $f(x) = -2|x| - 1; \{-3, -2, 3\}$

Name ______________________ Class ______________ Date ______________

Practice 5-2

Relations and Functions

Find the domain and range of each relation.

1. $\{(-3, -7), (-1, -3), (0, -1), (2, 3), (4, 7)\}$

2. $\{(-5, -4), (-4, 2), (0, 2), (1, 3), (2, 4)\}$

Determine whether each of the following relations is a function.

3. $\left\{(-4, -3), (-2, -2), (0, -1), \left(1, -\frac{1}{2}\right)\right\}$

4. $\{(0, 0), (1, 1), (4, 2), (1, -1)\}$

5.

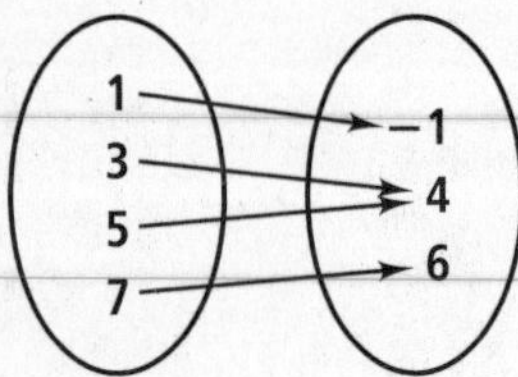

6.

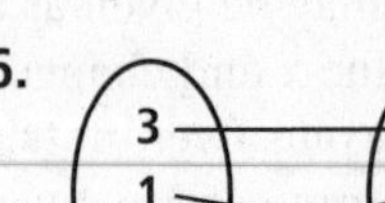

7.

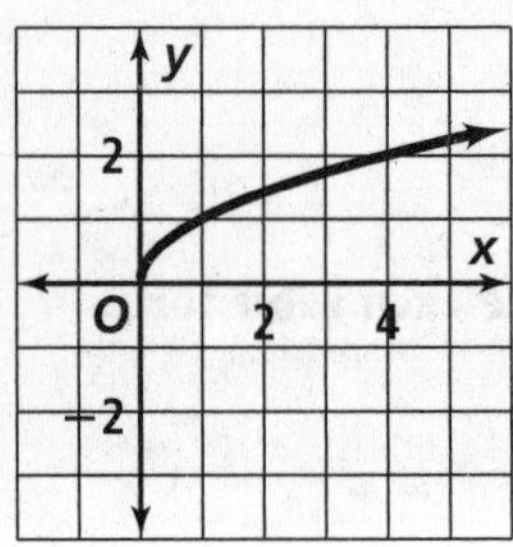

yes

8.

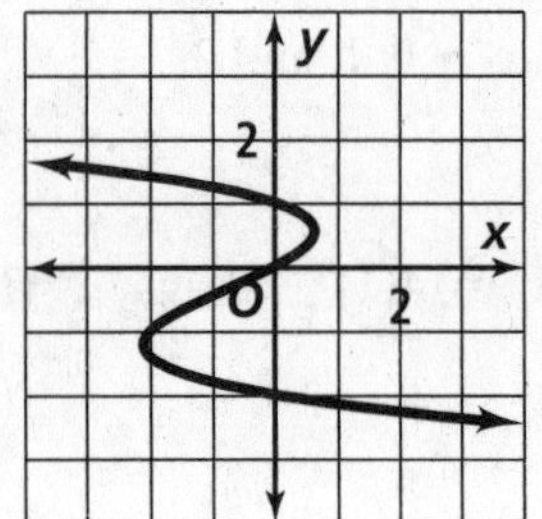

no

Evaluate each function rule for $x = 3$.

9. $f(x) = 2x - 15$

10. $f(x) = -x + 3$

11. $g(x) = \frac{2}{3}x - 1$

12. $h(x) = -\frac{1}{2}x - \frac{1}{2}$

13. $h(x) = -0.1x + 2.1$

14. $g(x) = -\frac{x}{6} + \frac{3}{2}$

Evaluate each function rule for $x = -\frac{1}{2}$.

15. $f(x) = 4x - 2$

16. $f(x) = -\frac{1}{2}x + 1$

17. $g(x) = -|x| + 3$

18. $h(x) = x - \frac{1}{2}$

Find the range of each function for the given domain.

19. $f(x) = -3x + 1; \{-2, -1, 0\}$

20. $f(x) = x^2 + x - 2; \{-2, 0, 1\}$

21. $h(x) = -x^2; \{-3, -1, 1\}$

22. $g(x) = -\frac{1}{2}|x| + 1; \{-2, -1, 1\}$

23. For a car traveling at a constant rate of 60 mi/h, the distance traveled is a function of the time traveled.

a. Express this relation as a function. $d = 60t$

b. Find the range of the function when the domain is $\{1, 5, 10\}$. $d(1) = 60(1)$, $d(1) = 60$; $d(5) = 60(5)$, $d(5) = 300$

c. What do the domain and range represent?

$(1, 60)\ (5, 300)\ (10, 600)$

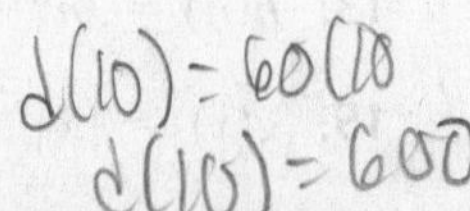

Name ______________________ Class ______________ Date ______________

Reteaching 5-3

Function Rules, Tables, and Graphs

OBJECTIVE: Graphing a function	**MATERIALS:** Graph paper

You can use a rule to model a function with a table and a graph.

Example

Graph the function $y = 2x + 3$.

Step 1: Choose four different values for x. Write these values in the first column of the table. Choose some negative values for x.

Step 2: Evaluate the function to find y for each value of x.

x	$y = 2x + 3$	(x, y)
-2	$y = 2(-2) + 3 = -1$	$(-2, -1)$
-1	$y = 2(-1) + 3 = 1$	$(-1, 1)$
3	$y = 2(3) + 3 = 9$	$(3, 9)$
5	$y = 2(5) + 3 = 13$	$(5, 13)$

Step 3: Plot the ordered pairs to graph the data.

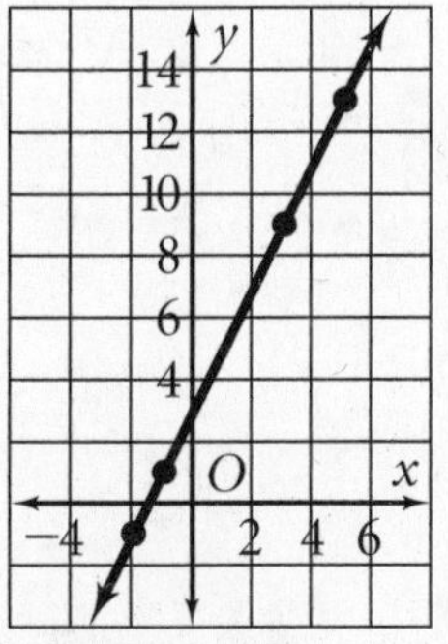

y(-3) = |-3| - 3
y(-3) = 0
y(-1) = |-1| - 3
y = 4 - 3

X	equation	(x, y)
-3	y = |-3| - 3	(-3, 0)
-1	y = |-1| - 3	(-1, -2)
-4	y = |-4| - 3	(-4, 1)
-2	y = |-2| - 3	(-5, -1)

Exercises

Use a table to graph each function. Choose an appropriate number of values for x. Choose some negative values for x.

1. $y = 4x + 1$

2. $y = x - 2$

3. $y = x + 5$

4. $y = |x| - 3$

5. $y = x^2 - 4$

6. $y = 3x + 3$

7. $y = -|x| + 3$

8. $y = -x^2 + 4$

Name ______________________ Class ______________ Date ______________

Practice 5-3

Function Rules, Tables, and Graphs

Model each rule with a table of values and a graph.

1. $f(x) = x + 1$

2. $f(x) = 2x$

3. $f(x) = 3x - 2$

4. $f(x) = \frac{3}{2}x - 2$

5. $f(x) = \frac{1}{2}x$

6. $f(x) = -\frac{2}{3}x + 1$

7. $f(x) = x^2 + 1$

8. $f(x) = -x^2 + 2$

9. $f(x) = x - 3$

10. Suppose a van gets 22 mi/gal. The distance traveled $D(g)$ is a function of the gallons of gas used.

a. Use the rule $D(g) = 22g$ to make a table of values and then a graph.

$D(10.5) = 22(10.5)$

b. How far did the van travel if it used 10.5 gallons of gas?

$D(10.5) = 231$

c. Should the points of the graph be connected by a line? Explain.

11. The admission to a fairgrounds is \$3.00 per vehicle plus \$.50 per passenger. The total admission is a function of the number of passengers.

$T(6) = 3 + 0.50(6)$

a. Use the rule $T(n) = 3 + 0.50n$ to make a table of values and then a graph.

$T(6) = 3 + 3$

b. What is the admission for a car with six people in it?

$T(6) = 6$

c. Should the points of the graph be connected by a line? Explain.

Graph each function.

12. $f(x) = 4x + 2$

13. $f(x) = |-2x|$

14. $f(x) = -3x + 7$

15. $f(x) = -|x| - 1$

16. $f(x) = 8 - \frac{3}{4}x$

17. $f(x) = \frac{2}{3}x - 7$

18. $f(x) = -\frac{2}{3}x + 6$

19. $f(x) = x^2 - 2x + 1$

20. $f(x) = -\frac{1}{2}x + 3$

21. $y = -x^2 + 1$

22. $y = 9 - x^2$

23. $y = 2x^2 + x - 2$

Make a table of values for each graph.

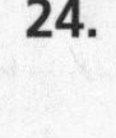

24.

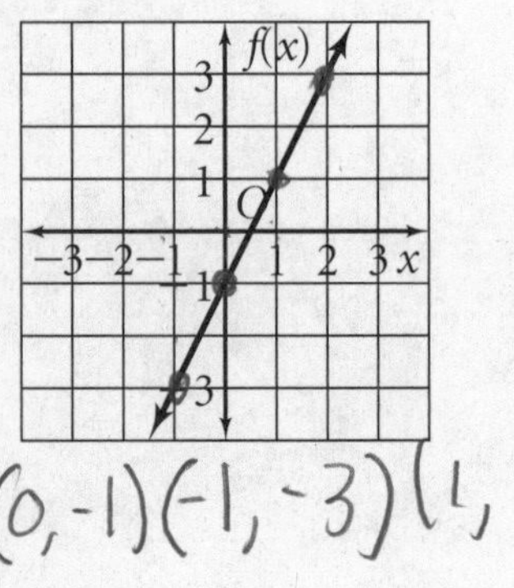

(0, −1) (−1, −3) (1, 1)

25.

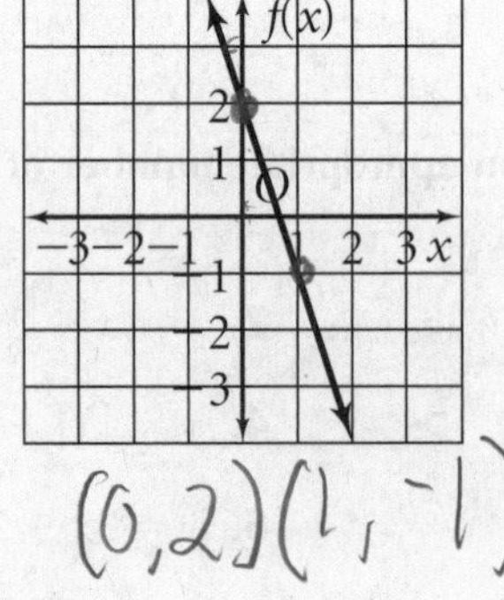

(0, 2) (1, −1)

26.

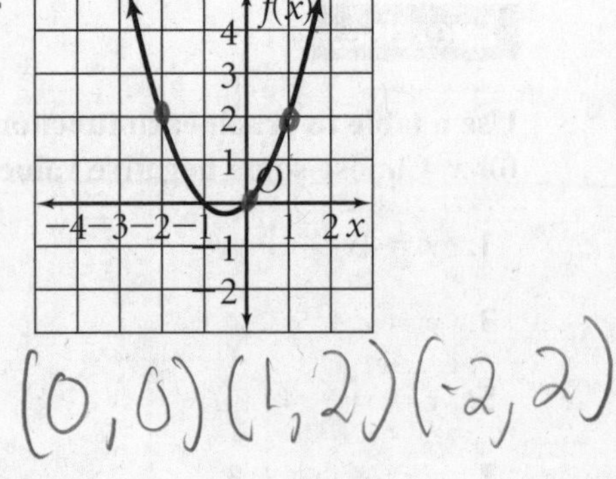

(0, 0) (1, 2) (−2, 2)

Name ______________________ Class ____________ Date ____________

Reteaching 5-4

OBJECTIVE: Writing rules for functions from tables and words

MATERIALS: None

You can write a rule for a function by analyzing a table of values. Look for a pattern in the data table. For each row, ask yourself, "What can I do to the first number to get the second number?" Write the patterns. Circle the pattern that works for all of the data in the table. This is the rule for the function.

Example

x	*f(x)*	
1	3	← (Add 2) or multiply by 3.
2	4	← (Add 2) or multiply by 2.
3	5	← (Add 2)

The function rule must be $f(x)$ equals x plus 2. The statement can be written as $f(x) = x + 2$.

Exercises

Analyze each table and then write the function rule.

1.

x	*f(x)*
0	0
1	3
2	6
3	9

2.

x	*f(x)*
0	−1
1	0
2	1
3	2

3.

x	*f(x)*
0	0
−1	1
3	9
5	25

Write a function rule for each situation.

4. the length $\ell(w)$ of a box that is two more than four times the width w.

5. the width $w(\ell)$ of a sheet of plywood that is one half the length ℓ.

6. the cost $c(a)$ of a pounds of apples at $.99 per pound

7. the distance $d(t)$ traveled at 65 miles per hour in t hours

8. the value $v(q)$ of a pile of q quarters

9. a worker's earnings $e(n)$ for n hours of work when the worker's hourly wage is $8.25

10. the distance $f(d)$ traveled in feet when you know the distance d in yards

Name ______________________ Class ______________ Date ____________

Practice 5-4

Writing a Function Rule

Write a function rule for each table.

1.

x	f(x)
0	3
2	5
4	7
6	9

2.

x	f(x)
0	0
1	3
3	9
5	15

3.

x	f(x)
5	0
10	5
15	10
20	15

4. a. Write a function rule to calculate the cost of buying bananas at \$.39 a pound.

b. How much would it cost to buy 3.5 pounds of bananas?

5. To rent a cabin, a resort charges \$50 plus \$10 per person.

a. Write a function rule to calculate the total cost of renting the cabin.

b. Use your rule to find the total cost for six people to stay in the cabin.

Write a function rule for each table.

6.

x	f(x)
−4	−2
−2	−1
6	3
8	4

7.

x	f(x)
−3	9
0	0
1	1
5	25

8.

x	f(x)
0	20
2	18
4	16
8	12

9. Pens are shipped to the office supply store in boxes of 12 each.

a. Write a function rule to calculate the total number of pens when you know the number of boxes.

b. Calculate the total number of pens in 16 boxes.

10. a. Write a function rule to determine the change you would get from a \$20 bill when purchasing items that cost \$1.25 each.

b. Calculate the change when five of these items are purchased.

c. Can you purchase 17 of these items with a \$20 bill?

11. You invest \$209 to buy shirts and then sell them for \$9.50 each.

a. Write a function rule to determine your profit.

b. Use your rule to find your profit after selling 24 shirts.

c. How many shirts do you need to sell to get back your investment?

Reteaching 5-5

Direct Variation

OBJECTIVE: Using constant of variation to solve problems

MATERIALS: Graph paper and a straight piece of wire or pipe cleaner

Example

Is the equation of the line joining the points (2, 3) and (4, 6) a direct variation? If it is, find the constant of variation.

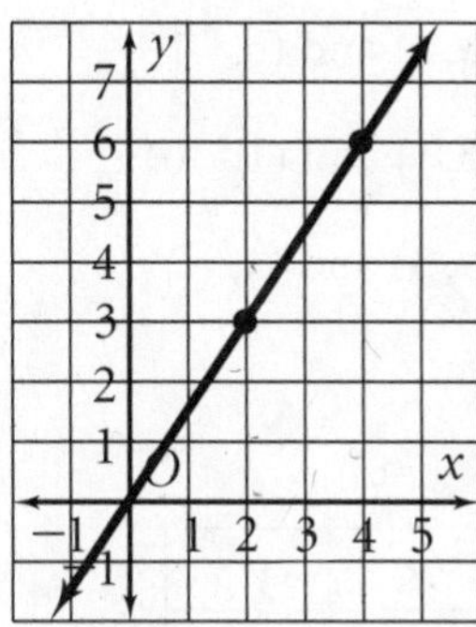

← **Graph the two points. Place the wire on the graph so that it passes through the two points given.**

a. Is the graph a straight line passing through the origin? Yes, it is.

b. Is the equation of this line a direct variation? Yes, since the line passes through the origin.

c. What is the constant of variation?

$y = kx$ ← **Write the general form of a direct variation.**

$3 = k(2)$ ← **Substitute the coordinates of either point.**

$k = \frac{3}{2}$ ← **Solve for k.**

The constant of variation is $\frac{3}{2}$.

Exercises

Work with a partner. Draw axes and label them and the origin on your graph paper. One partner places the wire on the graph so that it passes through the two points given. The other partner answers the questions. Exchange roles for each exercise.

Is the equation of the line joining each pair of points a direct variation? If it is a direct variation, what is the constant of variation?

1. $(-1, 3), (1, -3)$ **2.** $(0, 3), (-1, 1)$ **3.** $(1, -2), (4, -8)$

4. $(5, 5), (-5, -5)$ **5.** $(2, 4), (1, 2)$ **6.** $(2, 3), (3, 5)$

Name ______________________ Class ______________ Date ______________

Practice 5-5

Direct Variation

Is each equation a direct variation? If it is, find the constant of variation.

1. $y = 5x$
2. $8x + 2y = 0$
3. $y = \frac{3}{4}x - 7$
4. $y = 2x + 5$
5. $3x - y = 0$
6. $y = \frac{3}{5}x$
7. $-3x + 2y = 0$
8. $-5x + 2y = 9$
9. $8x + 4y = 12$
10. $6x - 3y = 0$
11. $x - 3y = 6$
12. $9x + 5y = 0$

The ordered pairs in each exercise are for the same direct variation. Find each missing value.

13. (3, 2) and (6, y)
14. (–2, 8) and (x, 12)
15. (4, y) and (16, 12)
16. (x, 8) and (6, –16)
17. (3, y) and (9, 15)
18. (2, y) and (10, 15)
19. (–4, 3) and (x, 6)
20. (3, y) and (1.5, 6)
21. $\left(\frac{2}{3}, 2\right)$ and (x, 6)
22. (2.5, 5) and (x, 9)
23. (4.8, 5) and (2.4, y)
24. (9, 3) and (x, –2)

For the data in each table, tell whether y varies directly with x. If it does, write an equation for the direct variation.

25.

x	y
4	8
7	14
10	20

26.

x	y
−3	−2
3	2
9	6

27.

x	y
4	3
5	4.5
11	13.5

28.

x	y
−2	−2.8
3	4.2
8	11.2

29. Charles's Law states that at constant pressure, the volume of a fixed amount of gas varies directly with its temperature measured in degrees Kelvin. A gas has a volume of 250 mL at 300° K.

   a. Write an equation for the relationship between volume and temperature.

   b. What is the volume if the temperature increases to 420° K?

30. Your percent grade varies directly with the number of correct answers. You got a grade of 80 when you had 20 correct answers.

   a. Write an equation for the relationship between percent grade and number of correct answers.

   b. What would your percent grade be with 24 correct answers?

31. The amount of simple interest earned in a savings account varies directly with the amount of money in the savings account. You have $1000 in your savings account and earn $50 in simple interest. How much interest would you earn if you had $1500 in your savings account?

Name ______________________ Class ______________ Date ____________

Reteaching 5-6

Describing Number Patterns

OBJECTIVE: Finding the common difference and writing the next several terms in a sequence

MATERIALS: None

When trying to determine the common difference of an arithmetic sequence or find the pattern, it is helpful to attempt to express each term in the sequence as an expression involving the same number.

Example

Find the common difference of the sequence: 4, 7, 10, 13, . . .

Let n = the term number in the sequence.
Let $A(n)$ = the value of the nth term of the sequence.

$A(1) = 4$

$A(2) = 7 = 4 + 1(3)$ ← **3 is the common difference.**

$A(3) = 10 = 4 + 6 = 4 + 2(3)$ ← **Notice that the 3 in each expression is multiplied by a number one less than the term number.**

$A(4) = 13 = 4 + 9 = 4 + 3(3)$

$$A(n) = 4 + \underbrace{3 + 3 + \ldots + 3}_{n\,-\,1 \text{ terms}} = 4 + (n - 1)3$$

The formula for the sequence is $A(n) = 4 + (n - 1)3$.

You could use the formula for the sequence to determine the next several terms simply by substituting a specific term in for n. For example:

Term:

5th term $A(5) = 4 + (5 - 1)3$
$A(5) = 16$

100th term $A(100) = 4 + (100 - 1)3$
$A(100) = 301$

Exercises

Find the common difference of each sequence.

1. 2, 9, 16, 23, . . .

2. 5, 1, −3, −7, . . .

3. −52, −41, −30, −19, . . .

Find the next two terms in each sequence.

4. 2, 0, −2, −4, . . .

5. −4, −1, 2, 5, . . .

6. −17, −22, −27, −32, . . .

Find a formula for the sequence in the exercise indicated and use it to determine the fifth and tenth terms of the sequence.

7. Exercise 1

8. Exercise 2

9. Exercise 3

Name ______________________ Class ______________ Date ______________

Practice 5-6

Describing Number Patterns

Find the common difference of each arithmetic sequence.

1. 10, 16, 22, 28, . . .

2. 9, 6, 3, 0, . . .

3. −12, −17, −22, −27, . . .

4. −11, −8, −5, −2, . . .

5. $4, 4\frac{1}{2}, 5, 5\frac{1}{2}, \ldots$

6. $7\frac{1}{2}, 7, 6\frac{1}{2}, 6, \ldots$

7. 9, 10.5, 12, 13.5, . . .

8. 1, −1.5, −4, −6.5, . . .

9. 8, 9.1, 10.2, 11.3, . . .

10. −9, −8.1, −7.2, −6.3, . . .

11. −3, −0.6, 1.8, 4.2, . . .

12. 6.2, 4.5, 2.8, 1.1, . . .

Find the next two terms in each sequence.

13. 1, 7, 13, 19, . . .

14. −8, −5, −2, 1, . . .

15. 1, −4, −9, −14, . . .

16. $\frac{1}{2}, -\frac{1}{2}, -\frac{3}{2}, -\frac{5}{2}, \ldots$

17. 2.7, 4, 5.3, 6.6, . . .

18. 9.8, 0.7, −8.4, −17.5, . . .

19. $6\frac{1}{3}, 4\frac{2}{3}, 3, 1\frac{1}{3}, \ldots$

20. $2\frac{1}{2}, \frac{3}{4}, -1, -2\frac{3}{4}, \ldots$

Find the fifth, tenth, and hundredth terms of each sequence.

21. 4, 14, 24, 34, . . .

22. 14, 6, −2, −10, . . .

23. 3, 10, 17, 24, . . .

24. −19, −22, −25, −28, . . .

25. $\frac{1}{4}, -\frac{1}{4}, -\frac{3}{4}, -\frac{5}{4}, \ldots$

26. −1.3, −0.3, 0.7, 1.7, . . .

27. 0, 101, 202, 303, . . .

28. −1, −100, −199, −298, . . .

29. 5, 3.9, 2.8, 1.7, . . .

30. $-3\frac{1}{2}, -3\frac{3}{4}, -4, -4\frac{1}{4}, \ldots$

Determine whether each sequence is arithmetic. Justify your answer.

31. 0.5, 0.3, 0.1, −0.1, . . .

32. −1, 1, −1, 1, . . .

33. 3, 6, 12, 24, . . .

34. 100, 81, 64, 49, . . .

35. Renting a backhoe costs a flat fee of \$65 plus an additional \$35 per hour.

a. Write the first four terms of a sequence that represents the total cost of renting the backhoe for 1, 2, 3, and 4 hours.

b. What is the common difference?

c. What are the 5th, 24th, 48th, and 72nd terms in the sequence?

Name ______________________ Class ______________ Date ______________

Reteaching 6-1

Rate of Change and Slope

OBJECTIVE: Calculating the slope of a line **MATERIALS:** None

Example

Calculate the slope of the line shown in the graph.

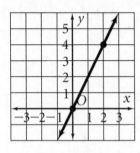

a. Pick any two points on the line. Write their coordinates. Underline the x-coordinates and circle the y-coordinates. This example uses $(\underline{0}, \textcircled{0})$, $(\underline{2}, \textcircled{4})$.

b. The difference of y-coordinates shows the vertical change or *rise*. Find the rise of the line by subtracting the y-coordinates.
vertical change $=$ rise $= 4 - 0 = 4$

c. The difference of x-coordinates shows the horizontal change or *run*. Find the run of the line by subtracting the x-coordinates. Be sure to subtract the x-coordinates in the same order as the y-coordinates.
horizontal change $=$ run $= 2 - 0 = 2$

d. Find the slope of the line through the two points by forming the ratio of rise to run.
slope $= \frac{\text{rise}}{\text{run}} = \frac{4}{2}$ or 2

Exercises

Use steps a–d from the example to find the slope of each line.

1.

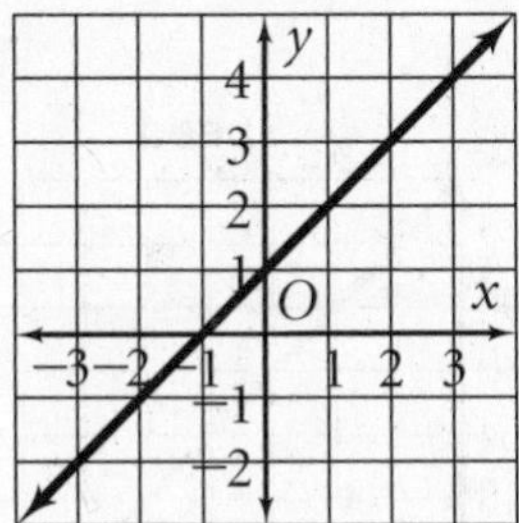

2.

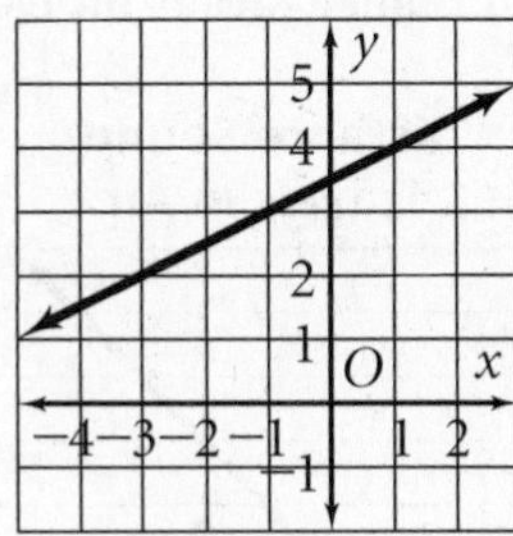

3.

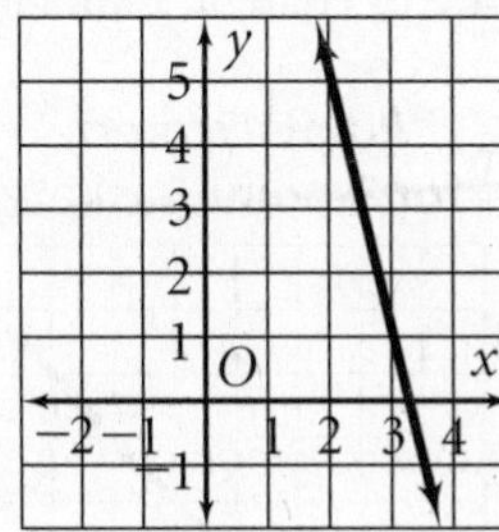

4. Draw a horizontal line. Find the slope of the line.

5. Draw a vertical line. Find the slope of the line.

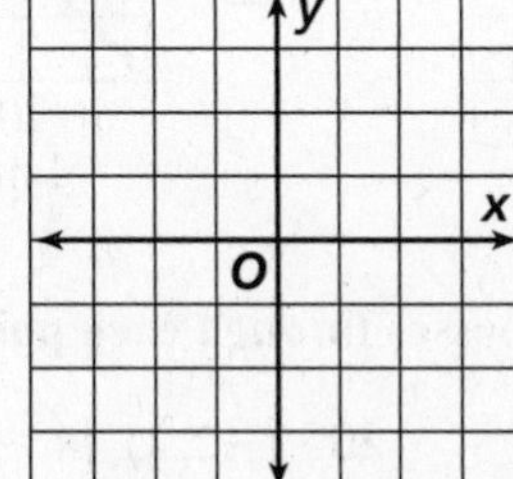

Name ______________________ Class ______________ Date ______________

Practice 6-1

Rate of Change and Slope

Find the slope of each line.

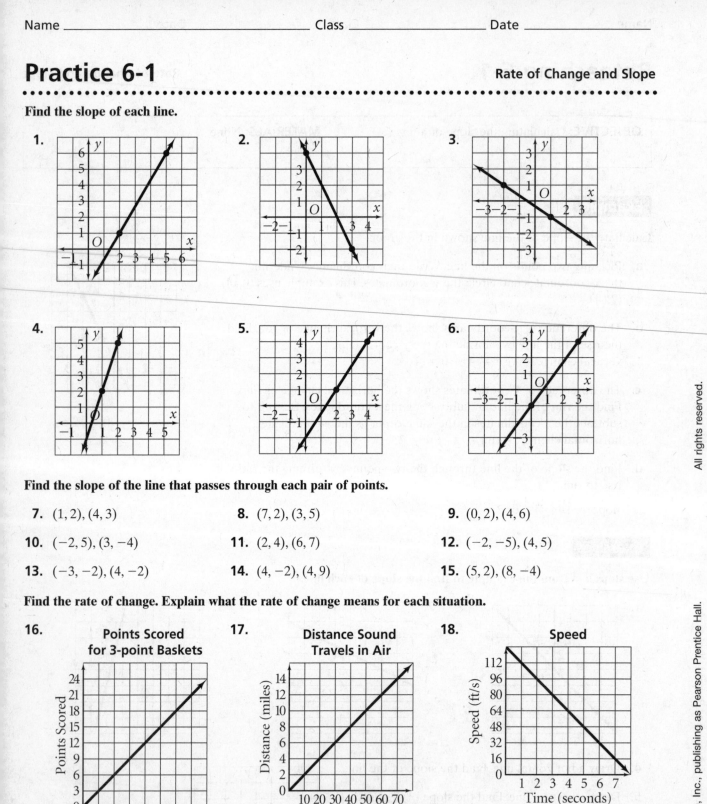

1. 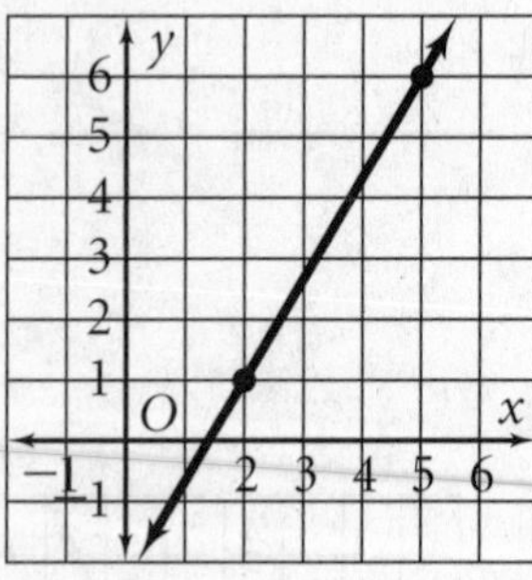

2. 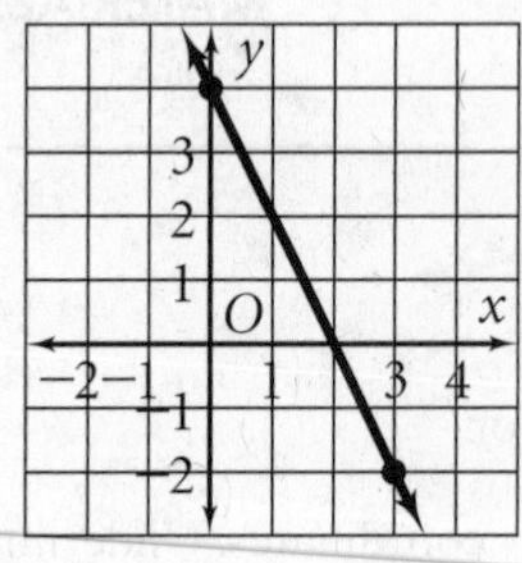

3. 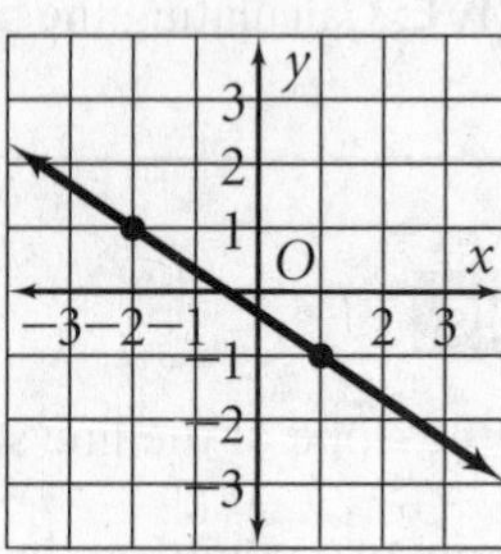

4. 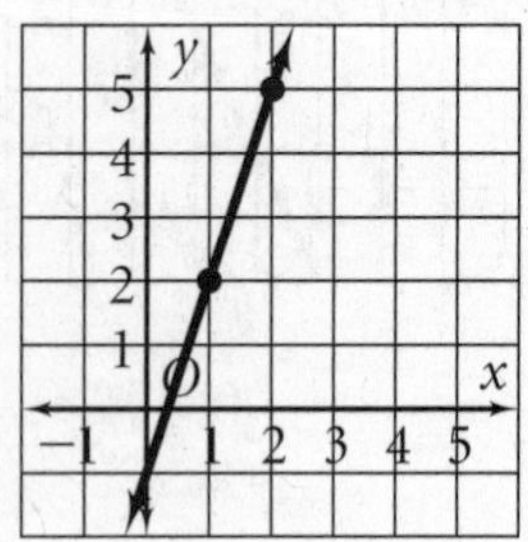

5. 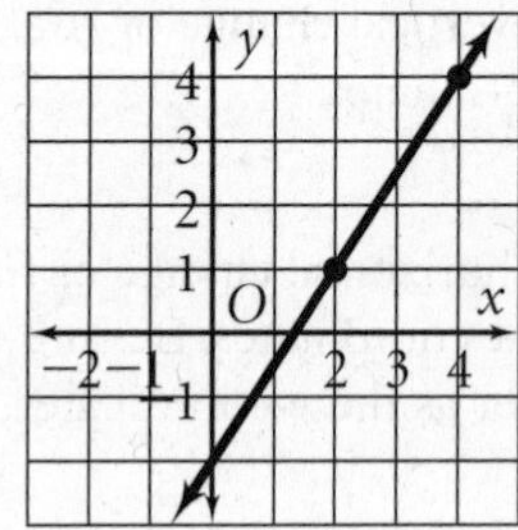

6. 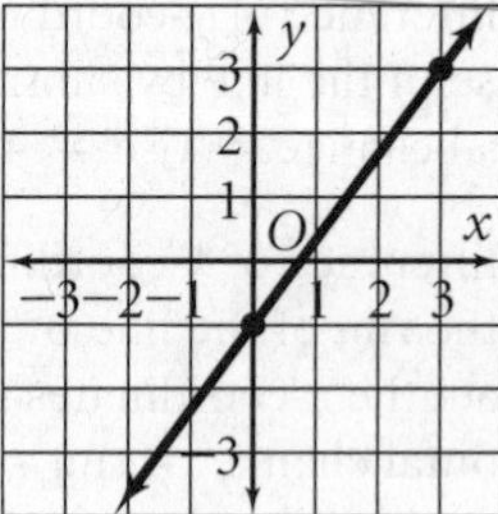

Find the slope of the line that passes through each pair of points.

7. (1, 2), (4, 3)
8. (7, 2), (3, 5)
9. (0, 2), (4, 6)
10. (−2, 5), (3, −4)
11. (2, 4), (6, 7)
12. (−2, −5), (4, 5)
13. (−3, −2), (4, −2)
14. (4, −2), (4, 9)
15. (5, 2), (8, −4)

Find the rate of change. Explain what the rate of change means for each situation.

16. 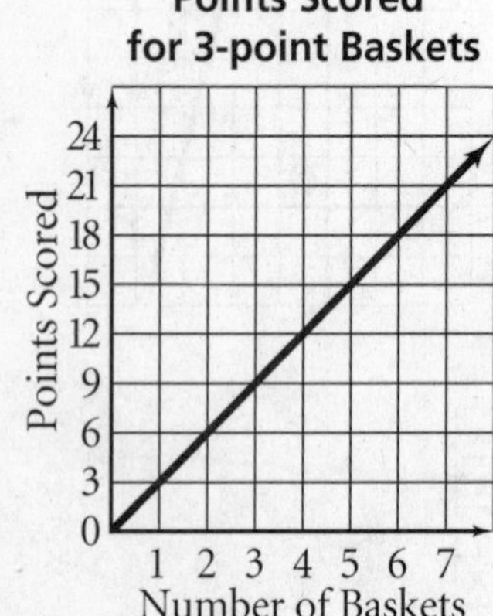

17. 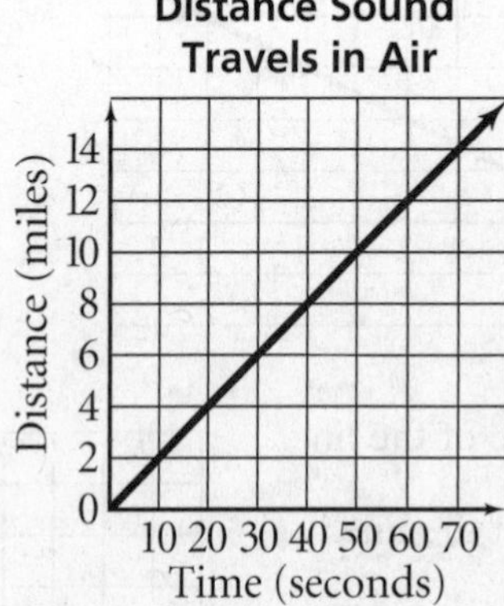

18. 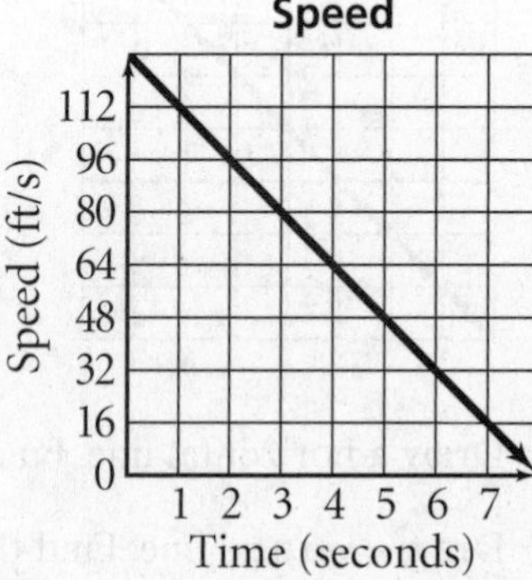

Find the slope of the line that passes through each pair of points.

19. (0, 0), (3, 7)
20. (−2, 4), (4, −1)
21. (−3, 6), (1, −2)
22. (2, 4), (4, −4)
23. (2, −10), (5, −6)
24. (5, 1), (11, 1)
25. (3, 7), (3, 5)
26. (7, 9), (2, 9)
27. (−5, −2), (−5, 3)

Name ______________________ Class ______________ Date ____________

Reteaching 6-2

OBJECTIVE: Using the slope and y-intercept to draw graphs and write equations

MATERIALS: Graph paper, counters, ten index cards

Write these numbers on the index cards, one number to a card: $1, -1, 2, -2, \frac{1}{2}, -\frac{1}{2}, 3, -3, \frac{1}{3}, -\frac{1}{3}$. These numbers represent different slopes.

- Draw a coordinate plane on the graph paper.
- Put a counter at any integer on the y-axis. Choose one of the index cards.
- Use the y-intercept shown by the counter and the slope shown on the card to write the equation of a line.
- Draw the graph of that line.

Example

Place the counter at -4. Choose the index card with the number 2.

$y = mx + b$ ⟵ **Write the slope-intercept form of the equation of a straight line. The counter shows that $b = -4$. The first card gives a slope of 2, so $m = 2$.**

$y = 2x + (-4)$ ⟵ **Substitute the values shown by the counter and the card.**

$y = 2x - 4$ ⟵ **Write the equation of the line in simplified form.**

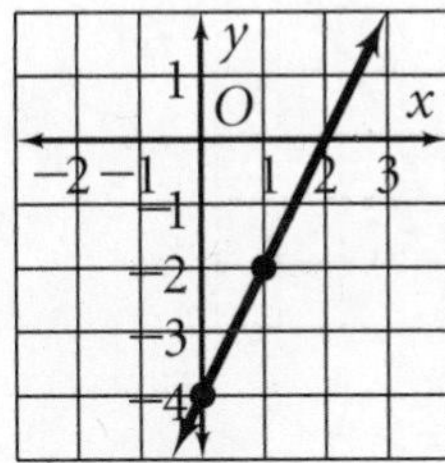

⟵ **Slope $= \frac{\text{vertical change}}{\text{horizontal change}}$, so rewrite 2 as $\frac{2}{1}$. Starting at the counter, move 2 units up and 1 unit to the right and place a second counter. Draw a straight line joining the two points for the graph of $y = 2x - 4$.**

Exercises

Place the counter. Then choose an index card.

1. Write the equation of the line.
2. Draw the graph.

Write an equation for each line.

3. 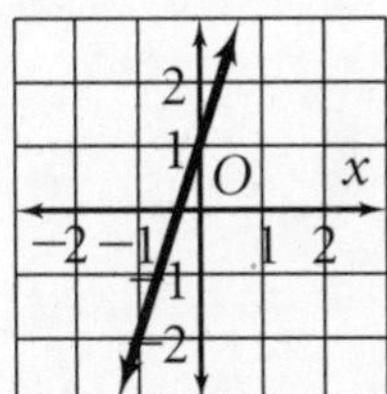
4. 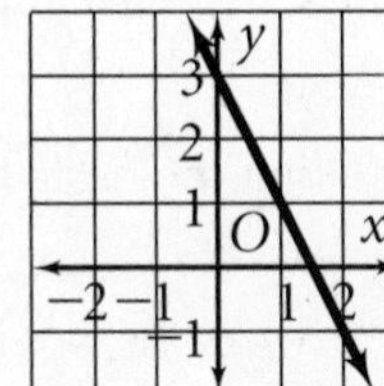
5. 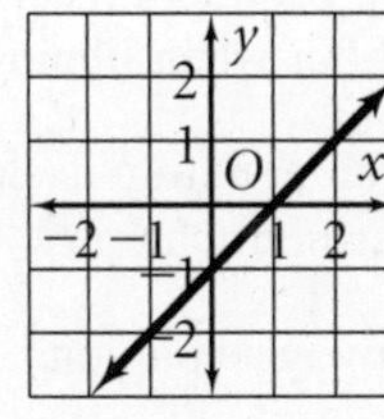

Name ______________________ Class ______________ Date ____________

Practice 6-2

Slope-Intercept Form

Find the slope and y-intercept of each equation. Then graph.

1. $y = x + 2$
2. $y + 3 = -\frac{1}{3}x$
3. $y = 2x - 1$
4. $y - \frac{3}{5}x = -1$
5. $y = \frac{1}{2}x - 4$
6. $y - 2x = -3$
7. $y = \frac{2}{5}x + 3$
8. $y + \frac{1}{3}x = -2$
9. $y = -x - 2$
10. $y - 6 = -2x$
11. $y = -5x - 2$
12. $y + x = 0$
13. $y + 4 = 2x$
14. $y = -5x + 5$
15. $y = -4 + x$
16. $y = -4x$
17. $y = \frac{4}{5}x + 2$
18. $y - \frac{3}{4}x = -5$
19. $y = -6$
20. $y - 3 = -\frac{2}{3}x$
21. $y = -\frac{7}{4}x + 6$
22. $y + 3x = 6$
23. $y + \frac{1}{5}x = -2$
24. $y = \frac{3}{7}x$

Write an equation of a line with the given slope and y-intercept.

25. $m = 4, b = 8$
26. $m = -2, b = -6$
27. $m = \frac{4}{3}, b = 0$
28. $m = -\frac{9}{5}, b = -7$
29. $m = -6, b = 1$
30. $m = \frac{3}{7}, b = -1$
31. $m = -\frac{1}{5}, b = -3$
32. $m = 9, b = 4$
33. $m = -8, b = 11$
34. $m = \frac{2}{9}, b = 0$
35. $m = -11, b = 13$
36. $m = -\frac{7}{2}, b = -6$

Write the slope-intercept form of the equation for each line.

37.
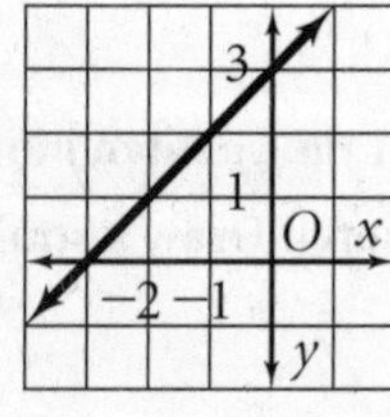

38.
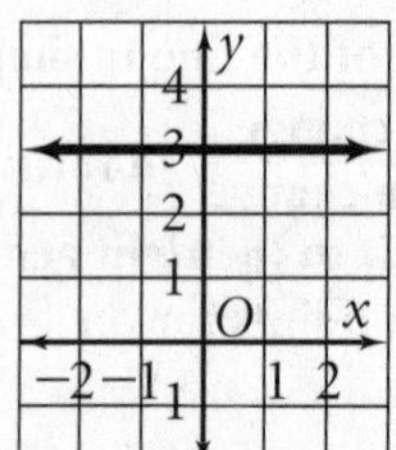

39.
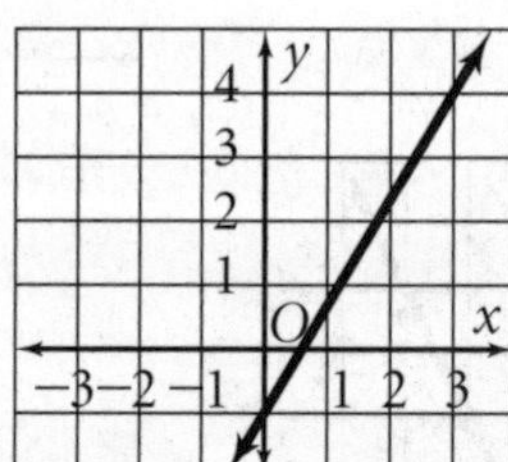

40.
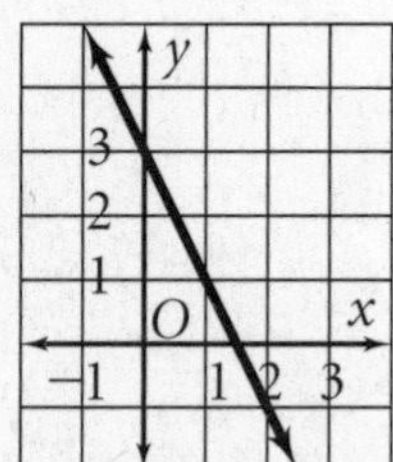

41.
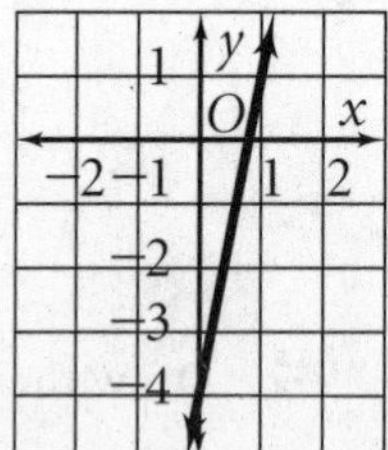

42.
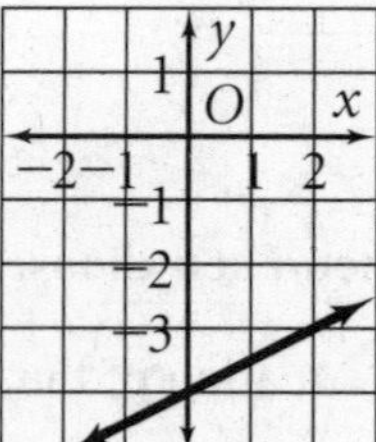

43. A television production company charges a basic fee of \$4000 and then \$2000 per hour when filming a commercial.

   a. Write an equation in slope-intercept form relating the basic fee and per-hour charge.

   b. Graph your equation.

   c. Use your graph to find the production costs if 4 hours of filming were needed.

Name ______________________ Class ______________ Date ____________

Reteaching 6-3

Standard Form

OBJECTIVE: Graphing equations using x- and y-intercepts

MATERIALS: Small self-stick removable notes

Example

Graph $4x + 5y = 20$ using x- and y-intercepts.

a. Write the equation in large figures so that each term is slightly smaller than a self-stick note.

b. Write a zero on a self-stick note.

c. Place the note over the $4x$. Solve the remaining equation.

$$0 + 5y = 20$$
$$5y = 20$$
$$y = 4$$

This gives us the point of the y-intercept: $(0, 4)$.

d. Place the note over the $5y$. Solve the remaining equation.

$$4x + 0 = 20$$
$$4x = 20$$
$$x = 5$$

This gives us the point of the x-intercept: $(5, 0)$.

e. Graph the two points. Draw the line between them.

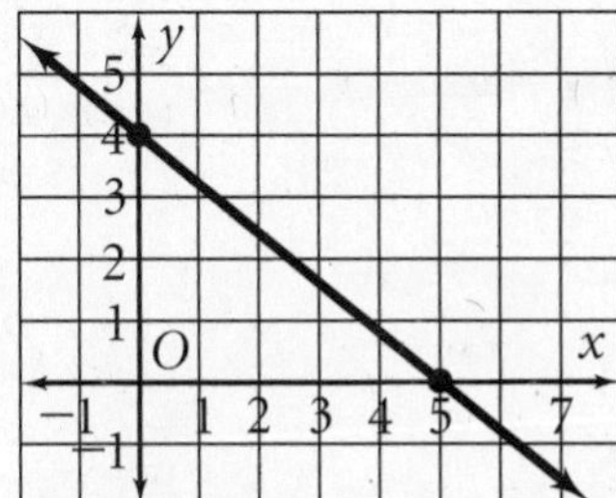

Exercises

Graph each equation using steps a–e.

1. $3x + 4y = 36$

2. $5x + 3y = 15$

3. $7x - 4y = 28$

4. $4x - 3y = 9$

5. $10x + 30y = 90$

6. $6x + 3y = 12$

Name ______________________ Class ______________ Date ______________

Practice 6-3

Standard Form

Graph each equation using x- and y-intercepts.

1. $x + y = 3$
2. $x + 3y = -3$
3. $-2x + 3y = 6$
4. $5x - 4y = -20$
5. $3x + 4y = 12$
6. $7x + 3y = 21$
7. $y = -2.5$
8. $2x - 3y = 4$
9. $x = 3$
10. $3x - 2y = -6$
11. $5x + 2y = 5$
12. $-7x + 2y = 14$
13. $3x + y = 3$
14. $-3x + 5y = 15$
15. $2x + y = 3$
16. $8x - 3y = 24$
17. $3x - 5y = 15$
18. $x + 4y = 4$
19. $x = -3.5$
20. $y = 6$

Write each equation in standard form using integers.

21. $y = 4x - 11$
22. $y = 2x - 6$
23. $y = -2x - 3$
24. $y = 5x - 32$
25. $y = \frac{2}{3}x - \frac{25}{3}$
26. $y = 43 - 4x$
27. $y = -\frac{4}{5}x + \frac{6}{5}$
28. $y = -\frac{x}{5}$
29. $y = \frac{5}{2}x - 22$
30. $y = \frac{7}{3}x + \frac{25}{3}$
31. $y = -\frac{x}{3} + \frac{2}{3}$
32. $y = -6x - 38$

33. The drama club sells 200 lb of fruit to raise money. The fruit is sold in 5-lb bags and 10-lb bags.
    a. Write an equation to find the number of each type of bag that the club should sell.
    b. Graph your equation.
    c. Use your graph to find two different combinations of types of bags.

34. The student council is sponsoring a carnival to raise money. Tickets cost $5 for adults and $3 for students. The student council wants to raise $450.
    a. Write an equation to find the number of each type of ticket they should sell.
    b. Graph your equation.
    c. Use your graph to find two different combinations of tickets sold.

35. Anna goes to a store to buy $70 worth of flour and sugar for her bakery. A bag of flour costs $5, and a bag of sugar costs $7.
    a. Write an equation to find the number of bags of each type Anna can buy.
    b. Graph your equation.

36. You have $50 to spend on cold cuts for a party. Ham costs $5.99/lb, and turkey costs $4.99/lb. Write an equation in standard form to relate the number of pounds of each kind of meat you could buy.

Name ______________________ Class ______________ Date ______________

Reteaching 6-4

Point-Slope Form and Writing Linear Equations

OBJECTIVE: Writing an equation given the graph of a line or two points on a line

MATERIALS: Graph paper

Example

Write an equation for the line shown in point-slope form.

a. Select any two points on the line. It is a good idea to select points whose coordinates are integers.
(0, 2) and (1, 4) lie on the line.

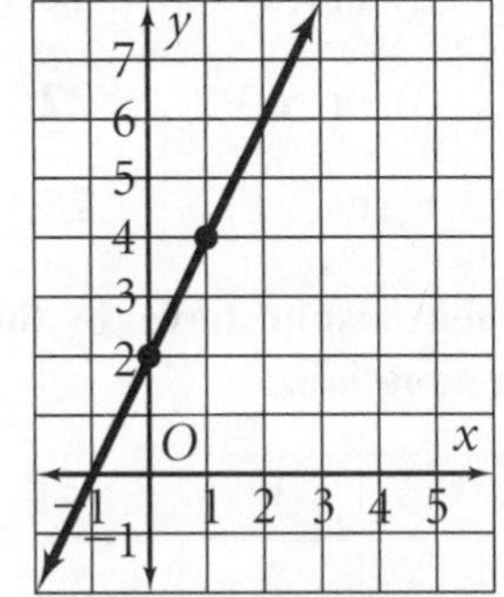

b. Use slope $= \frac{\text{rise}}{\text{run}}$ to find the slope.
From (0, 2), move up 2 units (rise = +2) and right 1 unit (run = +1) to get to (1, 4). So, $\frac{\text{rise}}{\text{run}} = \frac{+2}{+1} = 2$.
or
Use $m = \frac{y_2 - y_1}{x_2 - x_1}$ to find the slope.
If $(x_1, y_1) = (0, 2)$ and $(x_2, y_2) = (1, 4)$, then $m = \frac{4 - 2}{1 - 0} = \frac{2}{1} = 2$.

c. Use the point-slope form to write the equation.

Substitute $m = 2$ and $(x_1, y_1) = (0, 2)$.
$y - y_1 = m(x - x_1)$
$y - 2 = 2(x - 0)$
$y - 2 = 2x$

or

Substitute $m = 2$ and $(x_1, y_1) = (1, 4)$.
$y - y_1 = m(x - x_1)$
$y - 4 = 2(x - 1)$

Note: If you rewrite $y - 2 = 2x$ and $y - 4 = 2(x - 1)$ in slope-intercept form, you get $y = 2x + 2$. Although the two equations look different, they do represent the same line.

Exercises

Graph the line through the given points. Then follow steps a–c from the Example to write the equation of the line passing through the given points in point-slope form.

1. (6, 4), (4, 3) **2.** (0, −18), (5, 2) **3.** (−2, −2), (−4, 2) **4.** (−4, 5), (2, 5)

Write an equation for the line through the given points in point-slope form.

5. (2, −5), (0, −7) **6.** (4, 3), (3, −2) **7.** (2, −1), (−1, 8)

8. (−3, 4), (3, 8) **9.** (4, −1), (−8, 2) **10.** (5, −2), (−4, −2)

11. (−2, −6), (8, 4) **12.** (−4, 1), (−2, 2) **13.** (6, −6), (−3, −12)

14. (0, 0), (8, 7) **15.** (0, −2), (8, −6) **16.** (2, 7), (−6, −5)

17. (−1, −10), (5, 2) **18.** (0, 7), (−5, 12) **19.** (0, 1), (4, −7)

Name ______________________ Class ______________ Date ______________

Practice 6-4

Point-Slope Form and Writing Linear Equations

Write an equation in point-slope form for the line through the given points or through the given point with the given slope.

1. $(5, 7), (6, 8)$
2. $(-2, 3); m = -1$
3. $(1, 2), (3, 8)$
4. $(-2, 3); m = 4$
5. $(4, 7); m = \frac{3}{2}$
6. $(6, -2); m = -\frac{4}{3}$
7. $(0, 5), (-3, 2)$
8. $(8, 11), (6, 16)$
9. $(4, 2), (-4, -2)$
10. $(15, 16), (13, 10)$
11. $(0, -7); m = -4$
12. $(-3, 4), (1, 6)$
13. $(1, 2)$; m undefined
14. $(-6, 7); m = -\frac{1}{2}$
15. $(21, -2), (27, 2)$
16. $(7, 5); m = 0$
17. $(8, -2), (14, 1)$
18. $(4, 8), (2, 12)$
19. $(-5, 13), (-10, 9)$
20. $(6, 2); m = \frac{3}{4}$
21. $(5, -3); m = -2$
22. $(4, 3.5); m = 0.5$
23. $(-6, 2); m = \frac{5}{3}$
24. $(100, 90), (80, 120)$
25. $(-3, 6), (3, -6)$
26. $(11, 7), (9, 3)$
27. $(2, 7); m = \frac{5}{2}$
28. $(-9, 8); m = -\frac{5}{3}$

Is the relationship shown by the data linear? If it is, model the data with an equation.

29.

x	y
2	3
3	7
4	11
5	15

30.

x	y
−3	4
−1	6
1	7
3	10

31.

x	y
−4	12
1	8
5	−4
10	−8

32.

x	y
−2	5
3	−5
7	−13
11	−21

33.

x	y
−6	−5
−2	1
0	4
8	16

34.

x	y
−6	11
−3	9
6	3
15	−3

35.

x	y
−7	−3
−5	0
−1	3
3	7

36.

x	y
−4	1
2	4
6	6
14	10

Write an equation of each line in point-slope form.

37. 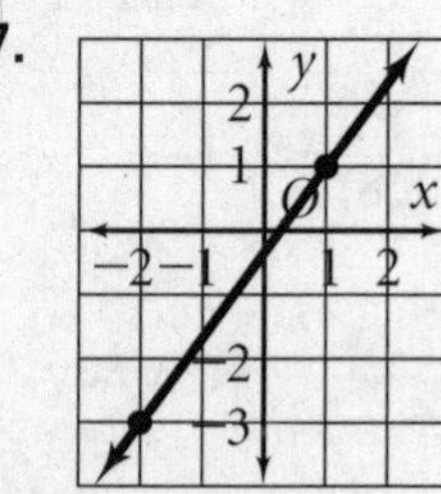

38. 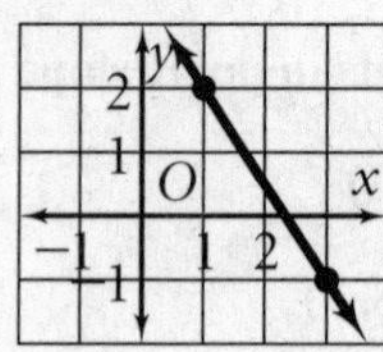

39. 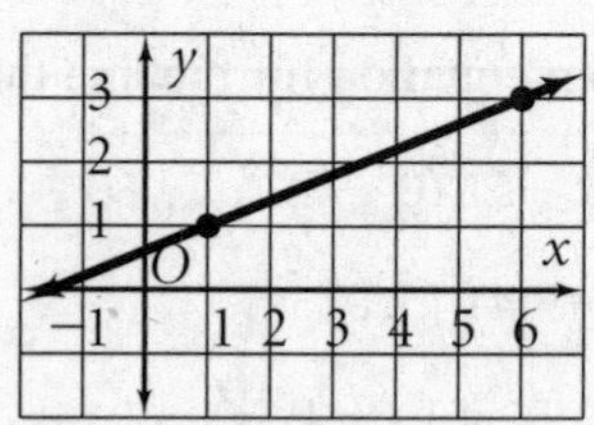

Name ______________________ Class ______________ Date ______________

Reteaching 6-5

Parallel and Perpendicular Lines

OBJECTIVE: Writing equations for parallel and perpendicular lines

MATERIALS: Graph paper and two items that can be used to represent lines such as pencils, straws, or coffee stirrers

Example

Write an equation for the line that is parallel to $y = 3x$, and contains $(0, -2)$. Then, write an equation for the line that is perpendicular to $y = 3x$ and contains $(0, -2)$.

On a piece of graph paper, draw a grid like the one shown below. Comparing $y = 3x$ to $y = mx + b$, we see that the line has y-intercept 0 and its slope is 3 or $\frac{3}{1}$. This means that the graph contains $(0, 0)$ and a point 3 units up and 1 unit right from there, $(1, 3)$. Place a pencil or other object on the grid that joins the points $(0, 0)$ and $(1, 3)$.

Place a second pencil on the grid so that it is parallel to the first pencil. Notice that you can move your second pencil to many other places on the grid and still have it parallel to your first pencil. Now, place your second pencil so that it contains $(0, -2)$, keeping it parallel to your first pencil. You have only one correct placement. Count units to verify that the slope of the line represented by your second pencil is also $\frac{3}{1}$ or 3. This line has slope $m = 3$ and y-intercept $b = -2$. So, its equation is $y = 3x - 2$.

Leaving your first pencil in place, move the second pencil so that it is perpendicular to the first. Now, place your second pencil so that it contains $(0, -2)$, keeping it perpendicular to the first pencil. You have only one correct placement. Count units to verify that the slope of the line represented by your second pencil is $-\frac{1}{3}$. Recall that the product of the slopes of perpendicular lines is -1, so $3(-\frac{1}{3}) = -1$. This line has slope $m = -\frac{1}{3}$ and y-intercept $b = -2$. So, its equation is $y = -\frac{1}{3}x - 2$.

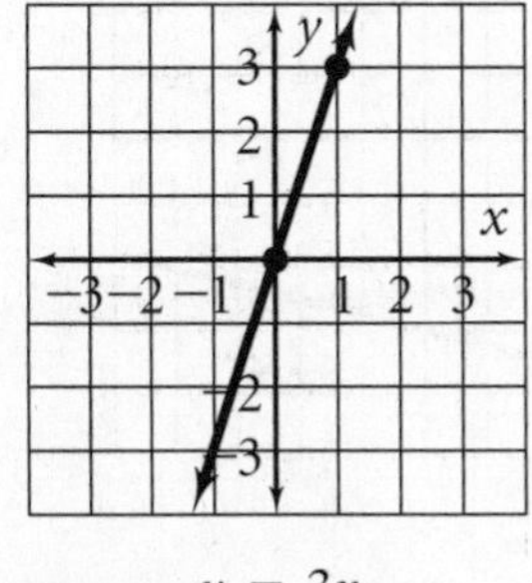

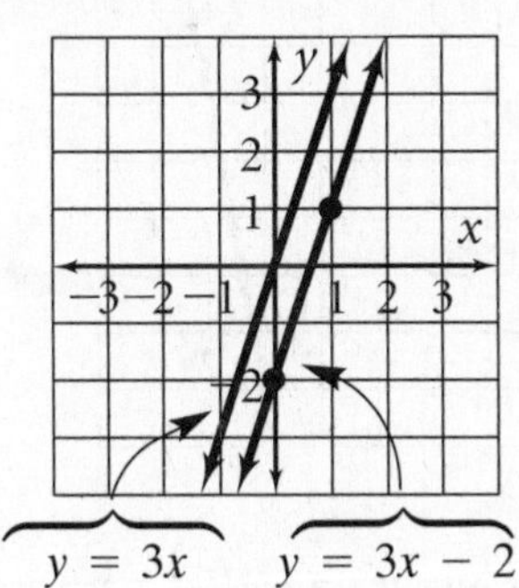

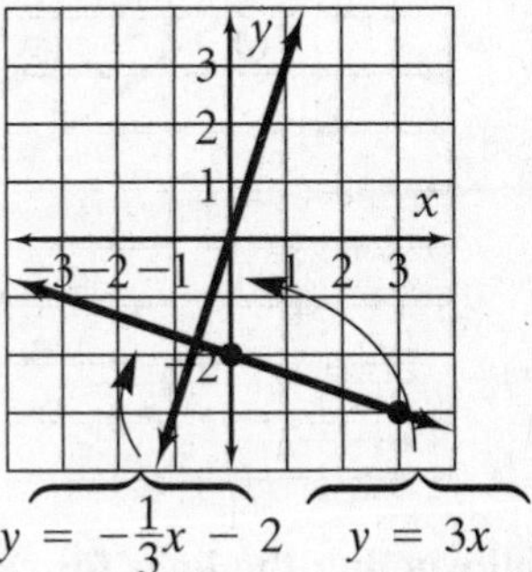

Exercises

Follow the steps above to find an equation of the line parallel to the given line that contains the given y-intercept. Then find an equation of the line perpendicular to the given line that contains the given y-intercept.

1. $y = 5x; (0, -1)$

2. $y = -3x; (0, 4)$

3. $y = 2x + 1; (0, -3)$

4. $y = -\frac{1}{4}x - 2; (0, 2)$

5. $y = \frac{1}{2}x + 2; (0, -1)$

6. $y = -\frac{1}{2}x; (0, 2)$

7. $y = -3x - 1; (0, 2)$

8. $y = \frac{2}{3}x + 1; (0, -2)$

9. $y = 3x - 4; (0, 6)$

Name ______________________ Class ______________________ Date ______________________

Practice 6-5

Parallel and Perpendicular Lines

Find the slope of a line parallel to the graph of each equation.

1. $y = 4x + 2$ **2.** $y = \frac{2}{7}x + 1$ **3.** $y = -9x - 13$ **4.** $y = -\frac{1}{2}x + 1$

5. $6x + 2y = 4$ **6.** $y - 3 = 0$ **7.** $-5x + 5y = 4$ **8.** $9x - 5y = 4$

9. $-x + 3y = 6$ **10.** $6x - 7y = 10$ **11.** $x = -4$ **12.** $-3x - 5y = 6$

Write an equation for the line that is perpendicular to the given line and that passes through the given point.

13. $(6, 4); y = 3x - 2$ **14.** $(-5, 5); y = -5x + 9$ **15.** $(-1, -4); y = \frac{1}{6}x + 1$

16. $(1, 1); y = \frac{1}{4}x + 7$ **17.** $(12, -6); y = 4x + 1$ **18.** $(0, -3); y = \frac{4}{3}x - 7$

19.

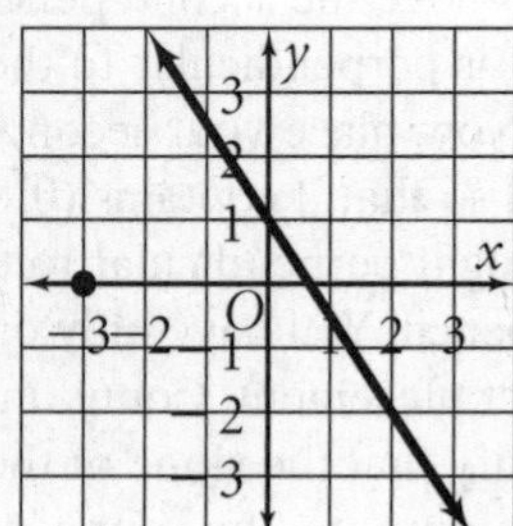

20.

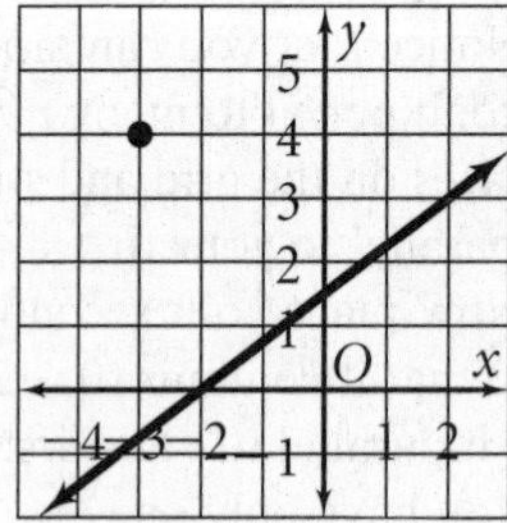

21.

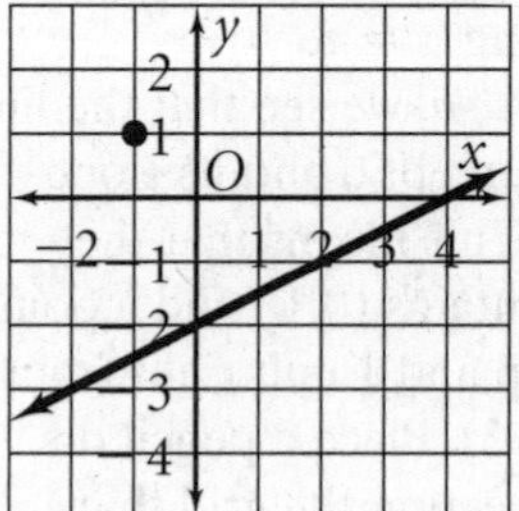

Write an equation for the line that is parallel to the given line and that passes through the given point.

22. $(3, 4); y = 2x - 7$ **23.** $(1, 3); y = -4x + 5$ **24.** $(4, -1); y = x - 3$

25. $(4,0); y = \frac{3}{2}x + 9$ **26.** $(-8, -4); y = -\frac{3}{4}x + 5$ **27.** $(9, -7); -7x - 3y = 3$

28.

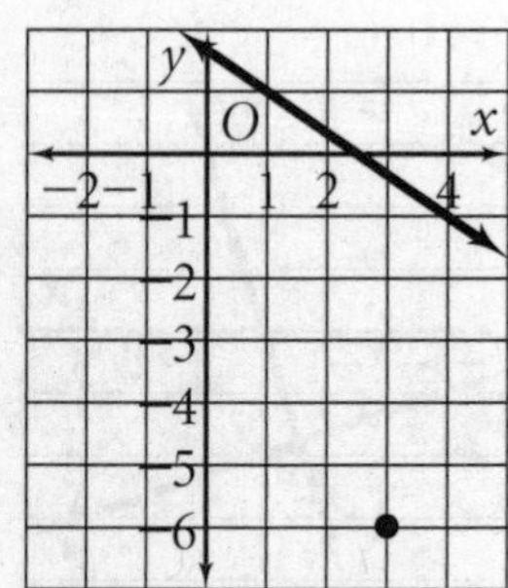

29.

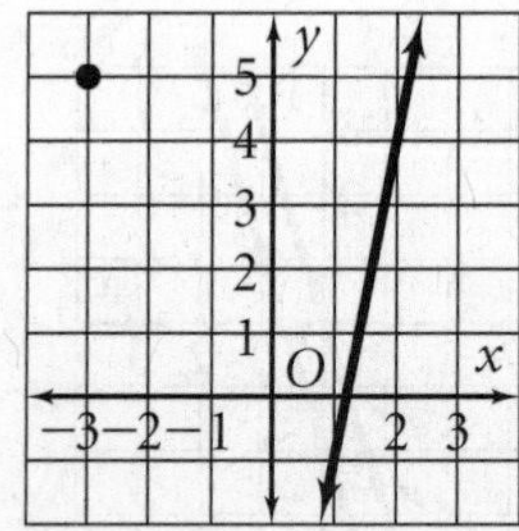

30.

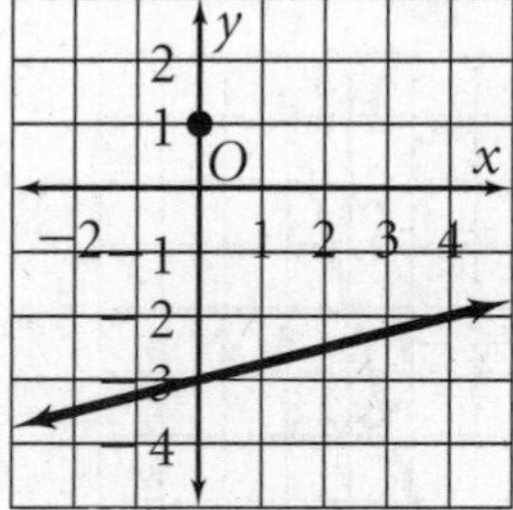

Tell whether the lines for each pair of equations are *parallel, perpendicular,* or *neither.*

31. $y = 3x - 8$
$3x - y = -1$

32. $3x + 2y = -5$
$y = \frac{2}{3}x + 6$

33. $y = -\frac{5}{2}x + 11$
$-5x + 2y = 20$

34. $9x + 3y = 6$
$3x + 9y = 6$

35. $y = -4$
$y = 4$

36. $x = 10$
$y = -2$

Name ______________________ Class ______________ Date ______________

Reteaching 6-6

Scatter Plots and Equations of Lines

OBJECTIVE: Finding the equation of a trend line **MATERIALS:** None

Example

Find an equation of a reasonable trend line for the data.

Rise in Minimum Wage

Year	Minimum Wage
1950	\$.75
1963	\$1.25
1975	\$2.10
1980	\$3.10
1991	\$4.25
1996	\$4.75
1997	\$5.15

Source: *World Almanac 2001,* p. 150.

a. Graph the points and draw a trend line. Let 0 correspond to 1950.

b. Pick any two points that appear to lie on the trend line, for example, (30, 3) and (50, 5).

c. On a new grid, graph the two points you selected. Draw the line through these two points.

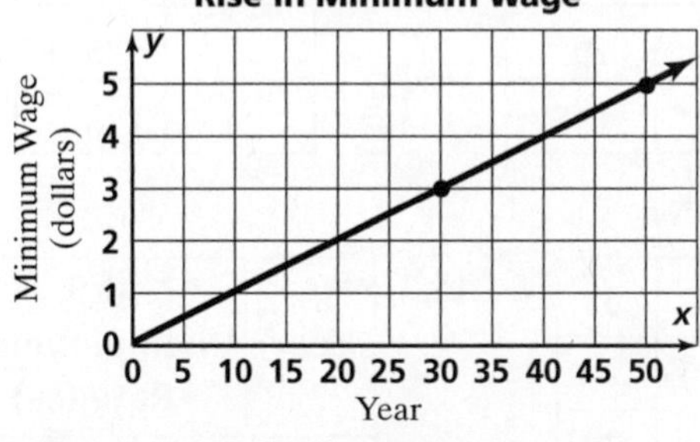

d. Find the slope of the trend line.

$$\text{slope} = \frac{\text{number of units up}}{\text{number of units across}} = \frac{\text{rise}}{\text{run}} = \frac{2}{20} = \frac{1}{10}$$

e. Make substitutions to obtain the equation of the line using either (30, 3) or (50, 2) as (x_1, y_1).

$y - y_1 = m(x - x_1)$ ⟵ **Use point-slope form.**

$y - 3 = \frac{1}{10}(x - 30)$ ⟵ **Substitute $\frac{1}{10}$ for m, 3 for y, and 30 for x.**

The equation $y - 3 = \frac{1}{10}(x - 30)$ models the rise in minimum wage.

Exercises

Find an equation of a reasonable trend line for each scatter plot.

1.

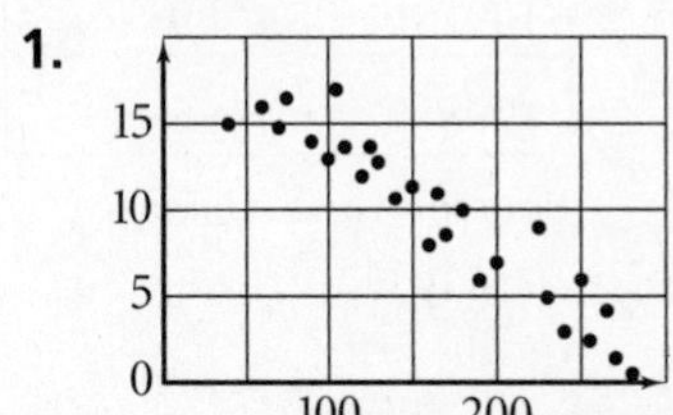

2.

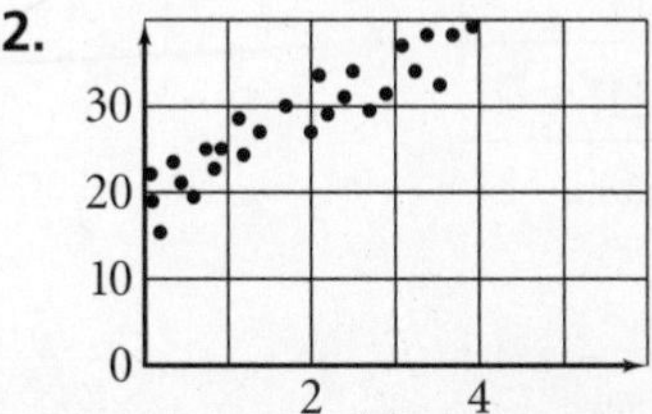

3.

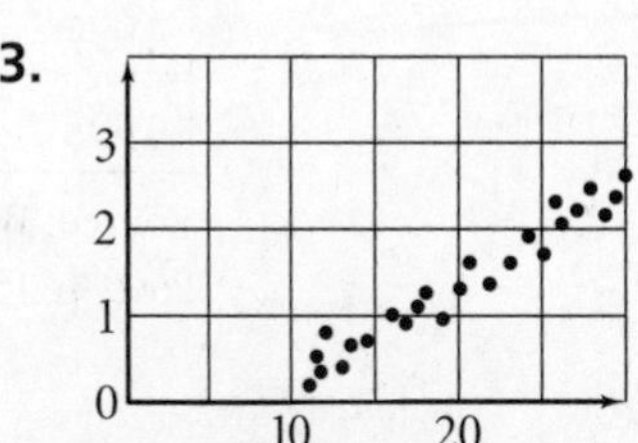

Name ______________________ Class ______________ Date ______________

Practice 6-6

Scatter Plots and Equations of Lines

Decide whether the data in each scatter plot follow a linear pattern. If they do, find the equation of a trend line.

1. 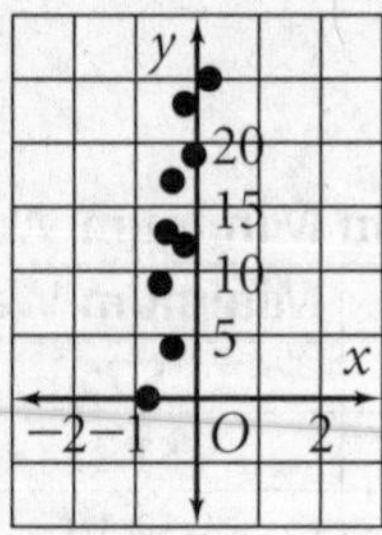

2. 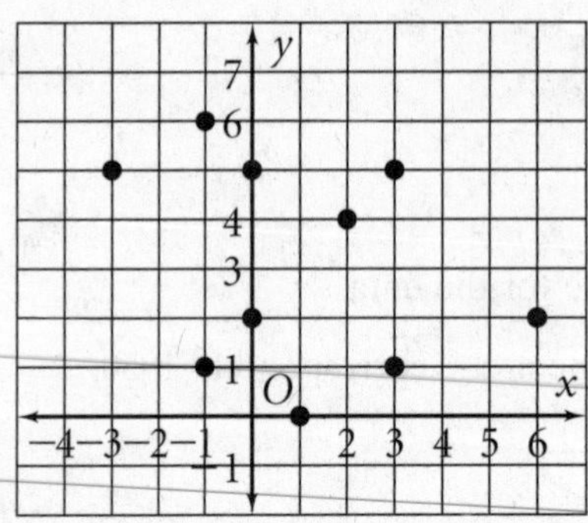

3. 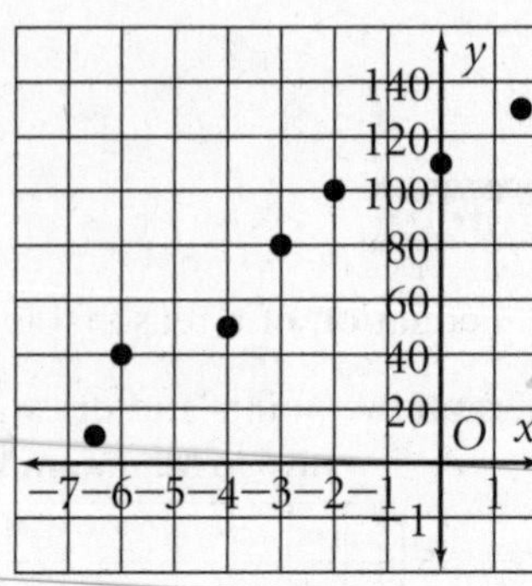

Use a graphing calculator to find the equation of the line of best fit for the following data. Find the value of the correlation coefficient *r* and determine if there is a strong correlation between the data.

4.

x	*y*
1	7
2	5
3	−1
4	3
5	−5

5.

x	*y*
1	6
2	15
3	−5
4	1
5	−2

6.

x	*y*
1	5
4	8
8	3
13	10
19	13

7.

x	*y*
12	28
15	50
18	14
21	28
24	36

Draw a scatter plot. Write the equation of the trend line.

8.

x	*y*
1	17
2	20
3	22
4	26
5	28
6	31

9.

Year	U.S. Union Membership (millions)
1988	17.00
1989	16.96
1990	16.74
1991	16.57
1992	16.39
1993	16.60
1994	16.75
1995	16.36
1996	16.27
1997	16.11
1998	16.21

Source: *World Almanac 2000,* p. 154.

10.

x	*y*
1	18
2	20
3	24
4	30
5	28
6	33

11.

Year	U.S. Unemployment Rate (%)
1988	5.5
1989	5.3
1990	5.6
1991	6.8
1992	7.5
1993	6.9
1994	6.1
1995	5.6
1996	5.4
1997	4.9
1998	4.5

Source: *World Almanac 2000,* p. 145.

Name ______________________ Class ______________ Date ____________

Reteaching 6-7

OBJECTIVE: To translate an absolute value equation

MATERIALS: None

An absolute value equation has a graph that looks like a *V* and it points either upward or downward.

A translation shifts a graph from its home position horizontally (left or right), vertically (up or down), or in some cases both. Translating a graph does not change its shape, but moves it to a different position.

Example

Graph $y = |x| + 1$.

Start with the graph of $y = |x|$.

Remember this is a *V*-shaped graph pointing upward with its vertex at the origin.
The + 1 tells us that the the graph will be shifted up 1 unit.
If the equation were $y = |x| - 1$, then the graph would be shifted down 1 unit.
You could also make a table of values.

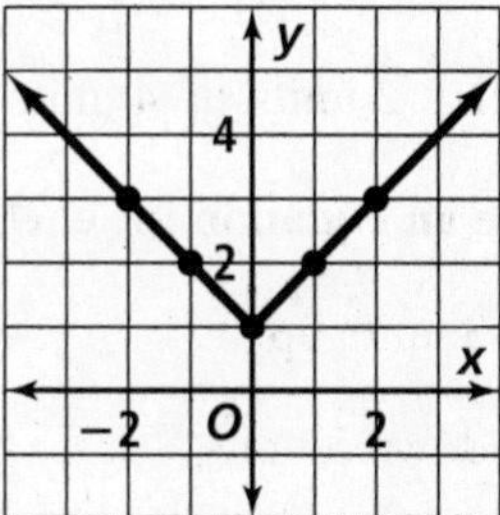

$y = \|x\| + 1$	
x	y
−2	3
−1	2
0	1
1	2
2	3

Substitute values for x and then plot the points.

Remember that an equation in the form $y = |x + 4|$ would be shifted horizontally. The shift would be the ***opposite*** of the sign inside the absolute value symbols.

For example, $y = |x - 3|$ would shift to the right (positive direction) 3 units.
$y = |x + 3|$ would shift to the left (negative direction) 3 units.

Exercises

In which direction would each absolute value equation shift and by how many units?

1. $y = |x| + 12$ **2.** $y = |x| - 15$ **3.** $y = |x + 13|$ **4.** $y = |x - 15|$

Graph each absolute value equation.

5. $y = |x| + 1$ **6.** $y = |x| - 2$ **7.** $y = |x - 3|$ **8.** $y = |x + 3|$

Name ______________________ Class ______________ Date ______________

Practice 6-7

Graphing Absolute Value Equations

Graph each equation by translating $y = |x|$.

1. $y = |x| - 3$
2. $y = |x| + 4$
3. $y = |x| - 1$
4. $y = |x| + \frac{1}{2}$
5. $y = |x| + 2\frac{1}{2}$
6. $y = |x| + 3$
7. $y = |x + 2|$
8. $y = |x - 4|$
9. $y = |3x|$
10. $y = |x + 3| - 2$
11. $y = |x - 2| + 1$
12. $y = |x - 3| + 2$

Graph each equation by translating $y = -|x|$.

13. $y = -|x| + 1$
14. $y = -|x + 2|$
15. $y = -|x| - 5$
16. $y = -|x - 4| + 2$
17. $y = -|x - 5|$
18. $y = -|x| + 4.5$
19. $y = -|x - 3| + 1$
20. $y = -|x + 1| + 3$
21. $y = -|x + 2| - 4$

Write an equation for each translation of $y = |x|$.

22. left 7 units
23. right 5 units
24. up 6 units
25. up 2 units, right 3 units
26. down 3 units, left 1 unit
27. down 1 unit, right 2 units
28. left 2 units, up 4 units
29. right 3 units, up 2 units
30. left 4 units, down 3.5 units

Write an equation for each translation of $y = -|x|$.

31. 3 units up
32. 3.5 units left
33. $\frac{3}{4}$ unit down
34. down 3 units
35. up 2 units, right 1 unit
36. down 5 units, left 1 unit
37. right 3 units, up 2 units
38. down 4 units, left 2 units
39. up 4 units, right 3 units

Write an equation for the given graphs.

40.

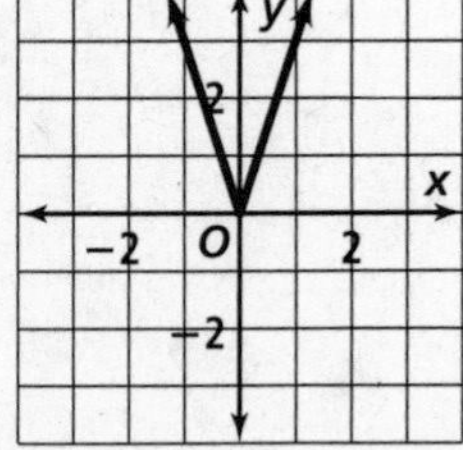

41.

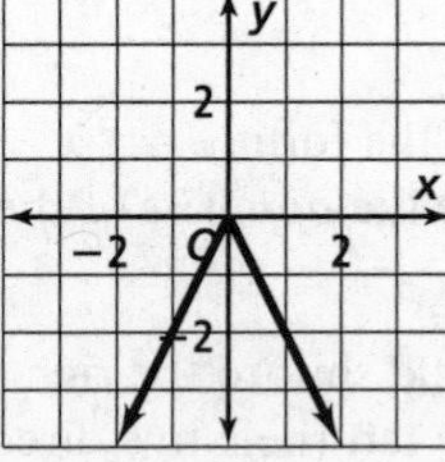

42.

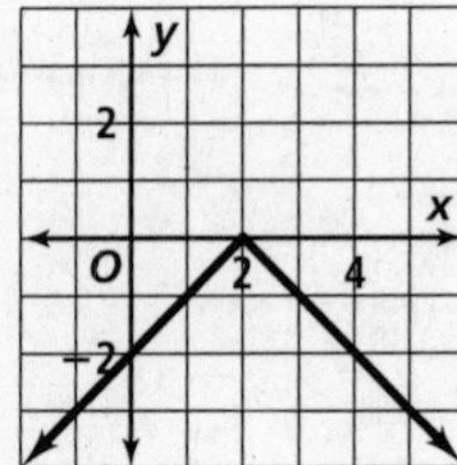

43.

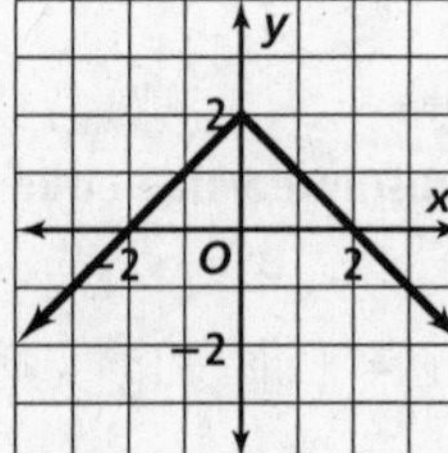

Name ______________________ Class ______________ Date ______________

Reteaching 7-1

Solving Systems by Graphing

OBJECTIVE: Solving systems of linear equations by graphing	**MATERIALS:** Graph paper, two toothpicks

- When you graph two equations, the point of intersection is the solution.
- To graph each equation, apply the slope-intercept form, $y = mx + b$.

Example

Solve by graphing.

$y = 3x - 9$

$y = -x - 1$

a. In the first equation, $b = -9$ and $m = 3$. Therefore, place one toothpick so that it intersects the y-axis at -9 and has a slope of 3.

b. Graph the second equation with $b = -1$ and $m = -1$ by placing another toothpick that intersects the y-axis at -1 and has a slope of -1.

c. Find the point where the two lines intersect. The lines intersect at $(2, -3)$. The solution of the system is $(2, -3)$.

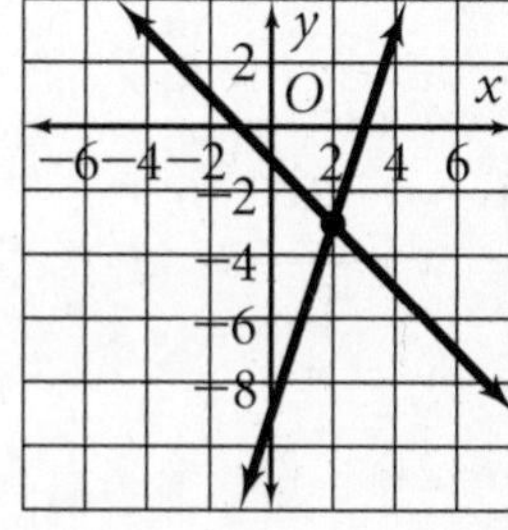

Check. See whether $(2, -3)$ makes both equations true.

$y = 3x - 9$		$y = -x - 1$
$\mathbf{-3} \stackrel{?}{=} 3(\mathbf{2}) - 9$	← **Substitute (2, −3) for (x, y).** →	$\mathbf{-3} \stackrel{?}{=} -(\mathbf{2}) - 1$
$-3 \stackrel{?}{=} 6 - 9$		$-3 = -3$ ✓
$-3 = -3$ ✓		

Exercises

Use graph paper, toothpicks, and steps a–c above to model and solve each system.

1. $y = 5x - 2$
$y = x + 6$

2. $y = 2x - 4$
$y = x + 2$

3. $y = x + 2$
$y = -x + 2$

Solve each system.

4. $y = 3x + 2$
$y = 3x - 4$

5. $y = 2x + 1$
$2y = 4x + 2$

6. $y = x - 3$
$y = -x + 3$

7. $y = 5x + 1$
$y = x - 3$

8. $y = x - 5$
$y = 4x + 1$

9. $y = 3x - 1$
$y = 3x - 4$

Name ______________________ Class ______________ Date ______________

Practice 7-1

Solving Systems by Graphing

Solve by graphing. Write *no solution* or *infinitely many solutions* where appropriate.

1. $y = 3x - 1$
$y = -2x + 4$

2. $y = x - 1$
$y = -x + 7$

3. $y = \frac{3}{4}x + 2$
$\frac{3}{4}x - y = 4$

4. $y = 4x + 7$
$y = -3x$

5. $y = x - 3$
$y = \frac{1}{7}x + 3$

6. $y = -3x - 4$
$3x + y = -4$

7. $y = -x - 3$
$y = -2x - 8$

8. $y = -x + 2$
$3x + 3y = 12$

9. $y = x$
$y = 3x + 2$

10. $y = 4x - 3$
$y = -3x - 3$

11. $y = \frac{5}{3}x - 4$
$y = 2x - 6$

12. $y = 3x + 2$
$2x + y = -8$

13. $x = y + 4$
$y = x + 4$

14. $x + y = 2$
$y = -2x - 1$

15. $2x - y = 3$
$y = x + 4$

16. $3x - 6y = 12$
$2x - 4y = 8$

17. $x - y = 1$
$y = \frac{3}{4}x + 1$

18. $y = x$
$x = 2y + 2$

19. $3x - y = 9$
$y = x + 1$

20. $2x + y = 0$
$y = 2x - 4$

21. $y = 2x - 6$
$x + y = 9$

22. $y = -x$
$y = 3x + 12$

23. $4x + y = 6$
$y = -4x - 1$

24. $y = 4x$
$y = -3x$

25. $y = x$
$2x + y = \frac{3}{2}$

26. $3x + y = 6$
$2x - y = \frac{3}{2}$

27. $x + 4y = -\frac{1}{2}$
$-2x - 3y = 1$

28. $x - y = -\frac{3}{2}$
$-2x + 5y = -4.5$

Solve each system by using a graphing calculator. Write *no solution* or *infinitely many solutions* where appropriate.

29. $y = x + 6$
$y = 2x - 7$

30. $y = \frac{7}{2}x - 6$
$y = 3x - 2$

31. $y = 2x - 20$
$y = -x + 34$

32. $y = \frac{2}{3}x + 4$
$2x - 3y = 3$

33. $y = -x - 5$
$y = 3x - 105$

34. $x + y = -10$
$2x + 3y = -30$

35. $3x - 4y = 0$
$2x + y = 110$

36. $y = \frac{1}{7}x + 10$
$x - 2y = 0$

37. $2x + y = 6$
$3y = -6x + 9$

38. $y = \frac{5}{6}x + 12$
$y = \frac{4}{3}x - 6$

39. $2x - y = 8$
$3x - 2y = 0$

40. $x + 2y = 2$
$3x + 4y = 22$

41. $y = 2x + 0.75$
$y = -4x - 8.25$

42. $1.25x + 3.25y = -5.75$
$0.5x - 1.5y = 0.5$

43. $x = -2y - 3.5$
$-5x + 3y = -15$

Name ______________________ Class ______________ Date ____________

Reteaching 7-2

Solving Systems Using Substitution

OBJECTIVE: Solving systems of linear equations by substitution

MATERIALS: None

Example

Solve using substitution.

$$-4x + y = -13$$
$$x - 1 = y$$

$y = 4x - 13$ ← **Rewrite each equation in the form $y = mx + b$.**

$y = x - 1$

$y = \boxed{4x - 13}$ ← **Circle the sides of the equations that do not contain y.**

$y = \boxed{x - 1}$

$4x - 13 = x - 1$ ← **Since both circled parts equal y, they are equal to each other.**

$3x = 12$ ← **Solve for x.**

$x = 4$

$y = 4x - 13$ ← **Substitute 4 for x in either equation. Solve for y.**

$y = 4(4) - 13$

$y = 3$

The solution is (4, 3).

Check to see whether (4, 3) makes both equations true. If it doesn't, then the system has no solution.

$-4(4) + 3 \stackrel{?}{=} -13$ $\qquad$ $4 - 1 \stackrel{?}{=} 3$

$-16 + 3 \stackrel{?}{=} -13$ $\qquad$ $3 = 3$ ✓

$-13 = -13$ ✓

Exercises

Solve each system using substitution. Check your solution.

1. $-3x + y = -2$
$y = x + 6$

2. $y + 4 = x$
$-2x + y = 8$

3. $y - 2 = x$
$-x = y$

4. $6y + 4x = 12$
$-6x + y = -8$

5. $3x + y = 5$
$2x - 5y = 9$

6. $x + 4y = 5$
$4x - 2y = 11$

7. $2y - 3x = 4$
$x = -2$

8. $3y + x = -1$
$x = -3y$

9. $2x + y = -1$
$6x = -3y - 3$

Name ______________ Class ______________ Date ______________

Practice 7-2

Solving Systems Using Substitution

Solve each system using substitution. Write *no solution* or *infinitely many solutions* where appropriate.

1. $y = x$
$y = -x + 2$
2. $y = x + 4$
$y = 3x$
3. $y = 3x - 10$
$y = 2x - 5$
4. $x = -2y + 1$
$x = y - 5$
5. $y = 5x + 5$
$y = 15x - 1$
6. $y = x - 3$
$y = -3x + 25$
7. $y = x - 7$
$2x + y = 8$
8. $y = 3x - 6$
$-3x + y = -6$
9. $x + 2y = 200$
$x = y + 50$
10. $3x + y = 10$
$y = -3x + 4$
11. $y = 2x + 7$
$y = 5x + 4$
12. $3x - 2y = 0$
$x + y = -5$
13. $4x + 2y = 8$
$y = -2x + 4$
14. $6x - 3y = 6$
$y = 2x + 5$
15. $2x + 4y = -6$
$x - 3y = 7$
16. $5x - 3y = -4$
$x + y = -4$
17. $y = -\frac{2}{3}x + 4$
$2x + 3y = -6$
18. $2x + 3y = 8$
$\frac{3}{2}y = 4 - x$
19. $3x - y = 4$
$2x + y = 16$
20. $x + y = 0$
$x = y + 4$
21. $5x + 2y = 6$
$y = -\frac{5}{2}x + 1$
22. $2x + 5y = -6$
$4x + y = -12$
23. $4x + 3y = -3$
$2x + y = -1$
24. $y = -\frac{2}{3}x + 1$
$4x + 6y = 6$
25. $5x - 6y = 19$
$4x + 3y = 10$
26. $2x + y = 6.6$
$5x - 2y = 0.3$
27. $2x - 4y = 3.8$
$3x - y = 17.7$
28. $3x + 4y = 8$
$4.5x + 6y = 12$
29. $3x - 4y = -5$
$x = y + 2$
30. $y = \frac{1}{3}x + 10$
$x = 3y + 6$
31. $2x + 5y = 62$
$3x - y = 23.3$
32. $-5x + y = 6$
$2x - 3y = 60$
33. $x = \frac{3}{4}y - 6$
$y = \frac{4}{3}x + 8$
34. $5x + 6y = -76$
$x + 2y = -44$
35. $3x - 2y = 10$
$y = \frac{3}{2}x - 1$
36. $-3x + 2y = -6$
$-2x + y = 6$
37. At an ice cream parlor, ice cream cones cost \$1.10 and sundaes cost \$2.35. One day, the receipts for a total of 172 cones and sundaes were \$294.20. How many cones were sold?
38. You purchase 8 gal of paint and 3 brushes for \$152.50. The next day, you purchase 6 gal of paint and 2 brushes for \$113.00. How much does each gallon of paint and each brush cost?

Name ______________________ Class ______________ Date ______________

Reteaching 7-3

Solving Systems Using Elimination

OBJECTIVE: Solving systems of linear equations using elimination

MATERIALS: At least 15 of each of three types or colors of objects, such as beans, colored cubes, or paper clips

When both linear equations of a system are in the form $Ax + By = C$, you can solve the system by elimination. You can use different objects (or, in the example below, symbols) to represent A, B, and C.

Example

Model each equation. Then solve the system of linear equations by elimination.

$$4x - 5y = -7$$
$$4x + y = -1$$

Use: ✱ for the coefficient of x, ■ for the coefficient of y, and ✦ for the constant.

a.

x y

✱✱✱✱ − ■■■■■ = −✦✦✦✦✦✦✦

✱✱✱✱ + ■ = −✦

b. Since there are an equal number of ✱s, subtract the second equation to eliminate x.

✱✱✱✱ − ■■■■■ = −✦✦✦✦✦✦✦

(−)✱✱✱✱ + (−)■ = (−)−✦

− ■■■■■■ = −✦✦✦✦✦✦

c. Since there are six items on the variable side of the equation, divide by 6 on each side to find that $y = 1$.

d. Now solve for the value of the eliminated variable in either equation.

$4x - 5(1) = -7$ ⟵ **Substitute 1 for *y*.**

$4x = -2$ ⟵ **Solve for *x*.**

$x = -\frac{1}{2}$

Since $x = -\frac{1}{2}$ and $y = 1$, the solution is $(-\frac{1}{2}, -1)$.

Check. See whether $(-\frac{1}{2}, 1)$ makes the other equation true.

$$4x + y = -1$$
$$4(-\tfrac{1}{2}) + 1 \stackrel{?}{=} -1$$
$$-1 = -1 \checkmark$$

Exercises

Use different objects that represent *A*, *B*, and *C* to model and solve each system by elimination.

1. $3x + 5y = 6$
$-3x + y = 6$

2. $2x + 4y = -4$
$2x + y = 8$

3. $y = x + 2$
$y = -x$

Name ______________________ Class ______________________ Date ______________

Practice 7-3

Solving Systems Using Elimination

Solve by elimination. Show your work.

1. $x + 2y = 7$
   $3x - 2y = -3$

2. $3x + y = 20$
   $x + y = 12$

3. $5x + 7y = 77$
   $5x + 3y = 53$

4. $2x + 5y = -1$
   $x + 2y = 0$

5. $3x + 6y = 6$
   $2x - 3y = 4$

6. $2x + y = 3$
   $-2x + y = 1$

7. $9x - 3y = 24$
   $7x - 3y = 20$

8. $2x + 7y = 5$
   $2x + 3y = 9$

9. $x + y = 30$
   $x - y = 6$

10. $4x - y = 6$
    $3x + 2y = 21$

11. $x + 2y = 9$
    $3x + 2y = 7$

12. $3x + 5y = 10$
    $x - 5y = -10$

13. $2x - 3y = -11$
    $3x + 2y = 29$

14. $8x - 9y = 19$
    $4x + y = -7$

15. $2x + 6y = 0$
    $-2x - 5y = 0$

16. $-2x + 3y = -9$
    $x + 3y = 3$

17. $4x - 3y = 11$
    $3x - 5y = -11$

18. $3x + 7y = 48$
    $5x - 7y = -32$

19. $-2x + 3y = 25$
    $-2x + 6y = 58$

20. $3x + 8y = 81$
    $5x - 6y = -39$

21. $8x + 13y = 179$
    $2x - 13y = -69$

22. $-x + 8y = -32$
    $3x - y = 27$

23. $2x + 7y = -7$
    $5x + 7y = 14$

24. $x + 6y = 48$
    $-x + y = 8$

25. $6x + 3y = 0$
    $-3x + 3y = 9$

26. $7x + 3y = 25$
    $-2x - y = -8$

27. $3x - 8y = 32$
    $-x + 8y = -16$

28. $4x - 7y = -15$
    $-4x - 3y = -15$

29. $5x + 7y = -1$
    $4x - 2y = 22$

30. $6x - 3y = 69$
    $7x - 3y = 76$

31. $x + 8y = 28$
    $-3x + 5y = 3$

32. $8x - 6y = -122$
    $-4x + 6y = 94$

33. $2x + 9y = 36$
    $2x - y = 16$

34. $-6x + 12y = 120$
    $5x - 6y = -48$

35. $-x + 3y = 5$
    $-x - 3y = 1$

36. $10x - 4y = 6$
    $10x + 3y = 13$

37. $6x + 3y = 27$
    $-4x + 7y = 27$

38. $6x - 8y = 40$
    $5x + 8y = 48$

39. $3x + y = 27$
    $-3x + 4y = -42$

40. $2x + 8y = -42$
    $-x + 8y = -63$

41. $5x + 9y = 112$
    $3x - 2y = 8$

42. $-3x + 2y = 0$
    $-3x + 5y = 9$

43. $8x - 2y = 58$
    $6x - 2y = 40$

44. $7x - 9y = -57$
    $-7x + 10y = 68$

45. $9x + 3y = 2$
    $-9x - y = 0$

46. Shopping at Savers Mart, Lisa buys her children four shirts and three pairs of pants for \$85.50. She returns the next day and buys three shirts and five pairs of pants for \$115.00. What is the price of each shirt and each pair of pants?

47. Grandma's Bakery sells single-crust apple pies for \$6.99 and double-crust cherry pies for \$10.99. The total number of pies sold on a busy Friday was 36. If the amount collected for all the pies that day was \$331.64, how many of each type were sold?

Name ______________________ Class ______________ Date ____________

Reteaching 7-4

Applications of Linear Systems

OBJECTIVE: Writing and solving systems of linear equations

MATERIALS: Graph paper or graphing calculator

As you solve multi-step systems of linear equations, remember these strategies:

- Determine which form each equation is in:

  $Ax + By = C$ or $y = mx + b$
- If the equations are in the form $Ax + By = C$ and a variable can easily be eliminated, use elimination.
- If the equations are in $y = mx + b$ form, use graphing or substitution.

Example

Last year, Zach received \$469.75 in interest from two investments. The interest rates were 7.5% on one account and 8% on the other. If the total amount invested was \$6000, how much was invested at each rate?

Define x = investment in first account; y = investment in second account

Relate The total amount invested was \$6000.

Write

$$x + y = 6000$$
$$0.075x + 0.08y = 469.75$$

← **Determine the form of each equation: $Ax + By = C$**

$$y = -x + 6000$$

← **Since a variable cannot easily be eliminated, rewrite one equation in the form $y = mx + b$.**

$$0.075x + 0.08(-x + 6000) = 469.75$$

← **Substitute $-x + 6000$ for y.**

$$-0.005x = -10.25$$

← **Solve for x.**

$$x = 2050$$
$$2050 + y = 6000$$

← **Substitute 2050 for x in the first equation and solve for y.**

$$y = 3950$$

The amount invested in the first account was \$2050. The amount invested in the second account was \$3950.

Exercises

Model with a system of equations and solve using elimination, substitution, and graphing. Explain which is the best method, and why.

1. Mary ordered lunch for herself and several co-workers on Monday and Tuesday. On Monday, she paid \$7 for five sandwiches and four sodas. On Tuesday, she paid \$6 for four of each. Find the price of a sandwich and the price of a soda.

2. A local landscape company had a one-week sale. On Monday, Mrs. Jones had \$82 to spend. After purchasing 5 trees, she had just enough money left to purchase 1 shrub. Later in that same week, she purchased 2 trees. She had \$37 with her, so she again had enough money left to purchase 1 shrub. Find the cost of a tree and the cost of a shrub.

Name ______________________ Class ______________ Date ______________

Practice 7-4

Applications of Linear Systems

Use a system of linear equations to solve each problem.

1. Your teacher is giving you a test worth 100 points containing 40 questions. There are two-point and four-point questions on the test. How many of each type of question are on the test?

2. Suppose you are starting an office-cleaning service. You have spent $315 on equipment. To clean an office, you use $4 worth of supplies. You charge $25 per office. How many offices must you clean to break even?

3. The math club and the science club had fundraisers to buy supplies for a hospice. The math club spent $135 buying six cases of juice and one case of bottled water. The science club spent $110 buying four cases of juice and two cases of bottled water. How much did a case of juice cost? How much did a case of bottled water cost?

4. On a canoe trip, Rita paddled upstream (against the current) at an average speed of 2 mi/h relative to the riverbank. On the return trip downstream (with the current), her average speed was 3 mi/h. Find Rita's paddling speed in still water and the speed of the river's current.

5. Kay spends 250 min/wk exercising. Her ratio of time spent on aerobics to time spent on weight training is 3 to 2. How many minutes per week does she spend on aerobics? How many minutes per week does she spend on weight training?

6. Suppose you invest $1500 in equipment to put pictures on T-shirts. You buy each T-shirt for $3. After you have placed the picture on a shirt, you sell it for $20. How many T-shirts must you sell to break even?

7. A light plane flew from its home base to an airport 255 miles away. With a head wind, the trip took 1.7 hours. The return trip with a tail wind took 1.5 hours. Find the average airspeed of the plane and the average windspeed.

8. Suppose you bought supplies for a party. Three rolls of streamers and 15 party hats cost $30. Later, you bought 2 rolls of streamers and 4 party hats for $11. How much did each roll of streamers cost? How much did each party hat cost?

9. A new parking lot has spaces for 450 cars. The ratio of spaces for full-sized cars to compact cars is 11 to 4. How many spaces are for full-sized cars? How many spaces are for compact cars?

10. While on vacation, Kevin went for a swim in a nearby lake. Swimming against the current, it took him 8 minutes to swim 200 meters. Swimming back to shore with the current took half as long. Find Kevin's average swimming speed and the speed of the lake's current.

Name ______________________ Class ______________ Date ______________

Reteaching 7-5

Linear Inequalities

OBJECTIVE: Graphing linear inequalities

MATERIALS: Graph paper

To graph inequalities, use the same strategies used to graph equations. Remember that the boundary line is solid if the inequality has an equal sign (indicating that the points on the boundary line are part of the solution) and dashed if the inequality does not have an equal sign (indicating that the points on the boundary line are not part of the solution).

Example

Graph the inequality $y - 3 < x$.

a. The equation of the boundary line is $y - 3 = x$. Rewrite the equation in the form $y = mx + b$.

$y = x + 3$

b. Graph the boundary line, $y = x + 3$. Since coordinates of points on the boundary line do not make the inequality true, graph a dashed line.

c. Use these guidelines for shading: If the inequality sign is less than (<), then shade the lower region of the graph (or the left region, for the vertical lines). Otherwise, shade the upper region of the graph (or the right region, for vertical lines).

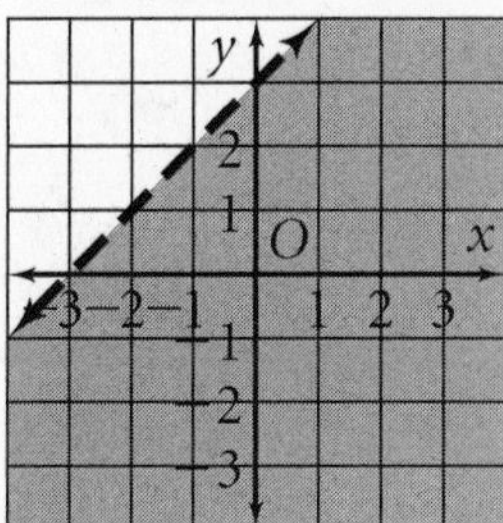

d. Test the point (0, 0) from the shaded region. See whether (0, 0) satisfies the original inequality.

$y - 3 < x$

$0 - 3 < 0$

$-3 < 0$ **True**

The inequality is true for (0, 0). So the shaded region is correct.

Exercises

Follow steps a–d above to graph each linear inequality.

1. $y < x + 2$

2. $y \leq 2x + 1$

3. $y > x$

Name ______________________ Class ______________ Date ______________

Practice 7-5

Linear Inequalities

Graph each linear inequality.

1. $y \geq -4$
2. $x + y < -2$
3. $y < x$
4. $x > 2$
5. $4x + y > -6$
6. $-3x + y \leq -3$
7. $x + 4y \leq 8$
8. $y > 2x + 6$
9. $y > -x + 2$
10. $2x + 3y < -9$
11. $y \leq \frac{3}{7}x + 2$
12. $4x + 2y < -8$
13. $y \leq \frac{3}{4}x + 1$
14. $x - y > 4$
15. $y \geq -\frac{2}{5}x - 2$

16. Suppose your class is raising money for the Red Cross. You make $5 on each basket of fruit and $3 on each box of cheese that you sell. How many items of each type must you sell to raise more than $150?
    a. Write a linear inequality that describes the situation.
    b. Graph the inequality.
    c. Write two possible solutions to the problem.

17. Suppose you intend to spend no more than $60 buying books. Hardback books cost $12 and paperbacks cost $5. How many books of each type can you buy?
    a. Write a linear inequality that describes the situation.
    b. Graph the inequality.
    c. Write two possible solutions to the problem.

18. Suppose that for your exercise program, you either walk 5 mi/d or ride your bicycle 10 mi/d. How many days will it take you to cover a distance of at least 150 mi?
    a. Write a linear inequality that describes the situation.
    b. Graph the inequality.
    c. Write two possible solutions to the problem.

Graph each linear inequality.

19. $6x - 4y > -16$
20. $y \geq -\frac{1}{4}x - 3$
21. $-5x + 4y < -24$
22. $y < -5x + 6$
23. $6x - 4y < -12$
24. $y \geq -\frac{9}{5}x + 7$
25. $y > \frac{5}{7}x - 3$
26. $y < -5x + 9$
27. $-7x + 3y < -18$
28. $y \geq \frac{6}{5}x - 8$
29. $-12x + 8y < 56$
30. $16x + 6y > 36$

Name ______________________ Class ______________ Date ______________

Reteaching 7-6

Systems of Linear Inequalities

OBJECTIVE: Solving systems of linear inequalities by graphing

MATERIALS: Graph paper, two highlighting markers in colors that combine to make a third color (pink and yellow, for example)

- When you graph the first inequality, mark the solution area with one color. Then graph the second inequality and mark the solution area with the other color. The common solution for the two inequalities appears where the two colors combine to make a third color.
- To graph inequalities, use the same strategies you use to graph equations.
- The boundary line is solid if the inequality has an equal sign (indicating that the points on the line are part of the solution) and dashed if the inequality does not have an equal sign.

Example

Solve by graphing.

$y - x < 5$
$y + 6 \geq 2x$

a. Rewrite the inequalities in slope-intercept form.
$y < x + 5$
$y \geq 2x - 6$

b. Graph the boundary line, $y = x + 5$ using a dashed line.

c. Test the inequality $y - x < 5$ using the point $(0, 0)$. Since the inequality is true for $(0, 0)$, shade the region containing $(0, 0)$ yellow.

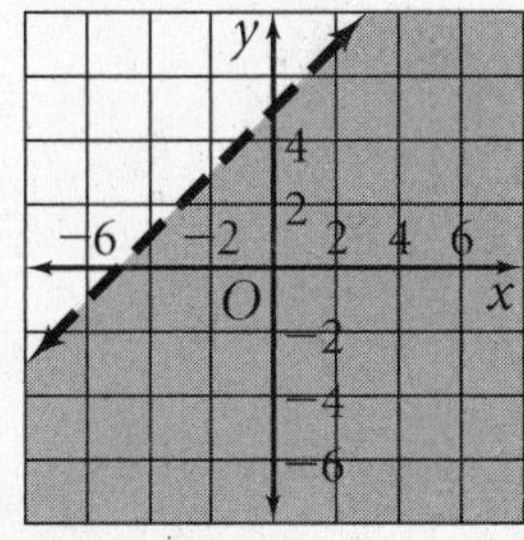

d. Graph the boundary line, $y = 2x - 6$ using a solid line.

e. Test the inequality $y + 6 \geq 2x$ using the point $(0, 0)$. It is true; therefore, shade the region containing $(0, 0)$ pink, including the boundary line.

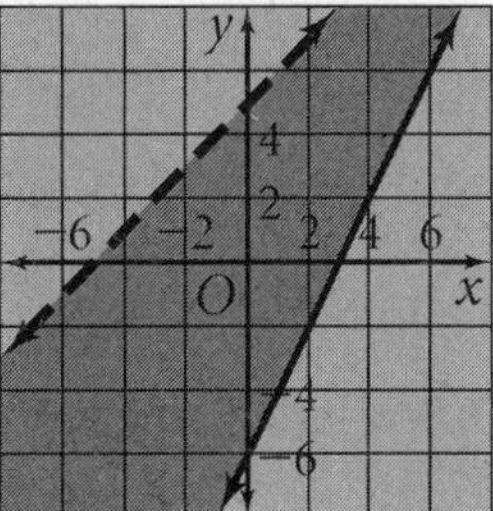

f. The region that appears orange is the solution region.

Exercises

Follow steps a–f above to graph each system of linear inequalities.

1. $y < 4x - 7$
$y > \frac{1}{2}x + 4$

2. $y - 4 < x$
$3y < x + 6$

3. $2x + 3y > 6$
$x - y \leq 0$

Name ______________________ Class ______________ Date ____________

Practice 7-6

Systems of Linear Inequalities

Solve each system by graphing. Show your work.

1. $y < 6$, $y > 3$
2. $x < 7$, $y > 2$
3. $x < 2$, $x > 5$
4. $x + y > -2$, $-x + y < 1$
5. $x + y < 2$, $x + y > 5$
6. $y < -5x + 6$, $y > 2x - 1$
7. $y < 2x - 3$, $-2x + y > 5$
8. $-x + 3y < 12$, $y \geq -x + 4$
9. $y \leq -\frac{1}{2}x + 3$, $y \geq -\frac{5}{3}x + 2$
10. $y \geq \frac{3}{4}x + 1$, $y \geq -\frac{2}{3}x - 1$
11. $6x + 4y > 12$, $-3x + 4y > 12$
12. $3x + y < 6$, $-2x + y < 6$
13. $-4x + 2y < -2$, $-2x + y > 3$
14. $-5x + y > -2$, $4x + y < 1$
15. $y < \frac{9}{5}x - 8$, $-9x + 5y > 25$
16. $5x + 4y < 1$, $8y \geq -10x + 24$
17. $6x + 8y < 32$, $-4x + 6y < 24$
18. $x + 7y < 14$, $x - 6y > -12$

19. In basketball you score 2 points for a field goal and 1 point for a free throw. Suppose that you have scored at least 3 points in every game this season, and have a season high score of 15 points in one game. How many field goals and free throws could you have made in any one game?
    a. Write a system of two inequalities that describes this situation.
    b. Graph the system to show all possible solutions.
    c. Write one possible solution to the problem.

20. Suppose you need to use at least \$1.00 worth of stamps to mail a package. You have as many \$.03 stamps as you need but only four \$.32 stamps. How many of each stamp can you use?
    a. Write a system of two inequalities that describes this situation.
    b. Graph the system to show all possible solutions.
    c. Write one possible solution to the problem.

21. A grandmother wants to spend at least \$40 but no more than \$60 on school clothes for her grandson. T-shirts sell for \$10 and pants sell for \$20. How many T-shirts and pants could she buy?
    a. Write a system of two inequalities that describes this situation.
    b. Graph the system to show all possible solutions.
    c. Write two possible solutions to the problem.

Name ______________________ Class ______________ Date ______________

Reteaching 8-1

Zero and Negative Exponents

OBJECTIVE: Evaluating and simplifying expressions in which zero and negative numbers are used as exponents

MATERIALS: None

- When a nonzero number a has a zero exponent, then $a^0 = 1$.
- For any nonzero number a and any integer n, $a^{-n} = \frac{1}{a^n}$.

Example

Write each expression as an integer or a simple fraction.

a. 2.7^0

1 ⟵ **Rewrite, using the Property of Zero as an exponent.**

b. 5^{-2}

$\frac{1}{5^2}$ ⟵ **Rewrite as a fraction, using the Property of Negative Exponents.**

$\frac{1}{25}$ ⟵ **Simplify.**

Exercises

Write each expression as an integer, a simple fraction, or an expression that contains only positive exponents. Simplify.

1. 10^{-3}

2. 1.67^0

3. 5^{-4}

4. 7^{-3}

5. $\left(-\frac{3}{2}\right)^{-2}$

6. $(5x)^{-4}$

7. 4^{-1}

8. 376.5^0

9. b^{-5}

Write each expression so that it contains only positive exponents.

10. $\left(\frac{2}{7}\right)^{-4}$

11. $3ab^0$

12. -4^{-3}

13. $a^{-3}b^{-4}$

14. $\frac{3x^{-2}}{y}$

15. $12xy^{-3}$

16. $\frac{8}{4^{-2}}$

17. $\frac{(3x)^{-1}}{4}$

18. $\frac{(2x)^{-2}}{3y^{-1}}$

19. $\frac{(4x)^{-2}}{2^{-3}}$

20. $\frac{(3a)^2b^{-3}}{b^{-2}}$

21. $\frac{4^0 5^3}{2^{-3}}$

Name ______________________ Class ______________ Date ______________

Practice 8-1

Zero and Negative Exponents

Simplify each expression.

1. 16^0 **2.** 4^{-2} **3.** 3^{-3} **4.** 8^{-4}

5. $\frac{1}{2^{-5}}$ **6.** $\frac{4}{4^{-3}}$ **7.** $\frac{3}{6^{-1}}$ **8.** $\frac{2^{-1}}{2^{-5}}$

9. $3 \cdot 8^0$ **10.** $16 \cdot 2^{-2}$ **11.** 12^{-1} **12.** -7^{-2}

13. $16 \cdot 4^0$ **14.** 9^0 **15.** $\frac{32^{-1}}{8^{-1}}$ **16.** $\frac{9}{2^{-1}}$

17. $\frac{8^{-2}}{4^0}$ **18.** $\frac{9^{-1}}{3^{-2}}$ **19.** $5(-6)^0$ **20.** $(3.7)^0$

21. $(-9)^{-2}$ **22.** $(-4.9)^0$ **23.** $-6 \cdot 3^{-4}$ **24.** $\frac{7^{-2}}{4^{-1}}$

Evaluate each expression for $a = -2$ and $b = 6$.

25. b^{-2} **26.** a^{-3} **27.** $(-a)^{-4}$ **28.** $-b^{-3}$

29. $4a^{-3}$ **30.** $2b^{-2}$ **31.** $(3a)^{-2}$ **32.** $(-b)^{-2}$

33. $2a^{-1}b^{-2}$ **34.** $-4a^{-2}b^{-3}$ **35.** $3^{-2}a^{-2}b^{-1}$ **36.** $(3ab)^{-2}$

Simplify each expression.

37. x^{-8} **38.** xy^{-3} **39.** $a^{-5}b$ **40.** m^2n^{-9}

41. $\frac{1}{x^{-7}}$ **42.** $\frac{3}{a^{-4}}$ **43.** $\frac{5}{d^{-3}}$ **44.** $\frac{6}{r^{-5}s^{-1}}$

45. $3x^{-6}y^{-5}$ **46.** $8a^{-3}b^2c^{-2}$ **47.** $15s^{-9}t^{-1}$ **48.** $-7p^{-5}q^{-3}r^2$

49. $\frac{d^{-4}}{e^{-7}}$ **50.** $\frac{3m^{-4}}{n^{-8}}$ **51.** $\frac{6m^{-8}n}{p^{-1}}$ **52.** $\frac{a^{-2}b^{-1}}{cd^{-3}}$

Write each number as a power of 10 using a negative exponent.

53. $\frac{1}{10{,}000}$ **54.** $\frac{1}{1{,}000{,}000}$ **55.** $\frac{1}{10{,}000{,}000}$ **56.** $\frac{1}{1{,}000{,}000{,}000}$

Write each expression as a decimal.

57. 10^{-5} **58.** 10^{-8} **59.** $4 \cdot 10^{-1}$ **60.** $6 \cdot 10^{-4}$

Evaluate each expression for $m = 4$, $n = 5$, and $p = -2$.

61. m^p **62.** n^m **63.** p^p **64.** n^p

65. m^pn **66.** m^{-n} **67.** p^{-n} **68.** mn^p

69. p^{-m} **70.** $\frac{m}{n^p}$ **71.** $\frac{1}{n^{-m}}$ **72.** $-n^{-m}$

Reteaching 8-2

Scientific Notation

OBJECTIVE: Writing numbers in scientific notation

MATERIALS: None

To write a number in **scientific notation**, follow these steps:

- Move the decimal to the right of the first integer.
- If the original number is greater than 1, multiply by 10^n, where n represents the number of places the decimal was moved to the left.
- If the original number is less than 1, multiply by 10^{-n}, where n represents the number of places the decimal was moved to the right.

Examples

Write each number in scientific notation.

a. 9,040,000,000 ⟵ **standard form**

9.040 000 000. ⟵ **Move the decimal to the left nine places.**

9.04×10^9 ⟵ **Drop all insignificant 0's. Multiply by the appropriate power of 10.**

b. 0.000 000 8 ⟵ **standard form**

0.000 000 8. ⟵ **Move the decimal to the right seven places.**

8.0×10^{-7} ⟵ **Multiply by the appropriate power of 10.**

Exercises

Write each number in scientific notation.

1. 420,000 **2.** 5,100,000,000 **3.** 260 billion

4. 830 million **5.** 0.00075 **6.** 0.004005

Write each number in standard notation.

7. 6.345×10^8 **8.** 3.2×10^{-5} **9.** 4.081×10^6

10. 2.581×10^{-3} **11.** 3.07×10^{-2} **12.** 1.526×10^6

13. 8.04×10^{-4} **14.** 7.625×10^5 **15.** 6.825×10^4

16. 3.081×10^{-5} **17.** 8.3847×10^2 **18.** 3.6245×10^{-2}

Name ______________________ Class ______________ Date ______________

Practice 8-2

Scientific Notation

Write each number in standard notation.

1. 7×10^4
2. 3×10^{-2}
3. 2.6×10^5
4. 7.1×10^{-4}
5. 5.71×10^{-5}
6. 4.155×10^7
7. 3.0107×10^2
8. 9.407×10^{-5}
9. 31.3×10^6
10. 83.7×10^{-4}
11. 0.018×10^{-1}
12. 0.016×10^5
13. 8.0023×10^{-3}
14. 6.902×10^8
15. 1005×10^2
16. 0.095×10^{-1}

Write each number in scientific notation.

17. 51,000,000
18. 975,000,000,000
19. 0.00000012
20. 0.000005008
21. 1560 billion
22. 0.5 million
23. 2 thousandths
24. 1095 millionths
25. 194×10^3
26. 154×10^{-3}
27. 0.05×10^6
28. 0.031×10^{-4}
29. 790 thousand
30. 25 hundredths
31. 0.000000000159
32. 5,000,900,000,000

Order the numbers in each list from least to greatest.

33. $7 \times 10^{-7}, 6 \times 10^{-8}, 5 \times 10^{-6}, 4 \times 10^{-10}$
34. $5.01 \times 10^{-4}, 4.8 \times 10^{-3}, 5.2 \times 10^{-2}, 5.6 \times 10^{-2}$
35. $62{,}040, 6.2 \times 10^2, 6.207 \times 10^3, 6.34 \times 10^{-1}$
36. $10^{-3}, 5 \times 10^{-3}, 8 \times 10^{-2}, 4 \times 10^{-1}$

Simplify. Write each answer using scientific notation.

37. $4(3 \times 10^5)$
38. $5(7 \times 10^{-2})$
39. $8(9 \times 10^9)$
40. $7(9 \times 10^6)$
41. $3(1.2 \times 10^{-4})$
42. $2(6.1 \times 10^{-8})$
43. $3(1.2 \times 10^{-4})$
44. $3(4.3 \times 10^{-4})$
45. $3(3.2 \times 10^{-2})$

Complete the table.

	Units of Area in Square Feet		
	Unit	**Standard Form**	**Scientific Notation**
46.	1 in.^{2} =		6.9444×10^{-3}
47.	1 link^2 =	0.4356	
48.	1 rod^2 =	272.25	
49.	1 mi^2 =		2.78×10^7
50.	1 cm^2 =	0.001076	
51.	1 hectare =		1.08×10^7

Name ____________________ Class ____________ Date ____________

Reteaching 8-3

Multiplication Properties of Exponents

OBJECTIVE: Multiplying powers with the same base

MATERIALS: None

- A power is an expression in the form a^n.
- To multiply powers with the same base, add the exponents $a^m \cdot a^n = a^{m+n}$

Example

Simplify $4^6 \cdot 4^3$.

$4^6 \cdot 4^3$

$= 4^{6+3}$ ⟵ **Rewrite as one base with the exponents added.**

$= 4^9$ ⟵ **Add the exponents.**

So $4^6 \cdot 4^3 = 4^9$.

Exercises

Complete each equation.

1. $8^2 \cdot 8^3 = 8^{■}$

2. $2^{■} \cdot 2^6 = 2^9$

3. $a^{12} \cdot a^{■} = a^{15}$

4. $x^{■} \cdot x^5 = x^6$

5. $b^{-4} \cdot b^3 = b^{■}$

6. $6^4 \cdot 6^{■} = 6^2$

7. $3^4 \cdot 3^8 = 3^{■}$

8. $c^{■} \cdot c^{-7} = c^{11}$

9. $10^{-6} \cdot 10^{-3} = 10^{■}$

Simplify each expression.

10. $3x^2 \cdot 4x \cdot 2x^3$

11. $m^2 \cdot 3m^4 \cdot 6a \cdot a^{-3}$

12. $p^3q^{-1} \cdot p^2q^{-8}$

13. $5x^2 \cdot 3x \cdot 8x^4$

14. $x^2 \cdot y^5 \cdot 8x^5 \cdot y^{-2}$

15. $7y^2 \cdot 3x^2 \cdot 9$

16. $2y^2 \cdot 3y^2 \cdot 4y^5$

17. $x^4 \cdot x^{-5} \cdot x^4$

18. $x^{12} \cdot x^{-8} \cdot y^{-2} \cdot y^3$

19. $6a^2 \cdot b \cdot 2a^{-1}$

20. $r^6 \cdot s^{-3} \cdot r^{-2} \cdot s$

21. $3p^{-2} \cdot q^3 \cdot p^3 \cdot q^{-2}$

Name ________________ Class ________________ Date ________________

Practice 8-3

Multiplication Properties of Exponents

Simplify each expression.

1. $(3d^{-4})(5d^{8})$
2. $(-8m^{4})(4m^{8})$
3. $n^{-6} \cdot n^{-9}$
4. $a^{3} \cdot a$
5. $3^{8} \cdot 3^{5}$
6. $(3p^{-15})(6p^{11})$
7. $p^{7} \cdot q^{5} \cdot p^{6}$
8. $(-1.5a^{5}b^{2})(6a)$
9. $(-2d^{3}e^{3})(6d^{4}e^{6})$
10. $\dfrac{1}{b^{-7} \cdot b^{5}}$
11. $p^{5} \cdot q^{2} \cdot p^{4}$
12. $\dfrac{1}{n^{7} \cdot n^{-5}}$
13. $(8d^{4})(4d^{7})$
14. $x^{-9} \cdot x^{3} \cdot x^{2}$
15. $2^{3} \cdot 2^{2}$
16. $r^{7} \cdot s^{4} \cdot s \cdot r^{3}$
17. $b^{7} \cdot b^{13}$
18. $(7p^{4})(5p^{9})$
19. $2^{8} \cdot 2^{-9} \cdot 2^{3}$
20. $(6r^{4}s^{3})(9rs^{2})$
21. $4^{3} \cdot 4^{2}$
22. $m^{12} \cdot m^{-14}$
23. $s^{7} \cdot t^{4} \cdot t^{8}$
24. $(-3xy^{6})(3.2x^{5}y)$
25. $5^{-7} \cdot 5^{9}$
26. $\dfrac{1}{h^{7} \cdot h^{3}}$
27. $\dfrac{1}{t^{-5} \cdot t^{-3}}$
28. $f^{5} \cdot f^{2} \cdot f^{0}$
29. $r^{6} \cdot r^{-13}$
30. $5^{-6} \cdot 5^{4}$

Simplify each expression. Write each answer in scientific notation.

31. $(7 \times 10^{7})(5 \times 10^{-5})$
32. $(3 \times 10^{8})(3 \times 10^{4})$
33. $(9.5 \times 10^{-4})(2 \times 10^{-5})$
34. $(4 \times 10^{9})(4.1 \times 10^{8})$
35. $(7.2 \times 10^{-7})(2 \times 10^{-5})$
36. $(5 \times 10^{7})(4 \times 10^{3})$
37. $(6 \times 10^{-6})(5.2 \times 10^{4})$
38. $(4 \times 10^{6})(9 \times 10^{8})$
39. $(6.1 \times 10^{9})(8 \times 10^{14})$
40. $(2.1 \times 10^{-4})(4 \times 10^{-7})$
41. $(1.6 \times 10^{5})(3 \times 10^{11})$
42. $(9 \times 10^{12})(0.3 \times 10^{-18})$
43. $(4 \times 10^{9})(11 \times 10^{3})$
44. $(5 \times 10^{13})(9 \times 10^{-9})$
45. $(7 \times 10^{6})(4 \times 10^{9})$
46. $(6 \times 10^{-8})(12 \times 10^{-7})$
47. $(6 \times 10^{15})(3.2 \times 10^{2})$
48. $(5 \times 10^{8})(2.6 \times 10^{-16})$

49. In 1990, the St. Louis metropolitan area had an average of 82×10^{-6} g/m^3 of pollutants in the air. How many grams of pollutants were there in 2×10^{3} m^3 of air?

50. Light travels approximately 5.87×10^{12} mi in one year. This distance is called a light-year. Suppose a star is 2×10^{4} light-years away. How many miles away is that star?

51. The weight of 1 m^3 of air is approximately 1.3×10^{3} g. Suppose that the volume of air inside of a building is 3×10^{6} m^3. How much does the air inside the building weigh?

52. Light travels 1.18×10^{10} in. in 1 second. How far will light travel in 1 nanosecond or 1×10^{-9} s?

Name ______________________ Class ______________ Date ______________

Reteaching 8-4

OBJECTIVE: Using two more multiplication properties of exponents

MATERIALS: None

- To raise a power to a power, multiply the exponents.
- Every number and variable inside parentheses is being raised to the power to the right of the parentheses.

Example

Simplify $(4x^3)^2$.

$(4x^3)^2$	
$(4^1x^3)^2$	← **Rewrite each number and variable with an exponent.**
$(4^1x^3)^2$	← **Draw arrows from the exponent outside the parentheses to each exponent inside the parentheses.**
$4^{2 \cdot 1}x^{2 \cdot 3}$	← **Rewrite, showing the exponents to be multiplied.**
4^2x^6	← **Multiply the exponents.**
$16x^6$	← **Simplify.**

Exercises

Draw arrows from the exponent outside the parentheses to each exponent inside the parentheses. Then simplify each expression.

1. $(5^2)^4$ **2.** $(a^5)^4$ **3.** $(2^3)^2$ **4.** $(4x)^3$

5. $(7a^4)^2$ **6.** $(3g^2)^3$ **7.** $(g^2h^3)^5$ **8.** $(s^6)^2$

Simplify each expression.

9. $(x^2y^4)^3$ **10.** $(3r^5)^0$ **11.** $g^9 \cdot g^{-7}$

12. $(c^4)^7$ **13.** $(3.2)^5 \cdot (3.2)^{-5}$ **14.** $(8ab^6)^3$

15. $(x^2y^3)^2$ **16.** $(x^7)^2$ **17.** $(3x^2y)^2$

18. $(-2x^2)^3$ **19.** $(x^3y^4)^3$ **20.** $(3x^2y)^3$

21. $(-4x^2y^3)^3$ **22.** $(xyz)^0$ **23.** $x^5 \cdot x^{-7}$

Name ______________________ Class ______________ Date ______________

Practice 8-4

More Multiplication Properties of Exponents

Simplify each expression.

1. $(4a^5)^3$
2. $(2^{-3})^4$
3. $(m^{-3}n^4)^{-4}$
4. $(x^5)^2$
5. $2^5 \cdot (2^4)^2$
6. $(4x^4)^3(2xy^3)^2$
7. $x^4 \cdot (x^4)^3$
8. $(x^5y^3)^3(xy^5)^2$
9. $(5^2)^2$
10. $(a^4)^{-5} \cdot a^{13}$
11. $(3f^4g^{-3})^3(f^2g^{-2})^{-1}$
12. $x^3 \cdot (x^3)^5$
13. $(d^2)^{-4}$
14. $(a^3b^4)^{-2}(a^{-3}b^{-5})^{-4}$
15. $(x^2y)^4$
16. $(12b^{-2})^2$
17. $(m^{-5})^{-3}$
18. $(x^{-4})^5(x^3y^2)^5$
19. $(y^6)^{-3} \cdot y^{21}$
20. $n^6 \cdot (n^{-2})^5$
21. $(m^5)^{-3}(m^4n^5)^4$
22. $(a^3)^6$
23. $b^{-9} \cdot (b^2)^4$
24. $(4^{-1}s^3)^{-2}$
25. $(5a^3b^5)^4$
26. $(b^{-3})^6$
27. $(y^6)^3$
28. $a^{-4} \cdot (a^4b^3)^2$
29. $(x^4y)^3$
30. $d^3 \cdot (d^2)^5$

Simplify. Write each answer in scientific notation.

31. $10^{-9} \cdot (2 \times 10^2)^2$
32. $(3 \times 10^{-6})^3$
33. $10^4 \cdot (4 \times 10^6)^3$
34. $(9 \times 10^7)^2$
35. $10^{-3} \cdot (2 \times 10^3)^5$
36. $(7 \times 10^5)^3$
37. $(5 \times 10^5)^4$
38. $(2 \times 10^{-3})^3$
39. $(5 \times 10^2)^{-3}$
40. $(3 \times 10^5)^4$
41. $(4 \times 10^8)^{-3}$
42. $(1 \times 10^{-5})^{-5}$
43. $10^5 \cdot (8 \times 10^7)^3$
44. $(10^2)^3(6 \times 10^{-3})^3$
45. $10^7 \cdot (2 \times 10^2)^4$

46. The kinetic energy, in joules, of a moving object is found by using the formula $E = \frac{1}{2}mv^2$, where m is the mass and v is the speed of the object. The mass of a car is 1.59×10^3 kg. The car is traveling at 2.7×10^1 m/s. What is the kinetic energy of the car?

47. The moon is shaped somewhat like a sphere. The surface area of the moon is found by using the formula $S = 12.56r^2$. What is the surface area of the moon if the radius is 1.08×10^3 mi?

48. Because of a record corn harvest, excess corn is stored on the ground in a pile. The pile is shaped like a cone. The height of the pile is 25 ft, and the radius of the pile is 1.2×10^2 ft. Use the formula $V = \frac{1}{3}\pi r^2 h$ to find the volume.

49. Suppose the distance in feet that an object travels in t seconds is given by the formula $d = 64t^2$. How far would the object travel after 1.5×10^3 seconds?

Reteaching 8-5

Division Properties of Exponents

OBJECTIVE: Applying division properties of exponents

MATERIALS: None

To divide powers with the same base, subtract exponents.

Example

Simplify $\frac{4^3}{4^5}$.

Method 1

$\frac{4 \cdot 4 \cdot 4}{4 \cdot 4 \cdot 4 \cdot 4 \cdot 4}$ ⟵ **Expand the numerator and the denominator.**

$\frac{\not{4} \cdot \not{4} \cdot \not{4}}{\not{4} \cdot \not{4} \cdot \not{4} \cdot 4 \cdot 4}$ ⟵ **Draw lines through terms that are in both the numerator and the denominator.**

$\frac{1}{4 \cdot 4}$ ⟵ **Cancel.**

$\frac{1}{4^2}$ or 4^{-2} ⟵ **Rewrite with exponents.**

Method 2

$3 - 5 = -2$ ⟵ **Subtract the exponents from the original equation. Compare this to the exponent in the first answer.**

So $\frac{4^3}{4^5} = 4^{3-5} = 4^{-2}$. ⟵ **Subtract the exponents from the original equation. Compare this to the exponent in the first answer.**

$\frac{1}{4^2}$ ⟵ **Write with positive exponents.**

To raise a quotient to a power use repeated multiplication.

Exercises

Use both methods shown in the example to simplify each expression. Use only positive exponents.

1. $\frac{z^6}{z^3}$ **2.** $\left(\frac{3^2}{4}\right)^3$ **3.** $\frac{m^{-3}}{m^{-4}}$ **4.** $\frac{5^3}{5^4}$

5. $\left(\frac{b^7}{b^5}\right)^3$ **6.** $\frac{5a^5}{15a^2}$ **7.** $\frac{2^2}{2^5}$ **8.** $\frac{d^8}{d^3}$

9. $\frac{x^7}{x^5}$ **10.** $\left(\frac{10^8}{10^2}\right)^3$ **11.** $\frac{14x^{11}}{7x^{10}}$ **12.** $\frac{8x^9}{12x^6}$

13. $\frac{x^{12}}{x^5}$ **14.** $\frac{6x^4}{4x^2}$ **15.** $\frac{x^3}{x^8}$ **16.** $\left(\frac{x^5}{x^3}\right)^4$

Name ______________________ Class ______________ Date ______________

Practice 8-5

Division Properties of Exponents

Simplify each expression.

1. $\frac{c^{15}}{c^9}$
2. $\left(\frac{x^3y^{-2}}{z^{-5}}\right)^{-4}$
3. $\frac{x^7y^9z^3}{x^4y^7z^8}$
4. $\left(\frac{a^2}{b^3}\right)^5$
5. $\frac{3^7}{3^4}$
6. $\left(\frac{a^3}{b^2}\right)^4$
7. $\left(\frac{2}{3}\right)^{-2}$
8. $\left(\frac{p^{-3}q^{-2}}{q^{-3}r^5}\right)^4$
9. $\frac{a^6b^{-5}}{a^{-2}b^7}$
10. $\frac{7^{-4}}{7^{-7}}$
11. $\frac{a^7b^6}{a^5b}$
12. $\left(\frac{a^2b^{-4}}{b^2}\right)^5$
13. $\left(-\frac{3}{2^3}\right)^{-2}$
14. $\frac{z^7}{z^{-3}}$
15. $\left(\frac{5a^0b^4}{c^{-3}}\right)^2$
16. $\frac{x^4y^{-8}z^{-2}}{x^{-1}y^6z^{-10}}$
17. $\frac{m^6}{m^{10}}$
18. $\left(\frac{2^3m^4n^{-1}}{p^2}\right)^0$
19. $\left(\frac{s^{-4}}{t^{-1}}\right)^{-2}$
20. $\left(\frac{2a^3b^{-2}}{c^3}\right)^5$
21. $\left(\frac{x^{-3}y}{xz^{-4}}\right)^{-2}$
22. $\frac{h^{-13}}{h^{-8}}$
23. $\frac{4^6}{4^8}$
24. $\left(\frac{1}{3}\right)^3$
25. $\frac{x^5y^3}{x^2y^9}$
26. $\left(\frac{m^{-3}n^4}{n^{-2}}\right)^4$
27. $\frac{4^{-1}}{4^2}$
28. $\left(\frac{a^8b^6}{a^{11}}\right)^5$
29. $\frac{n^9}{n^{15}}$
30. $\left(\frac{r^3s^{-1}}{r^2s^6}\right)^{-1}$
31. $\frac{n^{-8}}{n^4}$
32. $\frac{m^8n^3}{m^{10}n^5}$

Simplify each quotient. Write each answer in scientific notation.

33. $\frac{3.54 \times 10^{-9}}{6.15 \times 10^{-5}}$
34. $\frac{9.35 \times 10^{-3}}{3.71 \times 10^{-5}}$
35. $\frac{\text{495 billion}}{\text{23.9 million}}$
36. $\frac{8 \times 10^9}{4 \times 10^5}$
37. $\frac{9.5 \times 10^9}{5 \times 10^{12}}$
38. $\frac{6.4 \times 10^9}{8 \times 10^7}$
39. $\frac{\text{298 billion}}{\text{49 million}}$
40. $\frac{1.8 \times 10^{-8}}{0.9 \times 10^3}$
41. $\frac{3.6 \times 10^6}{9 \times 10^{-3}}$
42. $\frac{8.19 \times 10^7}{4.76 \times 10^{-2}}$
43. $\frac{\text{65 million}}{\text{19.5 billion}}$
44. $\frac{4.9 \times 10^{12}}{7 \times 10^3}$
45. $\frac{\text{36.2 trillion}}{\text{98.5 billion}}$
46. $\frac{3.9 \times 10^3}{1.3 \times 10^8}$
47. $\frac{5.6 \times 10^{-5}}{8 \times 10^{-7}}$
48. $\frac{\text{40 million}}{\text{985 million}}$

49. The half-life of uranium-238 is 4.5×10^9 years. The half-life of uranium-234 is 2.5×10^5 years. How many times greater is the half-life of uranium-238 than that of uranium-234?

Name ______________________ Class ____________ Date ____________

Reteaching 8-6

Geometric Sequences

OBJECTIVE: Finding the next terms of a geometric sequence

MATERIALS: None

- Multiplying a term in the sequence by a fixed number to find the next term forms a geometric sequence.
- The fixed number is called the common ratio.

Example

Find the next three terms of the sequence 3, −9, 27, −81, . . .

3, −9, 27, −81, . . .

$-\frac{9}{3} = -3$

The common ratio is −3.

Note that each term in the given sequence is −3 times the previous term.

Let A(n) = the value of the nth term in the sequence.

A(5) = −3 · −81 = 243 ⟵ **the common ratio times the fourth term**

A(6) = −3 · 243 = −729 ⟵ **the common ratio times the fifth term**

A(7) = −3 · −729 = 2187 ⟵ **the common ratio times the sixth term**

The next three terms in the sequence are 243, −729, 2187.

Exercises

Find the next three terms in each of the following sequences.

1. 2, 8, 32, 128, . . .

2. −3, 6, −12, 24, . . .

3. 1, −1, 1, −1, . . .

4. 12, 6, 3, $\frac{3}{2}$, . . .

5. 20, −10, 5, $-\frac{5}{2}$, . . .

6. 100, 10, 1, 0.1, . . .

7. 3, 15, 75, 375, . . .

8. −8, −12, −18, −27, . . .

9. 1.5, 4.5, 13.5, 40.5, . . .

10. 8, $-\frac{8}{3}$, $\frac{8}{9}$, $-\frac{8}{27}$, . . .

11. 7, −14, 28, −56, . . .

12. 100, 50, 25, 12.5, . . .

13. 8, 32, 128, 512, . . .

14. 76, −38, 19, −9.5, . . .

Name ______________________ Class ______________ Date ______________

Practice 8-6

Geometric Sequences

Find the next three terms of each sequence.

1. $4, 12, 36, 108, \ldots$

2. $2, -8, 32, -128, \ldots$

3. $18, 9, \frac{9}{2}, \frac{9}{4}, \ldots$

4. $1, -\frac{1}{3}, \frac{1}{9}, -\frac{1}{27}, \ldots$

5. $-2, 20, -200, 2000, \ldots$

6. $30, -10, \frac{10}{3}, -\frac{10}{9}, \ldots$

7. $\frac{1}{3}, 1\frac{1}{3}, 5\frac{1}{3}, 21\frac{1}{3}, \ldots$

8. $20, 4, \frac{4}{5}, \frac{4}{25}, \ldots$

9. $-100, -40, -16, -6.4, \ldots$

10. $40, 20, 10, 5, \ldots$

Determine whether each sequence is arithmetic or geometric.

11. $-8, -10, -12.5, -15.625, \ldots$

12. $5, 1, -3, -7, \ldots$

13. $1, \frac{2}{5}, \frac{4}{25}, \frac{8}{125}, \ldots$

14. $-0.2, -0.02, -0.002, -0.0002, \ldots$

15. $-10, -5, 0, 5, \ldots$

16. $6, -3, \frac{3}{2}, -\frac{3}{4}, \ldots$

Write a rule for each sequence.

17. $4, 12, 36, 108, \ldots$

18. $2, -8, 32, -128, \ldots$

19. $18, 9, \frac{9}{2}, \frac{9}{4}, \ldots$

20. $1, -\frac{1}{3}, \frac{1}{9}, -\frac{1}{27}, \ldots$

21. $-2, 20, -200, 2000, \ldots$

22. $30, -10, \frac{10}{3}, -\frac{10}{9}, \ldots$

23. $1, 4, 16, 64, \ldots$

24. $6, 12, 24, 48, \ldots$

25. $125, 25, 5, 1, \ldots$

26. $50, 25, 12.5, 6.25, \ldots$

Find the first, fourth, and eighth terms of each sequence.

27. $A(n) = 2 \cdot 3^{n-1}$

28. $A(n) = 3 \cdot 4^{n-1}$

29. $A(n) = 3 \cdot 2^{n-1}$

30. $A(n) = -1 \cdot 5^{n-1}$

31. $A(n) = 4 \cdot 2^{n-1}$

32. $A(n) = \frac{1}{2} \cdot 2^{n-1}$

33. $A(n) = 0.1 \cdot 4^{n-1}$

34. $A(n) = -2.1 \cdot 3^{n-1}$

35. $A(n) = 10 \cdot 5^{n-1}$

Write a rule and find the given term in each geometric sequence described below.

36. What is the sixth term when the first term is 4 and the common ratio is 3?

37. What is the fifth term when the first term is -2 and the common ratio is $-\frac{1}{2}$?

38. What is the tenth term when the first term is 3 and the common ratio is -1.2?

39. What is the fourth term when the first term is 5 and the common ratio is 6?

40. Suppose a manufacturer invented a computer chip in 1978 that had a computational speed of *s*. The company improves its chips so that every 3 years, the chip doubles in speed. What would the chip's speed have been for the year 2002? Write your solution in terms of *s*.

Name ______________________ Class ______________ Date ______________

Reteaching 8-7

Exponential Functions

OBJECTIVE: Examining patterns in exponential functions

MATERIALS: None

To express exponential changes as a function of a variable, follow these steps:

Step 1 Make a table of the data.

Step 2 Find the pattern.

Step 3 Write an equation with exponents.

Example

You have ten CDs. That number doubles every year. How many CDs will you have at the end of 5 yr?

Step 1 Make a table.

Time	No. of CDs
0	10
1 yr	$10 \cdot 2$
2 yr	$10 \cdot 2 \cdot 2$
3 yr	$10 \cdot 2 \cdot 2 \cdot 2$

Step 2 Find the pattern.

$10 \cdot 2 \longrightarrow$ After 1 yr

$10 \cdot 2^2 \longrightarrow$ After 2 yr

$10 \cdot 2^3 \longrightarrow$ After 3 yr

$10 \cdot 2^n \longrightarrow$ After n yr

Step 3 Write an equation with exponents and solve.

$y = 10 \cdot 2^n \longleftarrow$ **Write the equation.**

$y = 10 \cdot 2^5 \longleftarrow$ **Substitute 5 for n.**

$y = 320 \longleftarrow$ **Use a calculator.**

You will have 320 CDs at the end of 5 yr.

Exercises

Follow the above steps to write and evaluate the function.

1. Your science class is collecting cans. You start with 150 cans. Your collection triples every week. How many cans will you have collected after 7 wk?

2. A population of 2500 triples in size every 10 yr. What will the population be in 30 yr?

3. Your parents invested $2000 in a college fund for you when you were 4 yr old. It has doubled in value every 4 yr. If you are now 16, how much is in your college fund?

4. A bacteria culture doubles in size every 8 h. The culture starts with 150 cells. How many will there be after 24 h? After 72 h?

Name ______________________ Class ______________ Date ______________

Practice 8-7

Exponential Functions

Complete the table for each exercise.

1. Investment increases by 1.5 times every 5 yr.

Time	Value of Investment
Initial	\$800
5 yr	\$1200
10 yr	\$1800
15 yr	\$2700
20 yr	■
25 yr	■
■	■
■	■

2. The number of animals doubles every 3 mo.

Time	Number of Animals
Initial	18
3 mo	36
6 mo	72
9 mo	■
12 mo	■
■	■
■	■
■	■

3. The amount of matter halves every year.

Time	Amount of Matter
Initial	3200 g
1 yr	1600 g
2 yr	800 g
3 yr	■
■	■
■	■
■	■
■	■

Evaluate each function for the domain {–2, 0, 1, 2, 4}.

4. $y = 2^x$
5. $y = 3.1^x$
6. $y = 0.8^x$
7. $y = 2 \cdot 4^x$
8. $y = 10 \cdot 3^x$
9. $y = 25 \cdot 5^x$
10. $y = \left(\frac{2}{3}\right)^x$
11. $y = 100 \cdot \left(\frac{1}{10}\right)^x$
12. $y = \frac{1}{4} \cdot 8^x$

Graph each function.

13. $y = 3^x$
14. $y = 6^x$
15. $y = 1.5^x$
16. $y = 7^x$
17. $y = 10 \cdot 5^x$
18. $y = 16 \cdot 0.5^x$
19. $y = \frac{1}{8} \cdot 2^x$
20. $y = \frac{1}{2} \cdot 4^x$
21. $y = 8 \cdot \left(\frac{5}{2}\right)^x$

Evaluate each function rule for the given values.

22. $y = 5.5^x$ for $x = 1, 3,$ and 4
23. $y = 4 \cdot 1.5^x$ for $x = 2, 4,$ and 5
24. $y = 3 \cdot 4^x$ for $x = 1, 3,$ and 5
25. $y = 6^x$ for $x = 2, 3,$ and 4
26. $y = 0.7^x$ for $x = 1, 3,$ and 4
27. $y = 3.1^x$ for $x = 1, 2,$ and 3
28. $y = 180 \cdot 0.5^x$ for $x = 0, -2,$ and $-\frac{1}{2}$
29. $y = 4.3^x$ for $x = -2, -1,$ and 0
30. $y = 100 \cdot 0.1^x$ for $x = -4, -1,$ and 2
31. $y = 5^x$ for $x = -2, -3,$ and 4

Solve each equation.

32. $5^x = 625$
33. $2 \cdot 4^x = 128$
34. $4^x = \frac{1}{64}$
35. $4 \cdot 5^x = \frac{4}{125}$

Name ______________________ Class ______________ Date ______________

Reteaching 8-8

Exponential Growth and Decay

OBJECTIVE: Modeling exponential growth and decay

MATERIALS: None

To write an exponential function to find growth, follow these steps.

Step 1 Find the initial amount a.

Step 2 Multiply by the growth factor b, which occurs over x time periods. Remember that if your growth factor b is $0 < b < 1$, then b is your decay factor, and the function expresses negative growth, that is, a decay function.

Step 3 After the x time periods, the new amount will be $a \times b^x$.

The function is written $y = a \cdot b^x$.

Example

The cost of a car is $10,000. Suppose the price increases 5% each year. What will the cost be at the end of 10 yr? What if the price decreases 7% each year? Use the table below to find the amounts.

a (initial amount)	*b* (growth factor)	*x* (number of increases)	*y* (new amount)
10,000	$100\% + 5\% = 105\%$ $= 1.05$	10	$10{,}000 \cdot 1.05^{10} = y$
10,000	$100\% - 7\% = 93\%$ $= 0.93$	10	$10{,}000 \cdot 0.93^{10} = y$

The cost at the end of 10 yr with a growth factor of 5% will be $16,289; with a decay factor of 7%, it will be $4839.82.

Exercises

Write an exponential function to model each situation. Find each amount at the end of the specified time. Round your answers to the nearest whole number.

1. A town with a population of 5,000 grows 3% per year. Find the population at the end of 10 yr.

2. The price of a bicycle is $100. It increases 8% per year. What will the price be at the end of 5 yr?

3. A 2 ft-tall tree grows 10% per year. How tall will the tree be at the end of 8 yr?

4. $1,000 purchase
10% loss in value each year
5 yr

5. $5,000 investment
13.5% loss each year
8 yr

6. 20,000 population
12.5% annual decrease
10 yr

Name ______________________ Class ______________ Date ____________

Practice 8-8

Exponential Growth and Decay

Write an exponential function to model each situation. Find each amount after the specified time.

1. Suppose one of your ancestors invested \$500 in 1800 in an account paying 4% interest compounded annually. Find the account balance in each of the following years.

   a. 1850 **b.** 1900 **c.** 2000 **d.** 2100

2. Suppose you invest \$1500 in an account paying 4.75% annual interest. Find the account balance after 25 yr with the interest compounded the following ways.

   a. annually **b.** semiannually **c.** quarterly **d.** monthly

3. The starting salary for a new employee is \$25,000. The salary for this employee increases by 8% per year. What is the salary after each of the following?

   a. 1 yr **b.** 3 yr **c.** 5 yr **d.** 15 yr

4. Carbon-14 has a half-life of 5,700 years. Scientists use this fact to determine the age of things made of organic material. Suppose the average page of a book containing approximately 0.5 mg of carbon-14 is put into a time capsule. How much carbon-14 will each page contain after each of the following numbers of years?

   a. 5700 **b.** 11,400 **c.** 22,800 **d.** 34,200

5. The tax revenue that a small city receives increases by 3.5% per year. In 1990, the city received \$250,000 in tax revenue. Determine the tax revenue in each of the following years.

   a. 1995 **b.** 1998 **c.** 2000 **d.** 2006

6. Suppose the acreage of forest is decreasing by 2% per year because of development. If there are currently 4,500,000 acres of forest, determine the amount of forest land after each of the following.

   a. 3 yr **b.** 5 yr **c.** 10 yr **d.** 20 yr

7. A \$10,500 investment has a 15% loss each year. Determine the value of the investment after each of the following.

   a. 1 yr **b.** 2 yr **c.** 4 yr **d.** 10 yr

8. A city of 2,950,000 people has a 2.5% annual decrease in population. Determine the city's population after each of the following.

   a. 1 yr **b.** 5 yr **c.** 15 yr **d.** 25 yr

9. A \$25,000 purchase decreases 12% in value per year. Determine the value of the purchase after each of the following.

   a. 1 yr **b.** 3 yr **c.** 5 yr **d.** 7 yr

Name ______________________ Class ______________ Date ______________

Reteaching 9-1

Adding and Subtracting Polynomials

OBJECTIVE: Adding and subtracting polynomials **MATERIALS:** Tiles

Example

Using tiles, simplify $(2a^2 + 4a - 6) + (a^2 - 2a + 4)$.

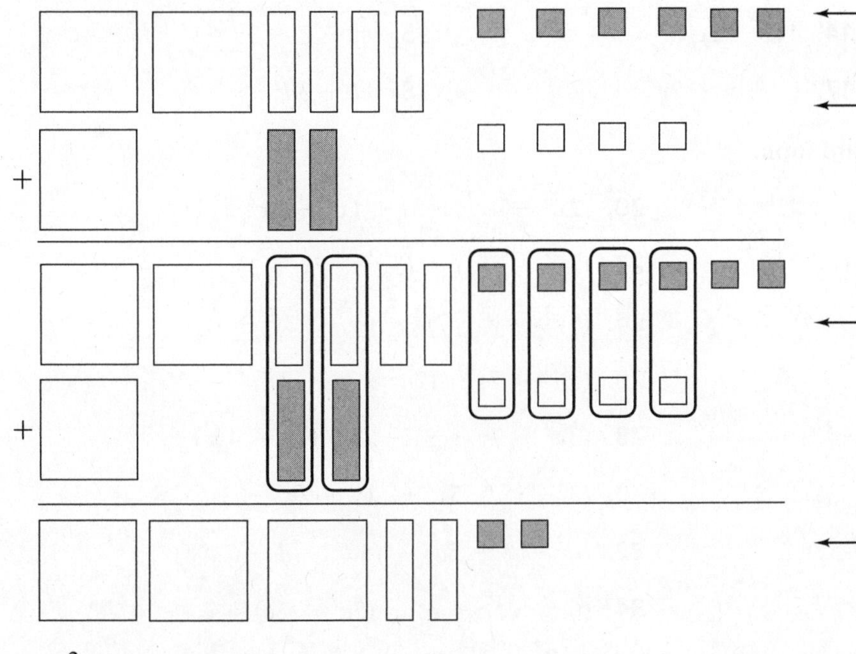

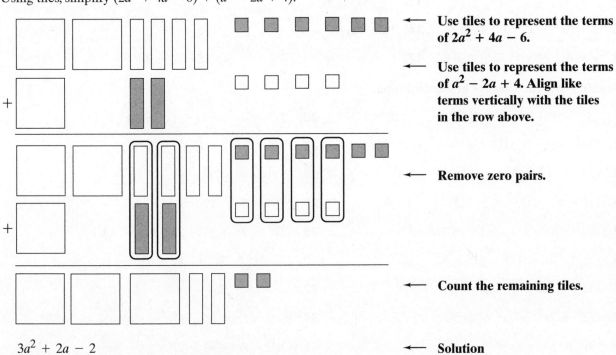

Use tiles to represent the terms of $2a^2 + 4a - 6$.

Use tiles to represent the terms of $a^2 - 2a + 4$. Align like terms vertically with the tiles in the row above.

Remove zero pairs.

Count the remaining tiles.

$3a^2 + 2a - 2$ ← **Solution**

Exercises

Use tiles to simplify each sum or difference.

1. $(4y^2 - 5y + 3) + (2y^2 + 7y - 7)$
2. $(3a^2 + 5a - 6) - (2a^2 - 3a - 9)$
3. $(6x^2 - 3x + 2) + (3x^2 + x - 5)$
4. $(4x^2 + 2x - 7) - (-3x^2 - 6x + 2)$
5. $(6z^2 - 5z + 1) + (8z^2 + 7z - 4)$
6. $(4x^2 + 2) - (-2x^2 + 5) + (x^2 + 4)$

Simplify. Write each answer in standard form.

7. $(2x^2 - 3x + 4) + (3x^2 + 2x - 3)$
8. $(7x^3 - 3x + 1) - (x^3 + x^2 - 2)$
9. $(3y^2 - 3y + 2) + (4y^2 + 3y - 1)$
10. $(5x^2 - 10) - (3x^2 + 7)$
11. $(2x^3 + x^2 + 1) + (3x^3 - x^2 + 2)$
12. $(4x^3 + 3x + 2) - (2x^2 - 3x + 7)$
13. $(3x^2 + 7x - 6) + (x^3 + x^2 - x - 1)$
14. $(4x^2 - x + 6) - (3x^2 - 4)$

Name ______________________ Class ______________________ Date ______________________

Practice 9-1

Adding and Subtracting Polynomials

Write each polynomial in standard form. Then name each polynomial based on its degree and number of terms.

1. $4y^3 - 4y^2 + 3 - y$
2. $x^2 + x^4 - 6$
3. $x + 2$
4. $2m^2 - 7m^3 + 3m$
5. $4 - x + 2x^2$
6. $7x^3 + 2x^2$
7. $n^2 - 5n$
8. $6 + 7x^2$
9. $3a^2 + a^3 - 4a + 3$
10. $5 + 3x$
11. $7 - 8a^2 + 6a$
12. $5x + 4 - x^2$
13. $2 + 4x^2 - x^3$
14. $4x^3 - 2x^2$
15. $y^2 - 7 - 3y$
16. $x - 6x^2 - 3$
17. $v^3 - v + 2v^2$
18. $8d + 3d^2$

Simplify. Write each answer in standard form.

19. $(3x^2 - 5x) - (x^2 + 4x + 3)$
20. $(2x^3 - 4x^2 + 3) + (x^3 - 3x^2 + 1)$
21. $(3y^3 - 11y + 3) - (5y^3 + y^2 + 2)$
22. $(3x^2 + 2x^3) - (3x^2 + 7x - 1)$
23. $(2a^3 + 3a^2 + 7a) + (a^3 + a^2 - 2a)$
24. $(8y^3 - y + 7) - (6y^3 + 3y - 3)$
25. $(x^2 - 6) + (5x^2 + x - 3)$
26. $(5n^2 - 7) - (2n^2 + n - 3)$
27. $(5n^3 + 2n^2 + 2) - (n^3 + 3n^2 - 2)$
28. $(3y^2 - 7y + 3) - (5y + 3 - 4y^2)$
29. $(2x^2 + 9x - 17) + (x^2 - 6x - 3)$
30. $(3 - x^3 - 5x^2) + (x + 2x^3 - 3)$
31. $(3x + x^2 - x^3) - (x^3 + 2x^2 + 5x)$
32. $(d^2 + 8 - 5d) - (5d^2 + d - 2d^3 + 3)$
33. $(3x^3 + 7x^2) + (x^2 - 2x^3)$
34. $(6c^2 + 5c - 3) - (3c^2 + 8c)$
35. $(3y^2 - 5y - 7) + (y^2 - 6y + 7)$
36. $(3c^2 - 8c + 4) - (7 + c^2 - 8c)$
37. $(4x^2 + 13x + 9) + (12x^2 + x + 6)$
38. $(2x - 13x^2 + 3) - (2x^2 + 8x)$
39. $(7x - 4x^2 + 11) + (7x^2 + 5)$
40. $(4x + 7x^3 - 9x^2) + (3 - 2x^2 - 5x)$
41. $(y^3 + y^2 - 2) + (y - 6y^2)$
42. $(x^2 - 8x - 3) - (x^3 + 8x^2 - 8)$
43. $(3x^2 - 2x + 9) - (x^2 - x + 7)$
44. $(2x^2 - 6x + 3) - (2x + 4x^2 + 2)$
45. $(2x^2 - 2x^3 - 7) + (9x^2 + 2 + x)$
46. $(3a^2 + a^3 - 1) + (2a^2 + 3a + 1)$
47. $(2x^2 + 3 - x) - (2 + 2x^2 - 5x)$
48. $(n^4 - 2n - 1) + (5n - n^4 + 5)$
49. $(x^3 + 3x) - (x^2 + 6 - 4x)$
50. $(7s^2 + 4s + 2) + (3s + 2 - s^2)$
51. $(6x^2 - 3x + 9) - (x^2 + 3x - 5)$
52. $(3x^3 - x^2 + 4) + (2x^3 - 3x + 9)$
53. $(y^3 + 3y - 1) - (y^3 + 3y + 5)$
54. $(3 + 5x^3 + 2x) - (x + 2x^2 + 4x^3)$
55. $(x^2 + 15x + 13) + (3x^2 - 15x + 7)$
56. $(7 - 8x^2) + (x^3 - x + 5)$
57. $(2x + 3) - (x - 4) + (x + 2)$
58. $(x^2 + 4) - (x - 4) + (x^2 - 2x)$

Name ____________________ Class ____________ Date ____________

Reteaching 9-2

Multiplying and Factoring

OBJECTIVE: Factoring a monomial from a polynomial

MATERIALS: None

- To factor a polynomial you must find the **G**reatest **C**ommon **F**actor. The **GCF** is the greatest factor that divides evenly into each term.

Example

Factor $18x^3 + 6x^2 - 12x$.

a. First find the GCF.

$18x^3 = (2)\ (3)\ 3\ (x)\ x\ x$ ⟵ **List the factors of each term. Circle the factors common to all terms.**

$6x^2 = (2)\ (3)\ x\ (x)$

$12x = (2)\ 2\ (3)\ (x)$

$2 \cdot 3 \cdot x = 6x$ ⟵ **Multiply the circled terms together to get the GCF.**

b. Factor out the GCF from each term.

$\frac{18x^3}{6x} = 3x^2$ ⟵ **Divide each term by the GCF.**

$\frac{6x^2}{6x} = x$

$\frac{-12x}{6x} = -2$

$6x(3x^2 + x - 2)$ ⟵ **Solution**

Exercises

Use the GCF to factor each polynomial.

1. $21x - 14$
2. $5y^3 - 10y^2 + 15y$
3. $x^3 + 3x^2 + x$
4. $3x^2 + 6x^4$
5. $18x^3 - 6x^2 + 24x$
6. $z^3 - 3z^2$
7. $12k^3 + 6k^2 - 18k$
8. $6x^3 - 4x^2 + 8x$
9. $8p^4 + 12p^2 + 4p$
10. $36x^2 - 18x$
11. $6x^2 + 18x$
12. $6x^3 - 2x^2 + 8x$
13. $6x^3 + 6x^2 - 6x$
14. $5x^3 + 5x^2$
15. $3x^2 + 6x + 3$
16. $10x^2 + 35x$
17. $8x^5 + 16x^4 - 8x^3$
18. $9x^3 - 6x^2 - 15x$

Name ______________________ Class ______________ Date ______________

Practice 9-2

Multiplying and Factoring

Simplify each product.

1. $4(a - 3)$
2. $-5(x - 2)$
3. $-3x^2(x^2 + 3x)$
4. $4x^3(x - 3)$
5. $-5x^2(x^2 + 2x + 1)$
6. $3x(x^2 - 5x - 3)$
7. $-x^2(-2x^2 + 3x - 2)$
8. $4d^2(d^2 - 3d - 7)$
9. $5m^3(m + 6)$
10. $a^2(2a + 4)$
11. $4(x^2 - 3) + x(x + 1)$
12. $4x(5x - 6)$

Find the GCF of the terms of each polynomial.

13. $8x - 4$
14. $15x + 45x^2$
15. $x^2 + 3x$
16. $4c^3 - 8c^2 + 8$
17. $12x - 36$
18. $12n^3 + 4n^2$
19. $14x^3 + 7x^2$
20. $8x^3 - 12x$
21. $9 - 27x^3$
22. $25x^3 - 15x^2$
23. $11x^2 - 33x$
24. $4n^4 + 6n^3 - 8n^2$
25. $8d^3 + 4d^2 + 12d$
26. $6x^2 + 12x - 21$
27. $8g^2 + 16g - 8$

Factor each polynomial.

28. $8x + 10$
29. $12n^3 - 8n$
30. $14d - 2$
31. $6h^2 - 8h$
32. $3z^4 - 15z^3 - 9z^2$
33. $3y^3 - 8y^2 - 9y$
34. $x^3 - 5x^2$
35. $8x^3 - 12x^2 + 4x$
36. $7x^3 + 21x^4$
37. $6a^3 - 12a^2 + 14a$
38. $6x^4 + 12x^2$
39. $3n^4 - 6n^2 + 9n$
40. $2w^3 + 6w^2 - 4w$
41. $12c^3 - 30c^2$
42. $2x^2 + 8x - 14$
43. $4x^3 + 12x^2 + 16x$
44. $16m^3 - 8m^2 + 12m$
45. $4a^3 - 20a^2 - 8a$
46. $18c^4 - 9c^2 + 7c$
47. $6y^4 + 9y^3 - 27y^2$
48. $6c^2 - 3c$
49. A circular pond will be placed on a square piece of land. The length of a side of the square is $2x$. The radius of the pond is x. The part of the square not covered by the pond will be planted with flowers. What is the area of the region that will be planted with flowers? Write your answer in factored form.
50. A square poster of length $3x$ is to have a square painting centered on it. The length of the painting is $2x$. The area of the poster not covered by the painting will be painted black. What is the area of the poster that will be painted black?
51. The formula for the surface area of a sphere is $A = 4\pi r^2$. A square sticker of side x is placed on a ball of radius $3x$. What is the surface area of the sphere not covered by the sticker? Write your answer in factored form.

Name ______________________ Class ______________ Date ____________

Reteaching 9-3

Multiplying Binomials

OBJECTIVE: Multiplying binomials

MATERIALS: None

To multiply two binomials, follow these steps:

- Multiply each term in one binomial by each term of the other binomial. Drawing arrows as a visual reminder of what to do is a helpful technique.
- Circle like terms and combine.

Example

Find the product $(x + 7)(x + 2)$.

$(x + 7)(x + 2)$	⟵ **Draw arrows from the first term in the first binomial to both terms in the second binomial.**
$x^2 + 2x$	⟵ **Multiply each term of the second binomial by x.**
$(x + 7)(x + 2)$	⟵ **Draw arrows from the second term in the first binomial to both terms in the second binomial.**
$7x + 14$	⟵ **Multiply each term of the second binomial by 7.**
$x^2 + 2x + 7x + 14$	⟵ **Add the two expressions.**
$x^2 + \circled{2x} + \circled{7x} + 14$	⟵ **Circle like terms and combine.**
$x^2 + 9x + 14$	⟵ **Solution**

Exercises

Use arrows as shown above to simplify each product.

1. $(x + 6)(x - 2)$ **2.** $(x - 8)(x - 4)$ **3.** $(x - 3)(x + 9)$

4. $(x + 2)(x - 7)$ **5.** $(2x + 3)(x + 4)$ **6.** $(x + 4)(2x + 5)$

Simplify each product.

7. $(7x + 4)(2x - 4)$ **8.** $(3x + 2)(3x + 2)$ **9.** $(5x + 1)(x + 1)$

10. $(2x + 1)(x + 1)$ **11.** $(4x + 1)(2x - 1)$ **12.** $(3x - 1)(x + 2)$

Name ______________________ Class ______________ Date ______________

Practice 9-3

Multiplying Binomials

Simplify each product. Write in standard form.

1. $(x + 3)(2x - 5)$
2. $(x^2 + x - 1)(x + 1)$
3. $(3w + 4)(2w - 1)$
4. $(x + 5)(x + 4)$
5. $(2b - 1)(b^2 - 3b + 4)$
6. $(a - 11)(a + 5)$
7. $(2g - 3)(2g^2 + g - 4)$
8. $(3s - 4)(s - 5)$
9. $(4x + 3)(x - 7)$
10. $(x + 6)(x^2 - 4x + 3)$
11. $(5x - 3)(4x + 2)$
12. $(3y + 7)(4y + 5)$
13. $(3x + 7)(x + 5)$
14. $(5x - 2)(x + 3)$
15. $(3m^2 - 7m + 8)(m - 2)$
16. $(a - 6)(a + 8)$
17. $(x + 2)(2x^2 - 3x + 2)$
18. $(a^2 + a + 1)(a - 1)$
19. $(x - 2)(x^2 + 4x + 4)$
20. $(2r + 1)(3r - 1)$
21. $(k + 4)(3k - 4)$
22. $(2n - 3)(n^2 - 2n + 5)$
23. $(p - 4)(2p + 3)$
24. $(3x + 1)(4x^2 - 2x + 1)$
25. $(2x^2 - 5x + 2)(4x - 3)$
26. $(x + 7)(x + 5)$
27. $(6x - 11)(x + 2)$
28. $(2x + 1)(4x + 3)$
29. $(3x + 4)(3x - 4)$
30. $(6x - 5)(3x + 1)$
31. $(n - 7)(n + 4)$
32. $(3x - 1)(2x + 1)$
33. $(d + 9)(d - 11)$
34. $(2x^2 + 5x - 3)(2x + 1)$
35. $(b + 8)(2b - 5)$
36. $(2x - 5)(x + 4)$
37. $(3x + 5)(5x - 7)$
38. $(x - 5)(2x^2 - 7x - 2)$
39. $(2x^2 - 9x + 11)(2x + 1)$
40. $(2x^2 + 5x - 4)(2x + 7)$
41. $(x^2 + 6x + 11)(3x + 5)$
42. $(5x + 7)(7x + 3)$
43. $(4x - 7)(2x - 5)$
44. $(x - 9)(3x + 5)$
45. $(2x - 1)(x^2 - 7x + 1)$

46. The width of a rectangular painting is 3 in. more than twice the height. A frame that is 2.5 in. wide goes around the painting.
    a. Write an expression for the combined area of the painting and frame.
    b. Use the expression to find the combined area when the height of the painting is 12 in.
    c. Use the expression to find the combined area when the height of the painting is 15 in.

47. The Robertsons put a rectangular pool with a stone walkway around it in their backyard. The total length of the pool and walkway is 3 times the total width. The walkway is 2 ft wide all around.
    a. Write an expression for the area of the pool.
    b. Find the area of the pool when the total width is 10 ft.
    c. Find the area of the pool when the total width is 9 ft.

48. The Cutting Edge frame shop makes a mat by cutting out the inside of a rectangular board. Use the diagram to find the length and width of the original board if the area of the mat is 184 in^2.

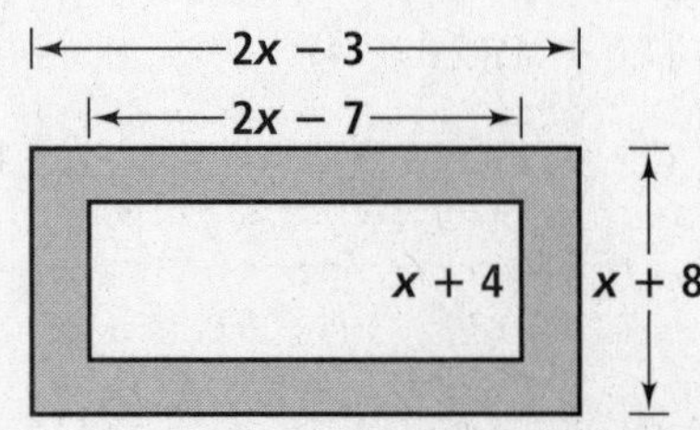

Name ______________________ Class ______________ Date ______________

Reteaching 9-4

Multiplying Special Cases

OBJECTIVE: Finding the square of a binomial and finding the difference of two squares.

MATERIALS: None

Examples

Finding the square of a binomial.

Remember:
- Square the first term.
- Double the product of the two terms.
- Square the last term.
- Write the sum of your three products.

$(x - 5)^2$	**Square the first term:**	x^2
	Double $(x)(-5)$:	$2 \cdot (-5x) = -10x$
	Square the last term:	$(-5)^2 = 25$
	Write the sum of your three products:	$x^2 - 10x + 25$

Finding the difference of two squares.

Remember:
- Square the first term.
- Square the last term.
- Write the difference of your first square and your second square.

$(3x - 2)(3x + 2)$	**Square the first term:**	$(3x)^2 = 9x^2$
	Square the last term:	$(2)^2 = 4$
	Write the difference of your first square and your second square:	$9x^2 - 4$

Exercises

Find each product.

1. $(x - 7)^2$

2. $(x + 1)^2$

3. $(x - 4)^2$

4. $(x - y)^2$

5. $(2x + 3)^2$

6. $(3x - 5)^2$

7. $(2x + 1)^2$

8. $(5x - 4)^2$

9. $(x + 7)(x - 7)$

10. $(x + 8)(x - 8)$

11. $(x - 3)(x + 3)$

12. $(x + y)(x - y)$

13. $(4x + 3)(4x - 3)$

14. $(2x + 5)(2x - 5)$

15. $(3x + 2)(3x - 2)$

16. $(7x - 1)(7x + 1)$

Name ____________________ Class ____________ Date ____________

Practice 9-4

Multiplying Special Cases

Simplify.

1. $(w - 2)^2$
2. $(y + 4)^2$
3. $(4w + 2)^2$
4. $(w - 9)^2$
5. $(3x + 7)^2$
6. $(3x - 7)^2$
7. $(2x - 9)^2$
8. $(x - 12)^2$
9. $(6x + 1)^2$
10. $(4x - 7)^2$
11. $(x + 8)(x - 8)$
12. $(x - 11)(x + 11)$
13. $(x - 12)(x + 12)$
14. $(y + w)(y - w)$
15. $(2x + 1)(2x - 1)$
16. $(5x - 2)(5x + 2)$
17. $(6x + 1)(6x - 1)$
18. $(2x - 4)(2x + 4)$
19. $(x^2 + y^2)^2$
20. $(2x^2 + y^2)^2$
21. $(a^2 - b^2)^2$
22. $(y^2 - 4w^2)^2$
23. $(3 - 6x^2)^2$
24. $(4a - 3y)^2$
25. $(3y + 2a)(3y - 2a)$
26. $(x^2 + 2y)(x^2 - 2y)$
27. $(3x^2 + 4w^2)(3x^2 - 4w^2)$
28. $(4x + 3w^2)(4x - 3w^2)$
29. $(2a + 7b)(2a - 7b)$
30. $(5a^2 - 6x)(5a^2 + 6x)$
31. 18^2
32. $(64)^2$
33. $(29)(31)$
34. $(97)(103)$
35. $(19)(42)$
36. $(95)(205)$

Find the area.

37.

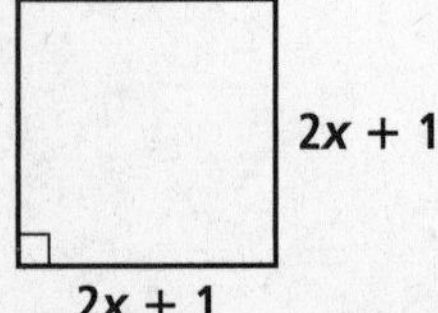

38.

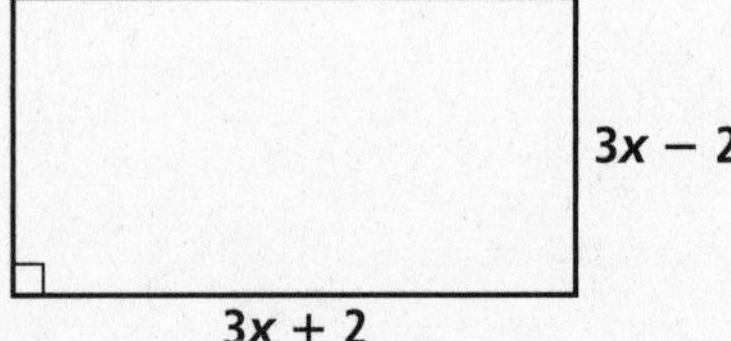

Find the area of the shaded region.

39.

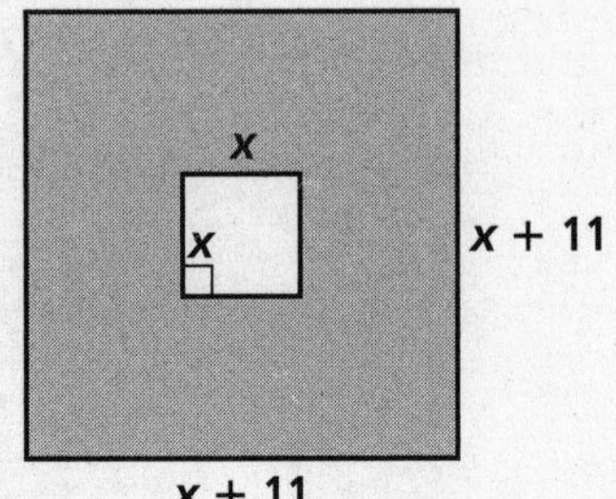

40.

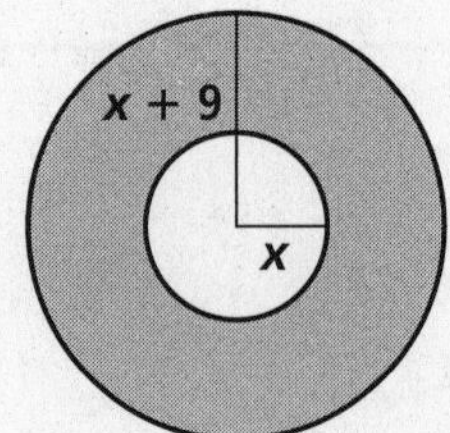

Reteaching 9-5

Factoring Trinomials of the Type $x^2 + bx + c$

OBJECTIVE: Factoring trinomials of the type $x^2 + bx + c$

MATERIALS: Tiles

Examples

Factor $x^2 + 6x + 8$.

$(x \quad)(x \quad)$ ← **Write factors of x^2, the first term of the trinomial, at the beginning of each set of parentheses. Note that the coefficient of x^2 is 1.**

$+1$ and $+8$ $\quad -1$ and -8 ← **List pairs of numbers that are factors of $+8$, which is the constant term of the trinomial. Choose the pair of factors that add to equal $+6$, the coefficient of the middle term of the trinomial.**

(+2) and (+4) $\quad -2$ and -4

$(x + 2)(x + 4)$ ← **Write those two factors, with their signs, at the end of each set of parentheses.**

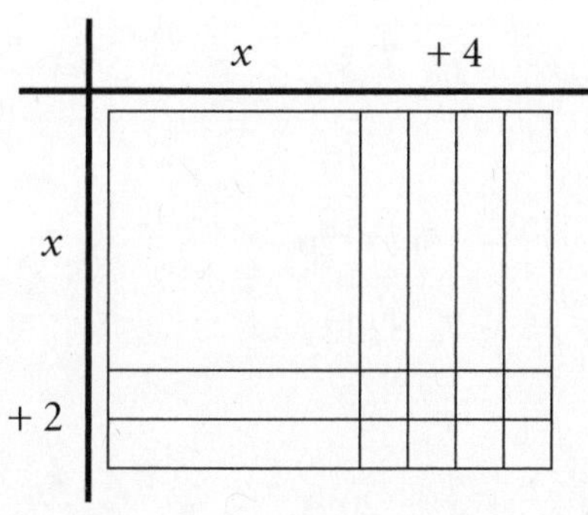

← **The trinomial $x^2 + 6x + 8$ represents the area of a rectangle with sides of length $(x + 4)$ and $(x + 2)$.**

Factor $x^2 + 4x - 21$.

$(x \quad)(x \quad)$

-1 and $+21$ $\quad +1$ and -21 ← **List pairs of numbers that are factors of -21.**

-3 and $+7$ $\quad +3$ and -7

$(x - 3)(x + 7)$ ← **Choose the pair of factors that add to equal $+4$.**

Exercises

Factor each expression.

1. $y^2 + 11y + 18$ **2.** $x^2 - 8x + 15$ **3.** $x^2 - 11x + 18$

4. $y^2 - 5y + 4$ **5.** $x^2 + 6x + 8$ **6.** $y^2 - 8y + 12$

7. $r^2 + 13r + 12$ **8.** $x^2 - 16x + 39$ **9.** $x^2 - 10x + 16$

10. $x^2 - x - 2$ **11.** $x^2 - 4x - 32$ **12.** $x^2 - 7x - 18$

13. $x^2 + 7x + 10$ **14.** $x^2 - 11x + 24$ **15.** $x^2 + 16x + 63$

Name ______________________________ Class ____________________ Date ____________

Practice 9-5

Factoring Trinomials of the Type $x^2 + bx + c$

Factor each expression.

1. $x^2 + 8x + 16$	**2.** $d^2 + 8d + 7$	**3.** $y^2 + 6y + 8$
4. $b^2 - 2b - 3$	**5.** $s^2 - 4s - 5$	**6.** $x^2 + 12x + 32$
7. $x^2 - 9x + 20$	**8.** $x^2 - 5x + 6$	**9.** $a^2 + 3a + 2$
10. $p^2 - 8p + 7$	**11.** $d^2 + 6d + 5$	**12.** $n^2 + n - 6$
13. $x^2 + 5x - 14$	**14.** $b^2 + 9b + 14$	**15.** $x^2 + 14x + 45$
16. $a^2 + 7a + 12$	**17.** $x^2 + 13x + 22$	**18.** $x^2 + 3x - 4$
19. $x^2 - 8x + 12$	**20.** $x^2 + 7x - 18$	**21.** $n^2 - 7n + 10$
22. $s^2 - 5s - 14$	**23.** $x^2 - 9x + 8$	**24.** $x^2 - 2x - 24$
25. $x^2 - 6x - 27$	**26.** $x^2 - 16x - 36$	**27.** $x^2 + 7x + 10$
28. $x^2 - 3x - 28$	**29.** $m^2 - 4m - 21$	**30.** $x^2 - 2x - 15$
31. $x^2 - 5x - 24$	**32.** $b^2 - 4b - 60$	**33.** $x^2 - 3x - 18$
34. $m^2 + 7m + 10$	**35.** $n^2 - n - 72$	**36.** $k^2 - 6k + 5$
37. $x^2 + 9x + 20$	**38.** $x^2 - 10x + 9$	**39.** $x^2 - 8x + 16$
40. $d^2 - 4d + 3$	**41.** $b^2 - 26b + 48$	**42.** $n^2 - 15n + 26$
43. $n^2 - n - 6$	**44.** $z^2 - 14z + 49$	**45.** $x^2 + 7x + 12$
46. $x^2 - 18x + 17$	**47.** $x^2 + 16x + 28$	**48.** $t^2 - 6t - 27$
49. $b^2 + 4b - 12$	**50.** $d^2 + 11d + 18$	**51.** $x^2 + x - 20$
52. $x^2 - 13x + 42$	**53.** $x^2 + x - 6$	**54.** $x^2 + 4x - 21$
55. $a^2 + 2a - 35$	**56.** $h^2 + 7h - 18$	**57.** $x^2 + 3x - 10$
58. $p^2 - 12p - 28$	**59.** $y^2 + 6y - 55$	**60.** $b^2 + 3b - 4$
61. $x^2 + 2x - 63$	**62.** $x^2 - 2x - 8$	**63.** $x^2 - 11x - 60$
64. $r^2 + 2r - 35$	**65.** $c^2 - 3c - 10$	**66.** $x^2 + 8x + 15$
67. $x^2 - 8x + 15$	**68.** $n^2 - 23n + 60$	**69.** $c^2 + 3c - 10$
70. $x^2 - 9x + 14$	**71.** $x^2 - 10x + 24$	**72.** $x^2 + 6x - 27$
73. $y^2 - 16y + 64$	**74.** $n^2 + 10n + 25$	**75.** $r^2 - 14r - 51$
76. $x^2 + 3x - 40$	**77.** $x^2 - x - 42$	**78.** $n^2 - 2n - 63$
79. $a^2 + 7a + 6$	**80.** $x^2 - 14x + 48$	**81.** $x^2 - 11x + 28$
82. $n^2 + 16n - 36$	**83.** $n^2 - 4n - 21$	**84.** $y^2 + 16y - 17$

Name ______________________ Class ______________ Date ______________

Reteaching 9-6

Factoring Trinomials of the Type $ax^2 + bx + c$

OBJECTIVE: Factoring trinomials of the type $ax^2 + bx + c$; $a > 1$

MATERIALS: None

A table can be helpful when factoring trinomials of the type $ax^2 + bx + c$.

Examples

Factor $2x^2 + 13x + 20$.

Write the first term in the top left box of the table. →

$2x^2$	
	20

Write the constant term in the bottom right box of the table. →

Find the product *ac*. → Since $a = 2$ and $c = 20$, $ac = 40$.

Find two numbers whose product is *ac* and sum is *b*. → Since $ac = 40$ and $b = 13$, the numbers are 8 and 5.

These numbers are the coefficients of the *x* terms that are written in the remaining boxes of the table. →

$2x^2$	$8x$
$5x$	20

(Note: Try repeating these steps, exchanging the locations of $5x$ and $8x$.)

Now, find the greatest common factors of the terms in each row and column. Write these above and to the left of the table. →

	x	4
$2x$	$2x^2$	$8x$
5	$5x$	20

Read across the top of the table to find one factor. → $x + 4$

Read down the left of the table to find the other factor. → $2x + 5$

So, $2x^2 + 13x + 20 = (x + 4)(2x + 5)$.

You can check your answer using FOIL.

Factor $3x^2 - 2x - 8$.

$ac = 3(-8) = -24$

$b = -2$

The numbers whose product is -24 and sum is -2 are -6 and 4. Write $-6x$ and $4x$ in the table and find the GCFs of each row and column.

	$3x$	4
x	$3x^2$	$4x$
-2	$-6x$	-8

$3x^2 - 2x - 8 = (3x + 4)(x - 2)$.

Exercises

Factor each expression.

1. $2x^2 + 11x + 14$

2. $4x^2 - 12x + 5$

3. $6x^2 - 13x + 2$

4. $6x^2 + 7x - 20$

5. $3x^2 + 4x - 4$

6. $8x^2 - 13x - 6$

7. $2x^2 - 5x + 3$

8. $5x^2 - 26x - 24$

9. $6x^2 - 7x - 3$

10. $6x^2 + 7x - 3$

Name ______________________ Class ______________ Date ______________

Practice 9-6

Factoring Trinomials of the Type $ax^2 + bx + c$

Factor each expression.

1. $2x^2 + 3x + 1$	**2.** $2x^2 + 5x + 3$	**3.** $2n^2 + n - 6$
4. $3x^2 - x - 4$	**5.** $2y^2 - 9y - 5$	**6.** $5x^2 - 2x - 7$
7. $7n^2 + 9n + 2$	**8.** $3c^2 - 17c - 6$	**9.** $3x^2 + 8x + 4$
10. $6x^2 - 7x - 10$	**11.** $3x^2 - 10x + 8$	**12.** $3y^2 - 16y - 12$
13. $5x^2 + 2x - 3$	**14.** $3x^2 + 7x + 2$	**15.** $7x^2 - 10x + 3$
16. $3x^2 + 8x + 5$	**17.** $2x^2 + 9x + 4$	**18.** $5x^2 - 7x + 2$
19. $5x^2 - 22x + 8$	**20.** $4x^2 + 17x - 15$	**21.** $5x^2 - 33x - 14$
22. $3x^2 - 2x - 8$	**23.** $3y^2 + 7y - 6$	**24.** $2x^2 + 13x - 24$
25. $4y^2 - 11y - 3$	**26.** $2y^2 + 9y + 7$	**27.** $5y^2 - 3y - 2$
28. $7y^2 + 19y + 10$	**29.** $7x^2 - 30x + 8$	**30.** $3x^2 + 17x + 10$
31. $2x^2 + 5x - 3$	**32.** $2x^2 - 5x + 3$	**33.** $3x^2 + 10x + 3$
34. $2x^2 - x - 21$	**35.** $5x^2 - 11x + 2$	**36.** $4x^2 + 4x - 15$
37. $6x^2 - 19x + 15$	**38.** $2x^2 - x - 15$	**39.** $3x^2 - 7x - 6$
40. $2x^2 - 5x - 12$	**41.** $6x^2 - 7x - 5$	**42.** $4x^2 + 7x + 3$
43. $12y^2 - 7y + 1$	**44.** $6y^2 - 5y + 1$	**45.** $6x^2 - 11x + 4$
46. $12x^2 + 19x + 5$	**47.** $7y^2 + 47y - 14$	**48.** $11x^2 - 54x - 5$
49. $15x^2 - 19x + 6$	**50.** $8x^2 - 30x + 25$	**51.** $14y^2 + 15y - 9$
52. $22x^2 + 51x - 10$	**53.** $14x^2 - 41x + 15$	**54.** $8y^2 + 17y + 9$
55. $8x^2 + 65x + 8$	**56.** $20x^2 + 37x + 15$	**57.** $24y^2 + 41y + 12$
58. $18x^2 - 27x + 4$	**59.** $10x^2 + 3x - 4$	**60.** $10y^2 - 29y + 10$

Name ______________________ Class ______________ Date ______________

Reteaching 9-7

Factoring Special Cases

OBJECTIVE: Factoring the difference of two squares	**MATERIALS:** None

- The difference of two squares is written $\boldsymbol{a^2 - b^2}$. Note that both terms must be perfect squares.
- The **factors** of the difference of two squares, $\boldsymbol{a^2 - b^2}$ are $\boldsymbol{(a + b)}$ and $\boldsymbol{(a - b)}$. Once you have determined that the binomial you want to factor is the difference of two squares, you can factor by using the formula $a^2 - b^2 = (a + b)(a - b)$.

Examples

Factor $a^2 - 16$.

$a^2 - 16$ ← **Both terms are perfect squares.**

$a^2 - 4^2$ ← **Rewrite 16 as 4^2.**

$a^2 - b^2 = (a + b)(a - b)$ ← **Write the formula.**

$a^2 - 4^2 = (a + 4)(a - 4)$ ← **Replace b with 4.**

$(a + 4)(a - 4)$ ← **Solution**

Factor $3a^2 - 75$.

$3a^2 - 75$ ← **Both terms are *not* perfect squares.**

$3(a^2 - 25)$ ← **Both $3a^2$ and 75 are divisible by 3. Factor out 3.**

$3(a^2 - 5^2)$ ← **25 is a perfect square. Rewrite 25 as 5^2.**

$a^2 - b^2 = (a + b)(a - b)$ ← **Write the formula.**

$3(a^2 - 5^2) = 3(a + 5)(a - 5)$ ← **Replace b with 5.**

$3(a + 5)(a - 5)$ ← **Solution**

Exercises

Factor each expression.

1. $a^2 - 36$ **2.** $x^2 - 64$ **3.** $y^2 - 49$

4. $4x^2 - 25$ **5.** $9y^2 - 16$ **6.** $25x^2 - 64$

7. $3x^2 - 12$ **8.** $2x^2 - 18$ **9.** $4x^2 - 16$

10. $x^2 - 225$ **11.** $x^2 - 144$ **12.** $16x^2 - 49$

13. $6x^2 - 54$ **14.** $7x^2 - 112$ **15.** $5x^2 - 125$

Name ______________________ Class ______________ Date ______________

Practice 9-7

Factoring Special Cases

Factor each expression.

1. $x^2 - 9$	**2.** $4m^2 - 1$	**3.** $a^2 + 2a + 1$
4. $4x^2 + 12x + 9$	**5.** $x^2 - 22x + 121$	**6.** $n^2 - 4$
7. $9x^2 - 4$	**8.** $16c^2 - 49$	**9.** $9x^2 - 30x + 25$
10. $4x^2 - 20x + 25$	**11.** $2a^2 - 18$	**12.** $x^2 - 24x + 144$
13. $3n^2 - 3$	**14.** $9h^2 + 60h + 100$	**15.** $9d^2 - 49$
16. $81a^2 - 400$	**17.** $r^2 - 36$	**18.** $3a^2 - 48$
19. $b^2 + 4b + 4$	**20.** $10x^2 - 90$	**21.** $25x^2 - 64$
22. $12w^2 - 27$	**23.** $g^3 - 25g$	**24.** $x^2 + 6x + 9$
25. $a^2 - 25$	**26.** $36s^2 - 225$	**27.** $4b^2 + 44b + 121$
28. $x^2 - 16x + 64$	**29.** $x^2 - 2x + 1$	**30.** $d^2 - 49$
31. $x^3 - 36x$	**32.** $9y^2 - 289$	**33.** $x^2 - 30x + 225$
34. $100a^2 - 9$	**35.** $2x^2 + 4x + 2$	**36.** $5n^3 - 20n$
37. $9n^2 + 12n + 4$	**38.** $d^2 - 169$	**39.** $4a^2 - 81$
40. $x^2 - 121$	**41.** $5x^2 + 40x + 80$	**42.** $16n^2 + 56n + 49$
43. $3n^2 - 30n + 75$	**44.** $a^2 + 26a + 169$	**45.** $25x^2 - 144$
46. $9d^2 - 64$	**47.** $n^2 - 28n + 196$	**48.** $49a^2 - 14a + 1$
49. $y^2 + 8y + 16$	**50.** $y^2 - 400$	**51.** $x^2 - 10x + 25$
52. $4x^2 - 60x + 225$	**53.** $3x^2 - 363$	**54.** $y^2 - 81$
55. $a^2 - 100$	**56.** $256a^2 - 1$	**57.** $n^2 + 34n + 289$
58. $2d^3 - 50d$	**59.** $y^2 + 22y + 121$	**60.** $144x^2 - 25$
61. $4x^2 - 169$	**62.** $x^2 - 12x + 36$	**63.** $64r^2 + 80r + 25$
64. $50m^3 - 32m$	**65.** $b^2 - 225$	**66.** $x^2 - 18x + 81$
67. $b^2 - 64$	**68.** $16x^2 - 72x + 81$	**69.** $b^2 - 256$
70. $x^2 + 24x + 144$	**71.** $225x^2 - 16$	**72.** $2x^3 + 40x^2 + 200x$
73. $4r^2 - 25$	**74.** $16x^2 + 8x + 1$	**75.** $b^2 - 14b + 49$
76. $x^2 + 30x + 225$	**77.** $m^2 - 28m + 196$	**78.** $9r^2 - 256$
79. $b^2 + 20b + 100$	**80.** $m^2 - 16$	**81.** $4x^2 - 32x + 64$
82. $x^2 - 196$	**83.** $8x^3 - 32x$	**84.** $25x^2 - 30x + 9$
85. $8m^2 - 16m + 8$	**86.** $9x^2 - 400$	**87.** $m^2 - 144$

Name ______________________ Class ______________ Date ______________

Reteaching 9-8

Factoring by Grouping

OBJECTIVE: Factoring by grouping **MATERIALS:** None

To factor a polynomial with four terms, we can sometimes group pairs of terms together, find the GCF of each pair, then factor a GCF from the resulting terms.

Examples

Factor $2x^3 - 8x^2 + 5x - 20$.

Group pairs of terms together. ⟶ $(2x^3 - 8x^2) + (5x - 20)$

Factor the GCF from each pair. ⟶ $2x^2(x - 4) + 5(x - 4)$

(Note: To proceed with this method, both sets of parentheses must contain the same expression.)

Replace the expressions in parentheses with ▲. ⟶ $2x^2$ ▲ + 5 ▲

Now, factor the common factor ▲ from both terms. ⟶ ▲ $(2x^2 + 5)$

Lastly, replace the ▲ with the expression it represents. ⟶ $(x - 4)(2x^2 + 5)$

So, $2x^3 - 8x^2 + 5x - 20 = (x - 4)(2x^2 + 5)$.

You can check your answer using FOIL.

It is sometimes possible to use this method to factor trinomials by first rewriting the middle term as a sum.

Factor $2x^2 + 13x + 15$.

Find two numbers whose product is *ac* and sum is *b*. ⟶ Since $a = 2$ and $c = 15$, $ac = 30$. Since $ac = 30$ and $b = 13$, the numbers are 10 and 3.

Rewrite the middle term as a sum of two terms whose coefficients are the two numbers you just found. ⟶ $13x = 10x + 3x$

Replace the middle term with this sum. ⟶ $2x^2 + (10x + 3x) + 15$

Regroup the terms and proceed as in the first example. ⟶ $(2x^2 + 10x) + (3x + 15)$

Factor the GCF from each pair. ⟶ $2x(x + 5) + 3(x + 5)$

Replace the common expression with ▲. ⟶ $2x$ ▲ + 3 ▲

Factor ▲ from both terms. ⟶ ▲$(2x + 3)$

Replace the ▲ with the expression. ⟶ $(x + 5)(2x + 3)$

So, $2x^2 + 13x + 15 = (x + 5)(2x + 3)$.

Exercises

Factor each polynomial by grouping.

1. $2x^3 + 4x^2 + x + 2$
2. $2x^3 + 6x^2 + 3x + 9$
3. $5x^3 - 25x^2 + 2x - 10$
4. $2x^3 + 12x^2 - 5x - 30$
5. $7x^3 - 4x^2 + 7x - 4$
6. $9x^3 - 12x^2 - 18x + 24$
7. $3x^2 + x - 2$
8. $2x^2 - x - 3$
9. $5x^2 + 34x - 7$

Name ______________________ Class ______________ Date ______________

Practice 9-8

Factoring by Grouping

Factor each expression.

1. $x(a + 2) - 2(a + 2)$
2. $3(x + y) + a(x + y)$
3. $m(x - 3) + k(x - 3)$
4. $a(y + 1) - b(y + 1)$
5. $x^2 + 3x + 2xy + 6y$
6. $y^2 - 5wy + 4y - 20w$
7. $xy + 4y - 2x - 8$
8. $ab + 7b - 3a - 21$
9. $ax + bx + ay + by$
10. $ax + bx - ay - by$
11. $2x^2 - 6xy + 5x - 15y$
12. $3x^2 - 6xy + 2x - 4y$
13. $2ax + 6xc + ba + 3bc$
14. $x^2y - 3x^2 - 2y + 6$
15. $6 + 2y + 3x^2 + x^2y$
16. $2x^2 - 3x + 1$
17. $2x^2 - 7x + 3$
18. $6x^2 + 7x + 2$
19. $4x^2 + 8x + 3$
20. $6x^2 - 7x + 2$
21. $4x^2 - 9x + 2$
22. $2x^2 - 3x - 2$
23. $12x^2 - x - 1$
24. $6x^2 + 19x + 3$
25. $12y^2 - 5y - 2$
26. $10y^2 + 21y - 10$
27. $5y^2 + 13y + 6$
28. $16y^2 + 10y + 1$
29. $16x^2 - 14x + 3$
30. $16x^2 + 16x + 3$
31. $10x^2 - 3x - 1$
32. $9x^2 + 25x - 6$
33. $14x^2 + 15x - 9$
34. $2x^3 + 8x^2 + x + 4$
35. $8x^4 + 6x - 28x^3 - 21$
36. $5x^3 - x^2 + 15x - 3$
37. $x^3 + 3x^2 + 4x + 12$
38. $6x^3 + 3x^2 + 2x + 1$
39. $3x^3 + 9x^2 + 2x + 6$
40. $9x^3 - 12x^2 + 3x - 4$
41. $10x^3 - 25x^2 + 4x - 10$
42. $4x^3 - 20x^2 + 3x - 15$

Find expressions for the possible dimensions of each rectangular prism.

43. The volume of the prism is given.

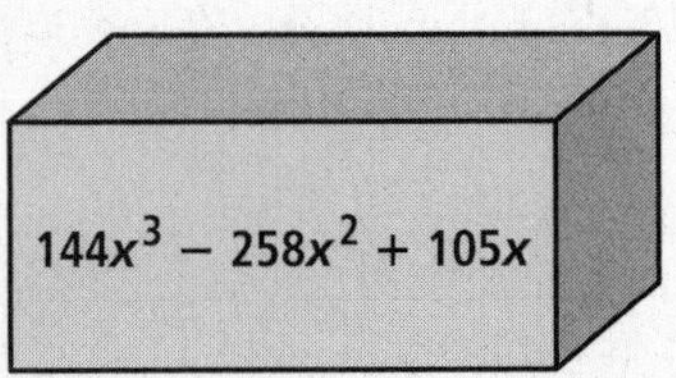

44. The volume of the prism is given.

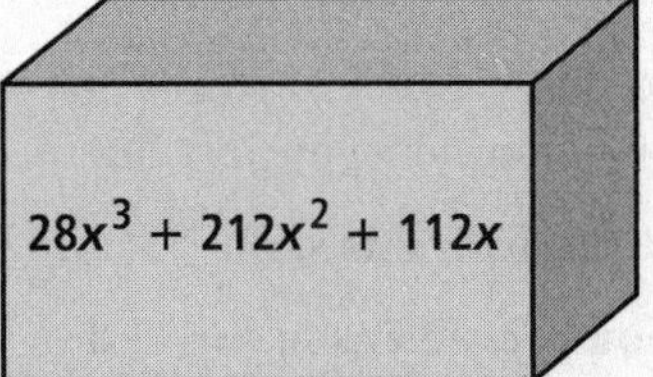

Name ____________________ Class ____________ Date ____________

Reteaching 10-1

Exploring Quadratic Graphs

OBJECTIVE: Graphing quadratic functions of the form $y = ax^2 + c$	**MATERIALS:** Graph paper

$y = ax^2$	Comparison	$y = ax^2 + c$
It forms a parabola.	Same	It forms a parabola.
It opens up if $a > 0$.	Same	It opens up if $a > 0$.
It opens down if $a < 0$.	Same	It opens down if $a < 0$.
Its line of symmetry is the y-axis.	Same	Its line of symmetry is the y-axis.
The vertex is the origin	Different	The vertex is shifted up c units from the origin if $c > 0$, down c units if $c < 0$.

Example

Sketch the graph of the equation $y = -x^2 + 5$.

Gather some information about the graph by looking closely at the equation.

opens *downward*

↓

$y = -x^2 + 5$

↑

The vertex is shifted *up* five units from the origin.

Make a table of values

x	y
−3	−4
−1	4
0	5
1	4
3	−4

Graph.

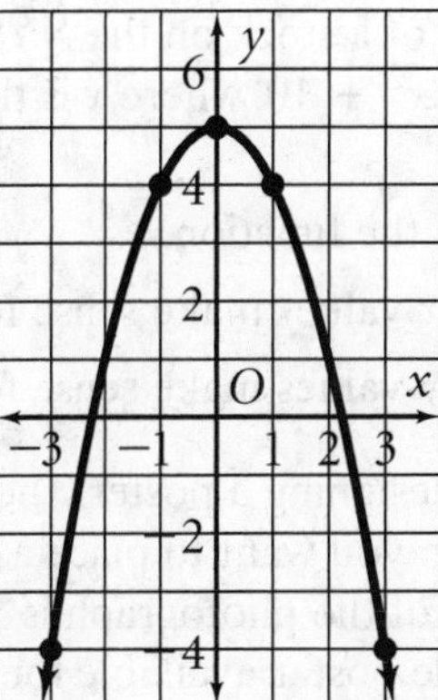

Exercises

Fill in the blanks for each equation. Make a table of values. Then graph each equation.

The parabola opens ____________.

The vertex is shifted ____________ unit(s) from the origin.

1. $y = x^2$

2. $y = 3x^2 + 1$

3. $y = -4x^2$

4. $y = \frac{1}{2}x^2$

5. $y = -\frac{1}{2}x^2 - 3$

6. $y = x^2 + \frac{1}{2}$

7. $y = 2x^2 - 4$

8. $y = -x^2 - 3$

9. $y = -4x^2 + 7$

10. $y = \frac{1}{4}x^2 - 2$

Name ________________________ Class ______________ Date ______________

Practice 10-1

Exploring Quadratic Graphs

Identify the vertex of each graph. Tell whether it is a minimum or a maximum.

1. $y = -3x^2$
2. $y = -7x^2$
3. $y = 0.5x^2$
4. $y = 5x^2$
5. $y = -4x^2$
6. $y = \frac{3}{2}x^2$

Order each group of quadratic functions from widest to narrowest graph.

7. $y = x^2, y = 5x^2, y = 3x^2$
8. $y = -8x^2, y = \frac{1}{2}x^2, y = -x^2$
9. $y = 5x^2, y = -4x^2, y = 2x^2$
10. $y = -\frac{1}{2}x^2, y = \frac{1}{3}x^2, y = -3x^2$
11. $y = 6x^2, y = -7x^2, y = 4x^2$
12. $y = \frac{3}{4}x^2, y = 2x^2, y = \frac{1}{5}x^2$

Graph each function.

13. $y = x^2$
14. $y = 4x^2$
15. $y = -3x^2$
16. $y = -x^2 - 4$
17. $y = 2x^2 - 2$
18. $y = 2x^2 + 3$
19. $y = \frac{1}{2}x^2 + 2$
20. $y = \frac{1}{2}x^2 - 3$
21. $y = \frac{1}{3}x^2 + 5$
22. $y = \frac{1}{3}x^2 - 4$
23. $y = 2.5x^2 + 3$
24. $y = 2.5x^2 + 5$
25. $y = 5x^2 + 8$
26. $y = 5x^2 - 8$
27. $y = -3.5x^2 - 4$

28. The price of a stock on the NYSE is modeled by the function $y = 0.005x^2 + 10$, where x is the number of months the stock has been available.
    a. Graph the function.
    b. What x-values make sense for the domain? Explain why.
    c. What y-values make sense for the range? Explain why.

29. You are designing a poster. The poster is 24 in. wide by 36 in. high. On the poster, you want to place a square photograph and some printing. If each side of the photograph is x in., the function $y = 864 - x^2$ gives the area of the poster available for printing.
    a. Graph the function.
    b. What x-values make sense for the domain? Explain why.
    c. What y-values make sense for the range? Explain why.

30. You are placing a circular drawing on a square piece of poster board. The poster board is 15 in. wide. The part of the poster board not covered by the drawing will be painted blue. If the radius of the drawing is r, the function $A = 225 - 3.14r^2$ gives the area to be painted blue.
    a. Graph the function.
    b. What x-values make sense for the domain? Explain why.
    c. What y-values make sense for the range? Explain why.

Name ______________________ Class ______________ Date ______________

Reteaching 10-2

Quadratic Functions

OBJECTIVE: Graphing quadratic functions of the form $y = ax^2 + bx + c$

MATERIALS: Graph paper

To graph the quadratic function $y = ax^2 + bx + c$:

- Find the axis of symmetry by substituting a and b values into the equation $x = -\frac{b}{2a}$. This is also the x-coordinate of the vertex.
- Find the y-coordinate of the vertex by substituting the x-value into the quadratic equation and solving for y.
- For graphs of inequalities, the curve is dashed for $<$ or $>$ and solid for $\leq$ or $\geq$.

Example

Sketch the graph of the equation $f(x) = -3 - 2x + x^2$.

Standard form: $y = x^2 - 2x - 3$

Axis of symmetry: $y = -\frac{b}{2a} = -\frac{(-2)}{2(1)} = \frac{2}{2(1)} = 1$

Vertex: Substitute $x = 1$ into the equation to get y.

$y = (1)^2 - 2(1) - 3 = -4$
vertex: $(1, -4)$

Table of Values		
x	$x^2 - 2x - 3$	y
−2	4 + 4 − 3	5
0	0 − 0 − 3	−3
2	4 − 4 − 3	−3

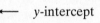

← y-intercept

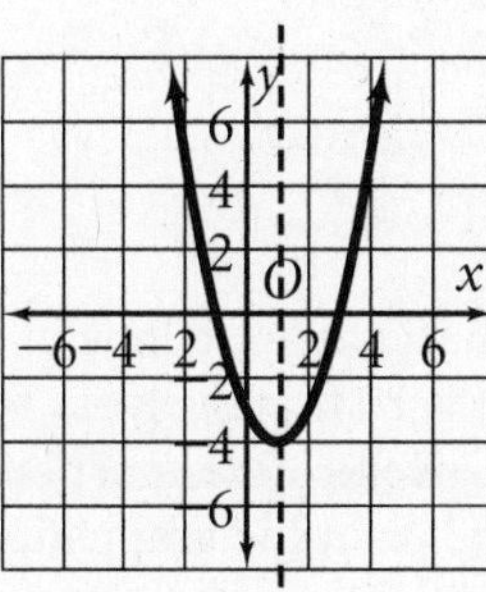

Exercises

Find the following to graph $y + x^2 = 16 + 4x$.

1. Standard form:
2. Axis of symmetry:
3. Vertex:
4. Table of values
5. Graph

Graph each function.

6. $y + x^2 = -1 + 2x$

7. $f(x) = -4x + 3 + x^2$

Name ____________________ Class ____________________ Date ____________________

Practice 10-2

Quadratic Functions

Find the equation of the axis of symmetry and the coordinates of the vertex of the graph of each function.

1. $y = x^2 - 10x + 2$
2. $y = x^2 + 12x - 9$
3. $y = -x^2 + 2x + 1$
4. $y = 3x^2 + 18x + 9$
5. $y = 3x^2 + 3$
6. $y = 16x - 4x^2$
7. $y = 0.5x^2 + 4x - 2$
8. $y = -4x^2 + 24x + 6$
9. $y = -1.5x^2 + 6x$

Graph each function. Label the axis of symmetry, the vertex, and the *y*-intercept.

10. $y = x^2 - 6x + 4$
11. $y = x^2 + 4x - 1$
12. $y = x^2 + 10x + 14$
13. $y = x^2 + 2x + 1$
14. $y = -x^2 - 4x + 4$
15. $y = -4x^2 + 24x + 13$
16. $y = -2x^2 - 8x + 5$
17. $y = 4x^2 - 16x + 10$
18. $y = -x^2 + 6x + 5$
19. $y = 4x^2 + 8x$
20. $y = -3x^2 + 6$
21. $y = 6x^2 + 48x + 98$

Graph each quadratic inequality.

22. $y > x^2 + 1$
23. $y \geq x^2 - 4$
24. $y < -x^2 + 1$
25. $y > x^2 + 6x + 3$
26. $y < x^2 - 4x + 4$
27. $y < -x^2 + 2x - 3$
28. $y \geq -2x^2 - 8x - 5$
29. $y \leq -3x^2 + 6x + 1$
30. $y \geq 2x^2 - 4x - 3$

Find the vertex of each function. Determine whether the vertex is a maximum or minimum.

31. $y = 2x^2 - 12x + 9$
32. $y = -2x^2 - 16x - 33$
33. $y = -4x^2 + 4x - 1$
34. $y = -3.5x^2 - 14x - 10$
35. $y = 0.05x^2 - 3.2x + 4$
36. $y = -1.8x^2 + 16.2x - 18.2$
37. You and a friend are hiking in the mountains. You want to climb to a ledge that is 20 ft above you. The height the grappling hook can be thrown is given by the function $h = -16t^2 - 32t + 5$. What is the maximum height the grappling hook can reach? Can you throw it high enough to reach the ledge?
38. The total profit made by an engineering firm is given by the function $p = x^2 - 25x + 5000$. Find the minimum profit made by the company.
39. You are trying to dunk a basketball. You need to jump 2.5 ft in the air to dunk the ball. The height that your feet are above the ground is given by the function $h = -16t^2 + 12t$. What is the maximum height your feet will be above the ground? Will you be able to dunk the basketball?

Name ______________________ Class ______________ Date ______________

Reteaching 10-3

Finding and Estimating Square Roots

OBJECTIVE: Finding square roots

MATERIALS: Calculator

- In decimal form, a rational number terminates or repeats.
- In decimal form, an irrational number continues without repeating.

Example

Complete the following table involving square roots.

Number	Principal Square Root	Negative Square Root	Rational/ Irrational	Perfect Square or $\sqrt{\ }$ Between Which Consecutive Integers
81	9	−9	rational	perfect square
0.25	0.5	−0.5	rational	perfect square
$\frac{4}{9}$	$\frac{2}{3}$	$-\frac{2}{3}$	rational	perfect square
7	2.645 . . .	−2.645 . . .	irrational	between 2 and 3
−17	undefined	undefined	undefined	undefined

Exercises

Complete the following table involving square roots.

1.

Number	Principal Square Root	Negative Square Root	Rational/ Irrational	Perfect Square or $\sqrt{\ }$ Between Which Consecutive Integers
$\frac{1}{64}$				
26				
23				
−36				
$\frac{81}{324}$				

Simplify each expression, and label it as rational or irrational.

2. $\sqrt{100}$

3. $\sqrt{12}$

4. $\sqrt{-14}$

5. $\sqrt{63}$

6. $-\sqrt{0}$

7. $\sqrt{\frac{1}{9}}$

Name ______________________ Class ______________ Date ______________

Practice 10-3

Finding and Estimating Square Roots

Tell whether each expression is *rational* or *irrational*.

1. $-\sqrt{64}$
2. $\sqrt{1600}$
3. $\pm\sqrt{160}$
4. $\sqrt{144}$
5. $\sqrt{125}$
6. $-\sqrt{340}$
7. $\sqrt{1.96}$
8. $-\sqrt{0.09}$

Use a calculator to find each square root to the nearest hundredth.

9. $\sqrt{20}$
10. $\sqrt{73}$
11. $-\sqrt{38}$
12. $\sqrt{130}$
13. $\sqrt{149.3}$
14. $-\sqrt{8.7}$
15. $\sqrt{213.8}$
16. $-\sqrt{320.7}$
17. $\sqrt{113.9}$
18. $-\sqrt{840.6}$
19. $-\sqrt{1348.9}$
20. $\sqrt{928.2}$

Simplify each expression.

21. $\sqrt{49}$
22. $-\sqrt{2.25}$
23. $\sqrt{\frac{1}{16}}$
24. $\sqrt{400}$
25. $\sqrt{6.25}$
26. $\pm\sqrt{\frac{36}{25}}$
27. $\sqrt{196}$
28. $\sqrt{2.56}$
29. $\sqrt{0.25}$
30. $\pm\sqrt{\frac{9}{100}}$
31. $\sqrt{576}$
32. $\pm\sqrt{\frac{121}{36}}$
33. $\sqrt{1600}$
34. $-\sqrt{0.04}$
35. $\sqrt{2500}$
36. $\sqrt{4.41}$

Between what two consecutive integers is each square root?

37. $\sqrt{40}$
38. $\sqrt{139}$
39. $-\sqrt{75}$
40. $\sqrt{93}$
41. $-\sqrt{105.6}$
42. $-\sqrt{173.2}$
43. $\sqrt{1123.7}$
44. $\sqrt{216.9}$

Solve the following problems. Round to the nearest tenth if necessary.

45. You are to put a metal brace inside a square shipping container. The formula $d = \sqrt{2x^2}$ gives the length of the metal brace, where x is the length of the side of the container. Find the length of the brace for each container side length.

    a. $x = 3$ ft **b.** $x = 4.5$ ft **c.** $x = 5$ ft **d.** $x = 8$ ft

46. You are designing a cone-shaped storage container. Use the formula $r = \sqrt{\frac{3V}{\pi h}}$ to find the radius of the storage container. Find the radius when $V = 10{,}000\text{ ft}^3$ and $h = 10$ ft.

Name ______________________ Class ______________ Date ____________

Reteaching 10-4

Solving Quadratic Equations

OBJECTIVE: Solving quadratic equations in $ax^2 = c$ form	**MATERIALS:** Calculator

Quadratic equations written in the form $x^2 = c$ can be solved by finding the square root of each side.

Value of c	No. of Real Solutions	x-Intercepts
$c > 0$	2	$(+\sqrt{c}, 0)(-\sqrt{c}, 0)$
$c = 0$	1	(0, 0)
$c < 0$	0	none

Note: Every parabola has two roots, but they are not always real number roots; they could be complex or a double root.

Example

Solve $3x^2 - 48 = 0$.

$3x^2 - 48 + 48 = 0 + 48$ ← **Add 48 to each side.**

$3x^2 = 48$

$x^2 = 16$ ← **Divide each side by 3.**

$x = \pm\sqrt{16}$ ← **Find the square roots.**

$x = \pm 4$ ← **Simplify.**

$3(4)^2 - 48 = 0$ $\quad$ $3(-4)^2 - 48 = 0$ ← **Check the results in the original equation.**

$3(16) - 48 = 0$ $\quad$ $3(16) - 48 = 0$

$48 - 48 = 0$ $\quad$ $48 - 48 = 0$

Exercises

Fill in the following chart to find the solutions to each equation.

	1. $4x^2 = 100$	**2.** $2x^2 - 6 = 0$	**3.** $x^2 + 4 = 0$	**4.** $81x^2 - 5 = 20$
Rewrite in $ax^2 = c$ form.				
Rewrite in $x^2 = \frac{c}{a}$ form.				
Find the square roots.				
Solutions				

Name ________________________ Class ________________ Date ____________

Practice 10-4

Solving Quadratic Equations

Solve each equation by finding square roots. If the equation has no real solution, write *no solution.* If the value is irrational, round to the nearest hundredth.

1. $x^2 = 16$	**2.** $x^2 - 144 = 0$	**3.** $3x^2 - 27 = 0$
4. $x^2 + 16 = 0$	**5.** $x^2 = 12$	**6.** $x^2 = 49$
7. $x^2 + 8 = -10$	**8.** $3x^2 = 300$	**9.** $2x^2 - 6 = 26$
10. $x^2 = 80$	**11.** $81x^2 - 10 = 15$	**12.** $2x^2 = 90$
13. $x^2 = 300$	**14.** $4x^2 + 9 = 41$	**15.** $2x^2 + 8 = 4$
16. $x^2 + 8 = 72$	**17.** $4x^2 + 6 = 7$	**18.** $x^2 = 121$
19. $5x^2 + 20 = 30$	**20.** $x^2 + 6 = 17$	**21.** $3x^2 + 1 = 54$
22. $2x^2 - 7 = 74$	**23.** $x^2 + 1 = 0$	**24.** $4x^2 - 8 = -20$
25. $9x^2 = 1$	**26.** $x^2 + 4 = 4$	**27.** $3x^2 = 1875$
28. $x^2 = 9$	**29.** $5x^2 - 980 = 0$	**30.** $x^2 - 10 = 100$
31. $4x^2 - 2 = 1$	**32.** $3x^2 - 75 = 0$	**33.** $x^2 + 25 = 0$
34. $2x^2 - 10 = -4$	**35.** $4x^2 + 3 = 3$	**36.** $4x^2 - 8 = 32$
37. $7x^2 + 8 = 15$	**38.** $x^2 + 1 = 26$	**39.** $6x^2 = -3$
40. $x^2 - 400 = 0$	**41.** $7x^2 - 8 = 20$	**42.** $2x^2 - 1400 = 0$
43. $5x^2 + 25 = 90$	**44.** $x^2 + 4x^2 = 20$	**45.** $5x^2 - 18 = -23$
46. $3x^2 - x^2 = 10$	**47.** $2x^2 + 6 - x^2 = 9$	**48.** $x^2 - 225 = 0$
49. $-3 + 4x^2 = 2$	**50.** $7x^2 - 1008 = 0$	**51.** $6x^2 - 6 = 12$

Solve each problem. If necessary, round to the nearest tenth.

52. You want to build a fence around a square garden that covers 506.25 ft^2. How many feet of fence will you need to complete the job?

53. The formula $A = 6s^2$ will calculate the surface area of a cube. Suppose you have a cube that has a surface area of 216 $in.^2$. What is the length of each side?

54. You drop a pencil out of a window that is 20 ft above the ground. Use the formula $V^2 = 64s$, where V is the speed and s is the distance fallen, to calculate the speed the pencil is traveling when it hits the ground.

55. Suppose you are going to construct a circular fish pond in your garden. You want the pond to cover an area of 300 ft^2. What is the radius of the pond?

56. During the construction of a skyscraper, a bolt fell from 400 ft. What was the speed of the bolt when it hit the ground? Use $V^2 = 64s$.

Name ______________________ Class ______________ Date ______________

Reteaching 10-5

Factoring to Solve Quadratic Equations

OBJECTIVE: Solving quadratic equations by factoring

MATERIALS: None

The Zero-Product Property can be used when factoring quadratic equations. It states that if the product of two numbers equals zero, then one of its factors is zero. For example, if $(x - 2)(x + 1) = 0$, then either $(x - 2) = 0$ or $(x + 1) = 0$. This property allows you to solve a quadratic equation.

Example

Solve $2x^2 - x = 3$ by factoring.

$2x^2 - x = 3$

$2x^2 - x - 3 = 0$ ⟵ **Subtract 3 from each side.**

$(2x - 3)(x + 1) = 0$ ⟵ **Factor $2x^2 - x - 3$.**

$2x - 3 = 0$ or $x + 1 = 0$ ⟵ **Use the Zero-Product Property.**

$2x = 3$ or $x = -1$ ⟵ **Solve for x.**

$x = \frac{3}{2}$ or $x = -1$

The solutions are $\frac{3}{2}$ and -1.

Check

Substitute $\frac{3}{2}$ for x.

$$\left(2\left(\frac{3}{2}\right) - 3\right)\left(\frac{3}{2} + 1\right) \stackrel{?}{=} 0$$

$$(3 - 3)\left(\frac{5}{2}\right) \stackrel{?}{=} 0$$

$$(0)\left(\frac{5}{2}\right) = 0 ✓$$

Substitute -1 for x.

$$(2(-1) - 3)(-1 + 1) \stackrel{?}{=} 0$$

$$(-2 - 3)(0) \stackrel{?}{=} 0$$

$$(-5)(0) = 0 ✓$$

Exercises

Solve by factoring.

1. $x^2 + 7x + 10 = 0$

2. $x^2 - x = 12$

3. $x^2 - 5x + 6 = 0$

4. $x^2 - 6x = -8$

5. $2x^2 + 5x + 3 = 0$

6. $3x^2 + 2x - 8 = 0$

7. $x^2 - 3x - 28 = 0$

8. $2x^2 - x - 10 = 0$

9. $6x^2 + 2x = 4$

Name ______________________ Class ______________ Date ____________

Practice 10-5

Factoring to Solve Quadratic Equations

Use the Zero-Product Property to solve each equation.

1. $(x + 5)(x - 3) = 0$

2. $(x - 2)(x + 9) = 0$

3. $(b - 12)(b + 12) = 0$

4. $(2n + 3)(n - 4) = 0$

5. $(x + 7)(4x - 5) = 0$

6. $(2x + 7)(2x - 7) = 0$

7. $(3x - 7)(2x + 1) = 0$

8. $(8y - 3)(4y + 1) = 0$

9. $(5x + 6)(4x + 5) = 0$

Solve by factoring.

10. $x^2 + 5x + 6 = 0$

11. $b^2 - 7b - 18 = 0$

12. $r^2 - 4 = 0$

13. $x^2 + 8x - 20 = 0$

14. $y^2 + 14y + 13 = 0$

15. $s^2 - 3s - 10 = 0$

16. $x^2 + 7x = 8$

17. $x^2 = 25$

18. $h^2 + 10h = -21$

19. $2t^2 + 8t - 64 = 0$

20. $3a^2 - 36a + 81 = 0$

21. $5x^2 - 45 = 0$

22. $2a^2 - a - 21 = 0$

23. $3n^2 - 11n + 10 = 0$

24. $2x^2 - 7x - 9 = 0$

25. $2n^2 - 5n = 12$

26. $3m^2 - 5m = -2$

27. $5s^2 - 17s = -6$

28. $6m^2 = 13m + 28$

29. $4a^2 - 4a = 15$

30. $4r^2 = r + 3$

31. Suppose you are building a storage box of volume 4368 in.^{3}. The length of the box will be 24 in. The height of the box will be 1 in. more than its width. Find the height and width of the box.

32. A banner is in the shape of a right triangle of area 63 in.^{2}. The height of the banner is 4 in. less than twice the width of the banner. Find the height and width of the banner.

33. A rectangular poster has an area of 190 in.^{2}. The height of the poster is 1 in. less than twice its width. Find the dimensions of the poster.

34. A diver is standing on a platform 24 ft above the pool. He jumps from the platform with an initial upward velocity of 8 ft/s. Use the formula $h = -16t^2 + vt + s$, where h is his height above the water, t is the time, v is his starting upward velocity, and s is his starting height. How long will it take for him to hit the water?

Solve each equation.

35. $(x - 9)(x + 8) = 0$

36. $x^2 - 9x - 10 = 0$

37. $(c - 21)(c + 21) = 0$

38. $(x - 12)(5x - 13) = 0$

39. $2a^2 - 21a - 65 = 0$

40. $x^2 + 6x - 91 = 0$

41. $a^2 + 6a - 72 = 0$

42. $4x^2 + 8x - 21 = 0$

43. $20d^2 - 82d + 80 = 0$

44. $3n^2 + 12n - 288 = 0$

45. $2s^2 - 13s - 24 = 0$

46. $x^2 + 5x = 150$

47. $3c^2 + 8c = 3$

48. $30a^2 + 121a - 21 = 0$

49. $c^2 - 81 = 0$

50. $x^2 + 306 = -35x$

51. $x^2 = 121$

52. $x^2 - 21x + 108 = 0$

Name ______________________ Class ______________ Date ______________

Reteaching 10-6

Completing the Square

OBJECTIVE: Solving quadratic equations by completing the square

MATERIALS: None

Remember that to complete the square, the coefficient of the squared term is 1 and the constant term is moved to the right side of the equation.

Example

Solve by completing the square: $2x^2 - 16x - 40 = 0$

$2x^2 - 16x - 40 = 0$

$x^2 - 8x - 20 = 0$ ← **Divide each side by 2.**

$x^2 - 8x = 20$ ← **Add 20 to each side.**

$x^2 - 8x + 16 = 20 + 16$ ← **Take $\frac{1}{2}$ the coefficient of x, square it, and add to both sides.**

$(x - 4)^2 = 36$ ← **Write the left hand side as a square.**

$\sqrt{(x - 4)^2} = \sqrt{36}$ ← **Take the square root of each side.**

$x - 4 = \pm 6$ ← **Simplify.**

$x - 4 = 6$ or $x - 4 = -6$ ← **Write as two equations.**

$x = 10$ or $x = -2$ ← **Solve.**

Check by substituting $x = 10$ and $x = -2$ into the original equation.

Exercises

Tell what is done in each step of the solution.

1. $3x^2 + 6x - 45 = 0$

a. $x^2 + 2x - 15 = 0$

b. $x^2 + 2x = 15$

c. $x^2 + 2x + 1 = 15 + 1$

d. $(x + 1)^2 = 16$

e. $\sqrt{(x + 1)^2} = \sqrt{16}$

f. $x + 1 = \pm 4$

g. $x + 1 = 4$ or $x + 1 = -4$

h. $x = 3$ or $x = -5$

Solve each equation by completing the square. Express all radicals to the nearest hundredth.

2. $x^2 - 10x + 16 = 0$

3. $x^2 - 12x + 32 = 0$

4. $x^2 - 12x + 3 = 0$

5. $x^2 + 8x - 5 = 0$

Name ______________________ Class ______________ Date ____________

Practice 10-6

Completing the Square

Find the value of c such that each expression is a perfect square trinomial.

1. $x^2 - 14x + c$
2. $x^2 - \frac{2}{9}x + c$
3. $x^2 - \frac{4}{9}x + c$
4. $x^2 - \frac{2}{6}x + c$

Solve each equation by completing the square.

5. $x^2 - 4x = 5$
6. $x^2 - x - 2 = 0$
7. $x^2 - 6x = 10$
8. $x^2 + 4x + 4 = 0$
9. $x^2 - 3x = 18$
10. $x^2 - 8x - 4 = 0$
11. $x^2 - 6x = 0$
12. $x^2 - 6x = 8$
13. $x^2 - 7x = 0$
14. $x^2 + 4x - 12 = 0$
15. $x^2 + 11x + 10 = 0$
16. $x^2 + 2x = 15$
17. $x^2 - 8x = 9$
18. $x^2 + 5x = -6$
19. $x^2 - 2x = 120$
20. $x^2 - 22x = -105$
21. $2x^2 = 3x + 9$
22. $2x^2 + 8x - 10 = 0$
23. $2x^2 - 3x - 2 = 0$
24. $2x^2 + 12x - 32 = 0$
25. $3x^2 + 17x - 6 = 0$
26. $2x^2 - x - 28 = 0$
27. $3x^2 - 4x + 1 = 0$
28. $2x^2 - 5x - 3 = 0$
29. $6x^2 - 2x = 28$
30. $2x^2 - 16x = -30$
31. $4x^2 = -2x + 12$
32. $9x^2 + 6x = 3$
33. $10x^2 + 3x = 4$
34. $12x^2 - 29x + 15 = 0$

Name ______________________ Class ______________ Date ______________

Reteaching 10-7

Using the Quadratic Formula

OBJECTIVE: Using the quadratic formula to solve quadratic equations

MATERIALS: Calculator

- The quadratic formula can be used to solve any quadratic equation.
- When the quadratic equation is in standard form ($ax^2 + bx + c = 0$), where $a \neq 0$, the solutions are found by the quadratic formula

$$x = \frac{-b \pm \sqrt{b^2 - 4ac}}{2a}.$$

Example

Solve $x^2 + 5x = 14$.

$x^2 + 5x = 14$

$x^2 + 5x - 14 = 0$ ← **Rewrite in standard form.**

$\overset{a}{x^2} + \overset{b}{5x} - \overset{c}{14} = 0$ ← **Write *a, b, c* above the appropriate numbers. ($a = 1, b = 5, c = -14$)**

$x = \frac{-b \pm \sqrt{b^2 - 4ac}}{2a}$ ← **Use the quadratic formula.**

$x = \frac{-5 \pm \sqrt{5^2 - 4(1)(-14)}}{2(1)}$ ← **Substitute 1 for *a*, 5 for *b*, and −14 for *c*.**

$x = \frac{-5 \pm \sqrt{25 + 56}}{2}$ ← **Solve.**

$x = \frac{-5 \pm \sqrt{81}}{2}$ ← **Simplify.**

$x = \frac{-5 \pm 9}{2}$

$x = \frac{-5 + 9}{2}$ or $x = \frac{-5 - 9}{2}$ ← **Write two equations.**

$x = 2$ or $x = -7$ ← **Solve for *x*.**

The solutions are $x = 2$ or $x = -7$.

Exercises

Use the quadratic formula to solve each equation. If necessary, round answers to the nearest hundredth.

1. $3x^2 + 7x + 2 = 0$
2. $x^2 + 3x + 2 = 0$
3. $4y^2 = 3 - 5y$
4. $2 = 11z - 5z^2$
5. $x^2 + 5x = 6$
6. $-3x^2 + x + 5 = 0$
7. $x^2 = 3x + 4$
8. $-4x^2 + x + 7 = 0$

Name ______________________ Class ______________ Date ______________

Practice 10-7

Using the Quadratic Formula

Use the quadratic formula to solve each equation. If the equation has no real solutions write *no real solutions.* If necessary, round your answers to the nearest hundredth.

1. $x^2 + 8x + 5 = 0$ **2.** $x^2 - 36 = 0$ **3.** $d^2 - 4d - 96 = 0$

4. $a^2 - 3a - 154 = 0$ **5.** $4p^2 - 12p - 91 = 0$ **6.** $5m^2 + 9m = 126$

7. $r^2 - 35r + 70 = 0$ **8.** $y^2 + 6y - 247 = 0$ **9.** $x^2 + 12x - 40 = 0$

10. $4n^2 - 81 = 0$ **11.** $x^2 + 13x + 30 = 0$ **12.** $a^2 - a = 132$

13. $6w^2 - 23w + 7 = 0$ **14.** $4x^2 + 33x = 27$ **15.** $7s^2 - 7 = 0$

16. $x^2 + 5x - 90 = 0$ **17.** $5b^2 - 20 = 0$ **18.** $4x^2 - 3x + 6 = 0$

19. $6h^2 + 77h - 13 = 0$ **20.** $5y^2 = 17y + 12$ **21.** $g^2 - 15g = 54$

22. $27f^2 = 12$ **23.** $4x^2 - 52x + 133 = 0$ **24.** $x^2 + 36x + 60 = 0$

25. $a^2 - 2a - 360 = 0$ **26.** $x^2 + 10x + 40 = 0$ **27.** $t^2 - 10t = 39$

28. $4x^2 + 7x - 9 = 0$ **29.** $2c^2 - 39c + 135 = 0$ **30.** $4x^2 + 33x + 340 = 0$

31. $m^2 - 40m + 100 = 0$ **32.** $8x^2 + 25x + 19 = 0$ **33.** $36w^2 - 289 = 0$

34. $4d^2 + 29d - 60 = 0$ **35.** $4z^2 + 43z + 108 = 0$ **36.** $3x^2 - 19x + 40 = 0$

37. $14x^2 = 56$ **38.** $32x^2 - 18 = 0$ **39.** $r^2 + r - 650 = 0$

40. $2y^2 = 39y - 17$ **41.** $5a^2 - 9a + 5 = 0$ **42.** $x^2 = 9x + 120$

43. $8h^2 - 38h + 9 = 0$ **44.** $20x^2 = 245$ **45.** $9h^2 - 72h = -119$

46. $x^2 + 3x + 8 = 0$ **47.** $6m^2 - 13m = 19$ **48.** $9x^2 - 81 = 0$

49. $4s^2 + 8s = 221$ **50.** $6p^2 + 25p - 119 = 0$ **51.** $2s^2 - 59s + 17 = 0$

52. A rectangular painting has dimensions x and $x + 10$. The painting is in a frame 2 in. wide. The total area of the picture and the frame is 900 in.^{2}. What are the dimensions of the painting?

53. A ball is thrown upward from a height of 15 ft with an inital upward velocity of 5 ft/s. Use the formula $h = -16t^2 + vt + s$ to find how long it will take for the ball to hit the ground.

54. Your community wants to put a square fountain in a park. Around the fountain will be a sidewalk that is 3.5 ft wide. The total area that the fountain and sidewalk can be is 700 ft^2. What are the dimensions of the fountain?

55. The Garys have a triangular pennant of area 420 in.^{2} flying from the flagpole in their yard. The height of the triangle is 10 in. less than 5 times the base of the triangle. What are the dimensions of the pennant?

Name ______________________ Class ______________ Date ______________

Reteaching 10-8

OBJECTIVE: Using the discriminant to find the number of solutions of a quadratic equation	**MATERIALS:** Calculator

In the quadratic formula $x = \frac{-b \pm \sqrt{b^2 - 4ac}}{2a}$, the discriminant is the expression under the radical sign, $b^2 - 4ac$. The discriminant determines how many solutions, or x-intercepts, a quadratic equation has.

- If the discriminant is positive, there are two real solutions.
- If the discriminant is 0, there is one real solution.
- If the discriminant is negative, there are no real solutions.

Example

Find the value of the discriminant and the number of real solutions for each quadratic equation.

$ax^2 + bx + c = 0$	Discriminant $(b^2 - 4ac)$	Number of Solutions	Number of x-intercepts
1. $x^2 + 2x + 3 = 0$	$(2)^2 - 4(1)(3) = -8$	none	none
2. $x^2 - 2x + 1 = 0$	$(-2)^2 - 4(1)(1) = 0$	one	one
3. $x^2 - 2x - 2 = 0$	$(-2)^2 - 4(1)(-2) = 12$	two	two

Exercises

Find the value of the discriminant and the number of solutions for each quadratic equation.

$ax^2 + bx + c = 0$	Discriminant $(b^2 - 4ac)$	Number of Solutions	Number of x-intercepts
1. $2x^2 + 3x + 3 = 0$			
2. $x^2 - 2x + 4 = 0$			
3. $3x^2 - 6x + 3 = 0$			

Find the value of the discriminant and the number of solutions of each equation.

4. $-2x^2 + 4x - 2 = 0$ **5.** $-\frac{1}{2}x^2 + x + 3 = 0$ **6.** $5x^2 - 2x + 3 = 0$

Name ______________________ Class ______________ Date ______________

Practice 10-8

Using the Discriminant

Find the number of real solutions of each equation.

1. $x^2 + 6x + 10 = 0$
2. $x^2 - 4x - 1 = 0$
3. $x^2 + 6x + 9 = 0$
4. $x^2 - 8x + 15 = 0$
5. $x^2 - 5x + 7 = 0$
6. $x^2 - 4x + 5 = 0$
7. $3x^2 - 18x + 27 = 0$
8. $4x^2 - 8 = 0$
9. $-5x^2 - 10x = 0$
10. $-x^2 = 4x + 6$
11. $4x^2 = 9x - 3$
12. $8x^2 + 2 = 8x$
13. $7x^2 + 16x + 11 = 0$
14. $12x^2 - 11x - 2 = 0$
15. $-9x^2 - 25x + 20 = 0$
16. $16x^2 + 8x = -1$
17. $-16x^2 + 11x = 11$
18. $12x^2 - 12x = -3$
19. $0.2x^2 + 4.5x - 2.8 = 0$
20. $-2.8x^2 + 3.1x = -0.5$
21. $0.5x^2 + 0.6x = 0$
22. $1.5x^2 - 15x + 2.5 = 0$
23. $-3x^2 + 27x = -40$
24. $2.1x^2 + 4.2 = 0$

25. One of the games at a carnival involves trying to ring a bell with a ball by hitting a lever that propels the ball into the air. The height of the ball is modeled by the equation $h = -16t^2 + 39t$. If the bell is 25 ft above the ground, will it be hit by the ball?

26. You are placing a rectangular picture on a square poster board. You can enlarge the picture to any size. The area of the poster board not covered by the picture is modeled by the equation $A = -x^2 - 10x + 300$. Is it possible for the area not covered by the picture to be 100 in.^{2}?

27. The equation $h = -16t^2 + 58t + 3$ models the height of a baseball t seconds after it has been hit.
    a. Was the height of the baseball ever 40 ft?
    b. Was the height of the baseball ever 60 ft?

28. A firefighter is on the fifth floor of an office building. She needs to throw a rope into the window above her on the seventh floor. The function $h = -16t^2 + 36t$ models how high above her she is able to throw a rope. If she needs to throw the rope 40 ft above her to reach the seventh-floor window, will the rope get to the window?

Find the number of x-intercepts of each function.

29. $y = x^2 + 10x + 16$
30. $y = x^2 + 3x + 5$
31. $y = x^2 - 2x - 7$
32. $y = 3x^2 - 3$
33. $y = 2x^2 + x$
34. $y = 3x^2 + 2x + 1$
35. $y = x^2 - 8x - 4$
36. $y = x^2 - 16x + 64$
37. $y = -2x^2 - 5x - 6$
38. $y = -4x^2 - 5x - 2$
39. $y = -x^2 + 12x - 36$
40. $y = -5x^2 + 11x - 6$

Name ______________________ Class ______________ Date ____________

Reteaching 10-9

Choosing a Linear, Quadratic, or Exponential Model

OBJECTIVE: Choosing a linear, quadratic, or exponential model

MATERIALS: None

When analyzing data to determine whether the model that best fits the data is linear, exponential, or quadratic, use the following guidelines.

Linear ($y = mx + b$)	The y-coordinates have a common difference.
Exponential ($y = a \cdot b^x$)	The y-coordinates have a common ratio.
Quadratic ($y = ax^2 + bx + c$)	The y-coordinates have a common second difference.

Example

Which kind of function best models the data below? Write an equation to model the data.

x	-2	-1	0	1	2
y	$\frac{3}{4}$	$\frac{3}{2}$	3	6	12

The y-coordinates have a common ratio, 2. Notice that each y-coordinate is equal to the previous y-coordinate multiplied by 2. The data is best modeled by an exponential function. To determine the function

$$y = a \cdot b^x,$$

let $a =$ the value of y when $x = 0$;

let $b =$ the common ratio, 2.

$$y = 3 \cdot 2^x$$

Exercises

Determine the function that best models the data. Write an equation to model the data.

1.

x	-2	-1	0	1	2
y	-7	-4	-1	2	5

2.

x	-2	-1	0	1	2
y	-8	-2	0	-2	-8

3.

x	0	1	2	3	4
y	2	$\frac{5}{2}$	3	$\frac{7}{2}$	4

4.

x	-2	-1	0	1	2
y	$-\frac{2}{9}$	$-\frac{2}{3}$	-2	-6	-18

5.

x	-4	-3	-2	-1	0
y	4	$\frac{9}{4}$	1	$\frac{1}{4}$	0

Name ______________________ Class ______________ Date ______________

Practice 10-9

Choosing a Linear, Quadratic, or Exponential Model

Which kind of function best models the data? Write an equation to model the data.

1. $(-1, 3), (1, 3), (3, 27), (5, 75), (7, 147)$
2. $(-2, 4), (-1, 2), (0, 0), (1, -2), (2, -4)$
3. $\left(-2, \frac{1}{16}\right), \left(-1, \frac{1}{4}\right), (0, 1), (1, 4), (2, 16)$
4. $(-6, -1), (-3, 0), (0, 1), (3, 2), (6, 3)$
5. $\left(-2, \frac{1}{3}\right), (-1, 1), (0, 3), (1, 9), (2, 27)$
6. $(-4, -32), (-2, -8), (0, 0), (2, -8), (4, -32)$

7.

x	y
-3	$\frac{9}{2}$
-2	2
-1	$\frac{1}{2}$
0	0

8.

x	y
-1	-2
0	-4
1	-6
2	-8

9.

x	y
-4	-4
-2	-1
0	0
2	-1

10.

x	y
0	-2
1	-8
2	-32
3	-128

11.

x	y
-7	-245
-5	-125
-3	-45
-1	-5

12.

x	y
-2	$\frac{3}{2}$
0	$\frac{1}{2}$
2	$-\frac{1}{2}$
4	$-\frac{3}{2}$

13. $\left(-2, \frac{1}{3}\right), \left(-1, \frac{1}{3}\right), \left(0, \frac{1}{3}\right), \left(1, \frac{1}{3}\right), \left(2, \frac{1}{3}\right)$

14. $\left(-1, -\frac{1}{4}\right), \left(0, -\frac{1}{2}\right), (1, -1), (2, -2), (3, -4)$

15. The cost of shipping computers from a warehouse is given in the table below.

Number of Computers	50	75	100	125
Cost (dollars)	1700	2500	3300	4100

a. Determine which kind of function best models the data.
b. Write an equation to model the data.
c. On the basis of your equation, what is the cost of shipping 27 computers?
d. On the basis of your equation, how many computers could be shipped for $5500?

16. During a scientific experiment, the bacteria count was taken at 5-min intervals. The data shows the count at several time periods during the experiment.

Time Interval	0	1	2	3
Count	110	132	159	190

a. Determine which kind of function best models the data.
b. Write an equation to model the data.
c. On the basis of your equation, what is the count 1 hr, 45 min after the start of the experiment?

Name ______________________ Class ______________ Date ______________

Reteaching 11-1

Simplifying Radicals

OBJECTIVE: Simplifying radicals involving products and quotients

MATERIALS: None

The following are three examples of simplifying radicals. Simplifying each radical makes it meet a condition that must be true to show that a radical expression is in its simplest form.

Example

Condition	Not in Simplest Form	How to Simplify	Simplest Form
The Multiplication Property of Square Roots is used to simplify the radical.			
The expression under the radical sign has no perfect square factors other than 1.	$\sqrt{20}$	Rewrite as a product of perfect squares and other factors. $= \sqrt{4 \cdot 5}$ $= \sqrt{4} \cdot \sqrt{5}$	$2\sqrt{5}$
The Division Property of Square Roots is used to simplify the radical.			
The expression under the radical sign is a fraction.	$\sqrt{\frac{16}{25}}$ $\frac{\sqrt{16}}{\sqrt{25}}$	Separate into two radical expressions. Simplify each separately.	$\frac{4}{5}$
The denominator contains a radical expression that is not a perfect square	$\frac{3}{\sqrt{2}}$	Rationalize the denominator by multiplying the fraction by a radical expression equal to 1. $= \frac{3}{\sqrt{2}} \cdot \frac{\sqrt{2}}{\sqrt{2}}$	$\frac{3\sqrt{2}}{2}$

Exercises

Simplify each radical expression.

1. $\sqrt{2} \cdot \sqrt{12}$
2. $3\sqrt{5} \cdot 2\sqrt{5}$
3. $4\sqrt{80}$
4. $\sqrt{3} \cdot \sqrt{36}$
5. $\sqrt{18}$
6. $\frac{5}{\sqrt{3}}$
7. $2\sqrt{28}$
8. $2\sqrt{\frac{4}{5}}$
9. $\sqrt{\frac{14}{25}}$
10. $\frac{\sqrt{5}}{\sqrt{64}}$
11. $2\sqrt{\frac{3}{8}}$
12. $\sqrt{\frac{16}{9}}$

Name ____________ Class ____________ Date ____________

Practice 11-1

Simplifying Radicals

Simplify each radical expression. Assume that all variables under radicals represent positive numbers.

1. $\sqrt{32}$
2. $\sqrt{22} \cdot \sqrt{8}$
3. $\sqrt{147}$
4. $\sqrt{\frac{17}{144}}$
5. $\sqrt{a^2b^5}$
6. $\frac{2}{\sqrt{6}}$
7. $\sqrt{80}$
8. $\sqrt{27}$
9. $\frac{\sqrt{256}}{\sqrt{32}}$
10. $\frac{8}{\sqrt{7}}$
11. $\sqrt{12x^4}$
12. $\frac{\sqrt{96}}{\sqrt{12}}$
13. $\sqrt{200}$
14. $\sqrt{\frac{12}{225}}$
15. $\sqrt{15} \cdot \sqrt{6}$
16. $\sqrt{120}$
17. $\frac{4}{\sqrt{2a}}$
18. $(3\sqrt{2})^3$
19. $\sqrt{250}$
20. $\frac{\sqrt{65}}{\sqrt{13}}$
21. $\sqrt{84}$
22. $\sqrt{\frac{18}{225}}$
23. $\sqrt{48s^3}$
24. $3\sqrt{24}$
25. $\sqrt{15} \cdot \sqrt{35}$
26. $\sqrt{160}$
27. $\frac{6}{\sqrt{3}}$
28. $\frac{\sqrt{48n^6}}{\sqrt{6n^3}}$
29. $\sqrt{136}$
30. $\sqrt{\frac{27x^2}{256}}$
31. $\sqrt{m^3n^2}$
32. $\frac{\sqrt{180}}{\sqrt{9}}$
33. $\sqrt{18} \cdot \sqrt{8}$
34. $(10\sqrt{3})^2$
35. $\sqrt{\frac{17}{64}}$
36. $\sqrt{50}$
37. $\sqrt{48}$
38. $\sqrt{20}$
39. $\sqrt{8}$
40. $\sqrt{25x^2}$
41. $\sqrt{\frac{7}{9}}$
42. $\sqrt{\frac{17}{64}}$
43. $\frac{\sqrt{48}}{\sqrt{8}}$
44. $\frac{\sqrt{120}}{\sqrt{10}}$
45. $\frac{5}{\sqrt{2}}$
46. $\sqrt{75}$
47. $\sqrt{300}$
48. $\sqrt{49a^3}$
49. $\sqrt{125}$
50. $\sqrt{28x^4}$
51. $\frac{7}{\sqrt{3}}$
52. $\sqrt{\frac{15}{49}}$
53. $\frac{\sqrt{60}}{\sqrt{12}}$
54. $\frac{3}{\sqrt{3}}$
55. $\frac{4}{\sqrt{8}}$
56. $\sqrt{72x^3}$
57. $\sqrt{50y^3}$
58. $\sqrt{45x^2y^3}$
59. $\sqrt{\frac{44x^3}{9x}}$
60. $\frac{\sqrt{4}}{\sqrt{3x}}$
61. $6\sqrt{20}$
62. $\sqrt{ab^3}$
63. $\sqrt{a^5b^6}$
64. $12\sqrt{60x^2}$
65. $(2\sqrt{3})^2$
66. $\sqrt{12} \cdot \sqrt{27}$
67. $(7\sqrt{5})^2$
68. $\sqrt{14} \cdot \sqrt{8}$
69. $(5\sqrt{5})^2$
70. $\sqrt{8x^6y^7}$
71. $\sqrt{16a^3} \cdot \sqrt{5a^2}$
72. $\sqrt{8} \cdot \sqrt{7}$
73. $\sqrt{3x} \cdot \sqrt{5x}$
74. $2\sqrt{5} \cdot 2\sqrt{5}$
75. $4\sqrt{3} \cdot 2\sqrt{2}$
76. $6\sqrt{3} \cdot 7\sqrt{8}$
77. $\frac{10}{\sqrt{x}}$
78. $\frac{\sqrt{9}}{\sqrt{2x}}$
79. $\frac{4}{\sqrt{20}}$
80. $\frac{\sqrt{12x}}{\sqrt{27x}}$
81. $\frac{3\sqrt{7}}{\sqrt{20x}}$
82. $\frac{4\sqrt{5}}{\sqrt{8y}}$

Name ______________________ Class ______________ Date ______________

Reteaching 11-2

The Pythagorean Theorem

OBJECTIVE: Finding the lengths of the sides of a right triangle

MATERIALS: None

As you solve problems using the Pythagorean Theorem, keep in mind these ideas.

- In the formula, *a* and *b* represent the *legs* of the right triangle.
- The *hypotenuse* is represented by *c*. This is the side *opposite* the right angle.
- Drawing a picture of the triangle each time is a good strategy for making sure you use the formula correctly.
- Writing *a, b,* and *c* on your picture with the values from your problem gives you a visual representation of your problem before you solve it.

Example

Find the length of the missing side: $a = 3, b = ■, c = 5$.

$c = 5$, $a = 3$, $b = ?$ ⟵ **Draw a triangle and include the values from the problem for *a, b,* and *c*.**

$a^2 + b^2 = c^2$ ⟵ **Use the Pythagorean Theorem.**

$3^2 + b^2 = 5^2$ ⟵ **Substitute 3 for *a* and 5 for *c*.**

$9 + b^2 = 25$ ⟵ **Simplify.**

$b^2 = 16$ ⟵ **Subtract 9 from each side.**

$\sqrt{b^2} = \sqrt{16}$ ⟵ **Take the square root of each side.**

$b = 4$ ⟵ **Use a calculator if necessary.**

Exercises

Draw and label a triangle. Find the length of the missing side to the nearest tenth.

1. $a = 6, b = ■, c = 10$
2. $a = ■, b = 4, c = 10$
3. $a = 5, b = 12, c = ■$

Find the length of the missing side to the nearest tenth.

4. $a = ■, b = 5, c = 7$
5. $a = 4, b = ■, c = 9$
6. $a = 7.5, b = 4, c = ■$
7. $a = 5, b = ■, c = 12$
8. $a = 8, b = ■, c = 17$
9. $a = 6, b = 8, c = ■$
10. $a = ■, b = 24, c = 25$
11. $a = 4, b = 3, c = ■$
12. $a = 9, b = ■, c = 15$

Name ______________________ Class ______________ Date ______________

Practice 11-2

The Pythagorean Theorem

Use the triangle at the right. Find the length of the missing side to the nearest tenth.

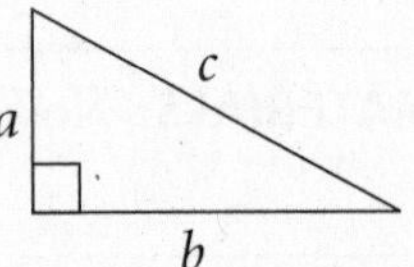

1. $a = 12, b = 35, c = ■$

2. $a = 10, b = ■, c = 26$

3. $a = 11, b = ■, c = 61$

4. $a = 36, b = 15, c = ■$

5. $a = 8, b = 15, c = ■$

6. $a = ■, b = 24, c = 40$

7. $a = 18, b = ■, c = 35$

8. $a = 17, b = ■, c = 49$

9. $a = 42, b = 37, c = ■$

10. $a = ■, b = 80, c = 90$

11. $a = 8, b = 8, c = ■$

12. $a = 19, b = ■, c = 26$

13. $a = ■, b = 27, c = 33$

14. $a = ■, b = 13, c = 24$

15. $a = 9, b = ■, c = 13$

16. $a = 19, b = 45, c = ■$

17. $a = ■, b = 24, c = 39$

18. $a = 14, b = 14, c = ■$

Determine whether the given lengths are sides of a right triangle.

19. 20, 21, 29

20. 16, 30, 34

21. 24, 60, 66

22. 23, 18, 14

23. 10, 24, 28

24. 45, 28, 53

25. $\frac{4}{5}, \frac{3}{5}, 1$

26. $\frac{2}{3}, \frac{4}{3}, \frac{1}{3}$

27. 3.5, 4.4, 5.5

28. 10.5, 11.3, 13.8

29. 3.3, 6.5, 5.6

30. 24, 70, 74

31. 4.2, 7.0, 5.6

32. 5.2, 6.5, 3.9

33. 2.1, 3.5, 2.8

34. 4.8, 7.5, 5.4

35. 7.5, 4.3, 6.7

36. $\frac{1}{9}, \frac{1}{15}, \frac{1}{18}$

37. $\frac{1}{2}, \frac{6}{5}, \frac{13}{10}$

38. $\frac{1}{5}, \frac{1}{4}, \frac{1}{3}$

Find the missing length to the nearest tenth.

39. A ladder is 25 ft long. The ladder needs to reach to a window that is 24 ft above the ground. How far away from the building should the bottom of the ladder be placed?

40. Suppose you are making a sail in the shape of a right triangle for a sailboat. The length of the longest side of the sail is 65 ft. The sail is to be 63 ft high. What is the length of the third side of the sail?

41. Suppose you leave your house and travel 13 mi due west. Then you travel 3 mi due south. How far are you from your house?

42. A wire is run between the tips of two poles. One pole is 23 ft taller than the other pole. The poles are 37 ft apart. How long does the wire need to be to reach between the two poles?

43. A 20-ft-long wire is used to support a television antenna. The wire is connected to the antenna 15 ft above the ground. How far away from the base of the tower will the other end of the wire be located?

Name ______________________ Class ______________ Date ______________

Reteaching 11-3

The Distance and Midpoint Formulas

OBJECTIVE: Finding the distance between two points in a coordinate plane; finding the coordinates of the midpoint of two points

MATERIALS: None

The following strategies may be used to help you apply the distance formula or the midpoint formula correctly.

- Underline the x-coordinates.
- Circle the y-coordinates.

Example

Find the distance between (2, 5) and (−1, −3). Round your answer to the nearest tenth.

$(\underline{2}, \textcircled{5}), (\underline{-1}, \textcircled{-3})$ ← **Underline the x-coordinates and circle the y-coordinates.**

$d = \sqrt{(x_2 - x_1)^2 + (y_2 - y_1)^2}$ ← **Write the distance formula.**

$d = \sqrt{(2 - (-1))^2 + (5 - (-3))^2}$ ← **Substitute the underlined numbers for x-coordinates and the circled numbers for the y-coordinates, in corresponding order.**

$d = \sqrt{3^2 + 8^2}$ ← **Simplify.**

$d = \sqrt{9 + 64}$

$d = \sqrt{73}$

$d = 8.5$ ← **Use a calculator. Round to the nearest tenth.**

Exercises

Find the distance between each pair of points. Round your answers to the nearest tenth.

1. (4, −2), (0, 4)
2. (2, 5), (−1, −3)
3. (4, −2), (−3, 5)
4. (−3, −2), (4, −1)

The midpoint of a line segment with endpoints $A(x_1, y_1)$ and $B(x_2, y_2)$ is $\left(\frac{x_1 + x_2}{2}, \frac{y_1 + y_2}{2}\right)$. Find the midpoint of $\overline{AB}$.

5. $A(2, 4)$ and $B(0, 6)$
6. $A(-6, -2)$ and $B(4, -1)$
7. $A(-2, 4)$ and $B(-6, 8)$
8. $A(-3, 6)$ and $B(-5, 0)$

Name ______________________ Class ______________ Date ______________

Practice 11-3

The Distance and Midpoint Formulas

Find the midpoint of $\overline{XY}$.

1. $X(8, 14)$ and $Y(2, 6)$
2. $X(11, 7)$ and $Y(3, 19)$
3. $X(-7, 6)$ and $Y(11, -2)$
4. $X(-3, -2)$ and $Y(7, 8)$
5. $X(-4, -1)$ and $Y(-8, 5)$
6. $X(6, 15)$ and $Y(4, 8)$
7. $X(-3, 5)$ and $Y(8, 9)$
8. $X(16, -8)$ and $Y(5, 9)$
9. $X(0, -15)$ and $Y(9, -15)$
10. $X(9\frac{1}{2}, 7)$ and $Y(7\frac{1}{2}, 5)$
11. $X(6, -2)$ and $Y(9, -1)$
12. $X(8, -13)$ and $Y(1, -7)$
13. $X(-7, -5)$ and $Y(-3, 16)$
14. $X(-7, -17)$ and $Y(11, 4)$
15. $X(11, 19)$ and $Y(6, -4)$
16. $X(3, -8)$ and $Y(-5, -13)$
17. $X(-2, 2)$ and $Y(6, -13)$
18. $X(-9, -4)$ and $Y(16, 12)$

Find the distance between each pair of points. If necessary, round to the nearest tenth.

19. $(3, 0), (0, 4)$
20. $(3, 5), (12, 17)$
21. $(-4, 2), (2, -6)$
22. $(5, -7), (9, -2)$
23. $(4, 9), (15, 4)$
24. $(-7, 4), (2, -9)$
25. $(6, -1), (-5, 5)$
26. $(9, 8), (1, 12)$
27. $(13, -8), (2, 15)$
28. $(16, -7), (-2, -3)$
29. $(9, 15), (5, 12)$
30. $(7, 5), (-9, -6)$
31. $(-7, 15), (19, 2)$
32. $(9, -1), (11, -28)$
33. $(14, -29), (10, -25)$
34. $(2, -8), (8, -1)$
35. $(-11, 1), (7, 13)$
36. $(-1, 9), (19, 23)$
37. $(-9, 33), (13, 31)$
38. $(7, 2), (1, -2)$

39. $\overline{AB}$ is a diameter of a circle. The coordinates of A are $(-1, 3)$, and the coordinates of B are $(-5, 9)$. Find the center of the circle.

40. $\overline{CD}$ is a diameter of a circle. The coordinates of C are $(-2, -3)$, and the coordinates of D are $(-12, -5)$. Find the center of the circle.

41. A quadrilateral is a parallelogram if the diagonals bisect each other. Quadrilateral $EFGH$ has vertices a $E(-4, 3)$, $F(2, 1)$, $G(4, 7)$, and $H(-2, 9)$. Find the midpoint of each diagonal. Is $EFGH$ a parallelogram? Explain.

42. A large building is on fire. Fire trucks from two different stations respond to the fire. One station is 1 mi east and 2 mi north of the fire. The other station is 2 mi west and 1 mi south of the fires. How far apart are the two fire stations?

43. The Anderson and McCready families decide to go to a concert together. The Andersons live 4 km west and 6 km north of the concert hall. The McCreadys live 5 km east and 2 km south of the concert hall. How far apart do the two families live?

44. According to the map, a ball field is 4 km west and 2 km north of where you live. A theater is 1 km east and 4 km south of where you live. How far apart are the ball field and the theater?

Name ______________________ Class ______________ Date ______________

Reteaching 11-4

Operations with Radical Expressions

OBJECTIVE: Simplifying radical expressions **MATERIALS:** None

- Underline radicals not in simplest form.
- Circle like terms. They can be combined.

Example

Simplify $\sqrt{27} + 2\sqrt{3}$.

$\sqrt{27} + 2\sqrt{3}$ ← **Underline radicals not in simplest form.**

$\sqrt{9 \cdot 3} + 2\sqrt{3}$ ← **Rewrite as a product of perfect squares and other factors. 9 is a perfect square and a factor of 27.**

$\sqrt{9} \cdot \sqrt{3} + 2\sqrt{3}$ ← **Use the Multiplication Property of Square Roots.**

$3\sqrt{3} + 2\sqrt{3}$ ← **Simplify $\sqrt{9}$.**

$3\sqrt{3} + 2\sqrt{3}$ ← **Circle like terms.**

$5\sqrt{3}$ ← **Combine like terms by adding the coefficients.**

Example

Simplify $\sqrt{5}(2 + \sqrt{10})$

$\sqrt{5}(2 + \sqrt{10}) = 2\sqrt{5} + \sqrt{50}$ ← **Use the Distributive Property.**

$= 2\sqrt{5} + \sqrt{25} \cdot \sqrt{2}$ ← **Use the Multiplication Property of Square Roots.**

$= 2\sqrt{5} + 5\sqrt{2}$ ← **Simplify.**

Exercises

Underline radicals not in simplest form and circle like terms. Simplify each expression.

1. $3\sqrt{24} - 2\sqrt{6}$
2. $6\sqrt{3} + 4\sqrt{3}$
3. $\sqrt{27} + \sqrt{3}$
4. $3\sqrt{12} - 2\sqrt{3}$
5. $10\sqrt{6} - 3\sqrt{6}$
6. $6\sqrt{7} - \sqrt{28}$

Simplify each expression.

7. $\sqrt{5}(\sqrt{5} + 2)$
8. $(\sqrt{2} + 1)(\sqrt{2} - 1)$
9. $\sqrt{2}(\sqrt{2} - \sqrt{3})$
10. $(2\sqrt{3} + \sqrt{5})^2$
11. $(3\sqrt{2} - \sqrt{5})(2\sqrt{5} + 4\sqrt{2})$
12. $(2\sqrt{3} + 1)(\sqrt{3})$

Name ______________ Class ______________ Date ______________

Practice 11-4

Operations with Radical Expressions

Simplify each expression.

1. $3\sqrt{7} + 5\sqrt{7}$
2. $10\sqrt{4} - \sqrt{4}$
3. $4\sqrt{2}(2 + 2\sqrt{3})$
4. $\sqrt{45} + 2\sqrt{5}$
5. $12\sqrt{11} + 7\sqrt{11}$
6. $\sqrt{2}(2\sqrt{3} - 4\sqrt{2})$
7. $\sqrt{28} + \sqrt{63}$
8. $3\sqrt{6} - 8\sqrt{6}$
9. $\sqrt{3}(\sqrt{6} - \sqrt{12})$
10. $\sqrt{18} - \sqrt{50}$
11. $4\sqrt{2} + 2\sqrt{8}$
12. $13\sqrt{15} - 11\sqrt{15}$
13. $3(8\sqrt{3} - 7)$
14. $8(2\sqrt{5} + 5\sqrt{2})$
15. $17\sqrt{21} - 12\sqrt{21}$
16. $\sqrt{6}(7 + 3\sqrt{3})$
17. $8(4 - 3\sqrt{2})$
18. $2\sqrt{12} + 6\sqrt{27}$
19. $19\sqrt{3} + \sqrt{12}$
20. $8\sqrt{26} + 10\sqrt{26}$
21. $\sqrt{10}(3 - 2\sqrt{6})$
22. $9\sqrt{2} - \sqrt{50}$
23. $10\sqrt{13} - 7\sqrt{13}$
24. $12\sqrt{6} - 4\sqrt{24}$
25. $5\sqrt{7} + \sqrt{28}$
26. $8\sqrt{13} - 12\sqrt{13}$
27. $13\sqrt{40} + 6\sqrt{10}$
28. $-3\sqrt{3}(\sqrt{6} + \sqrt{3})$
29. $12\sqrt{29} - 15\sqrt{29}$
30. $10\sqrt{6} - 2\sqrt{6}$
31. $8\sqrt{3} - \sqrt{75}$
32. $3\sqrt{6}(2\sqrt{3} + \sqrt{6})$
33. $17\sqrt{35} + 2\sqrt{35}$
34. $\sqrt{19} + 4\sqrt{19}$
35. $12\sqrt{9} - 4\sqrt{9}$
36. $\sqrt{8}(\sqrt{2} - 7)$
37. $\dfrac{1}{\sqrt{2} - \sqrt{3}}$
38. $\dfrac{5}{\sqrt{7} - \sqrt{3}}$
39. $\dfrac{3}{\sqrt{5} + 5}$
40. $(\sqrt{6} - 3)^2$
41. $(3\sqrt{5} + \sqrt{5})^2$
42. $\dfrac{7}{\sqrt{2} - \sqrt{7}}$
43. $\dfrac{3 - \sqrt{6}}{5 - 2\sqrt{6}}$
44. $\dfrac{-12}{\sqrt{6} - 3}$
45. $\dfrac{2\sqrt{3} - \sqrt{6}}{5\sqrt{3} + 2\sqrt{6}}$

Solve each exercise by using the golden ratio $(1 + \sqrt{5}) : 2$.

46. The ratio of the height : width of a window is equal to the golden ratio. The width of the window is 36 in. Find the height of the door. Express your answer in simplest radical form and in inches.

47. The ratio of the length : width of a flower garden is equal to the golden ratio. The width of the garden is 14 ft. Find the length of the garden. Express your answer is simplest radical form and in feet.

48. The ratio of the width : height of the front side of a building is equal to the golden ratio. The height of the building is 40 ft. Find the width of the building. Express your answer in simplest radical form and in feet.

Name ______________________ Class ______________ Date ______________

Reteaching 11-5

Solving Radical Equations

OBJECTIVE: Solving equations that contain radicals

MATERIALS: Index cards or pieces of paper of a similar size

A radical equation has a *variable* under the radical sign. The radical expression must be alone on one side of the equal sign before squaring.

Example

Jubal solved a radical equation, showing all the steps. He wrote each step on a separate index card. Then he dropped the pack of cards! Number each of his cards to show the correct order of his steps.

The number in the lower left corner shows the correct order for the steps.

$\sqrt{y} = 4$ **3.**	$3 + \sqrt{y} - 3 = 7 - 3$ **2.**	$y = 16$ **5.**
The solution of $3 + \sqrt{y} = 7$ is 16. **8.**	$(\sqrt{y})^2 = (4)^2$ **4.**	$3 + \sqrt{16} \stackrel{?}{=} 7$ **6.**
$3 + 4 = 7$ ✔ **7.**	$3 + \sqrt{y} = 7$ **1.**	

Exercises

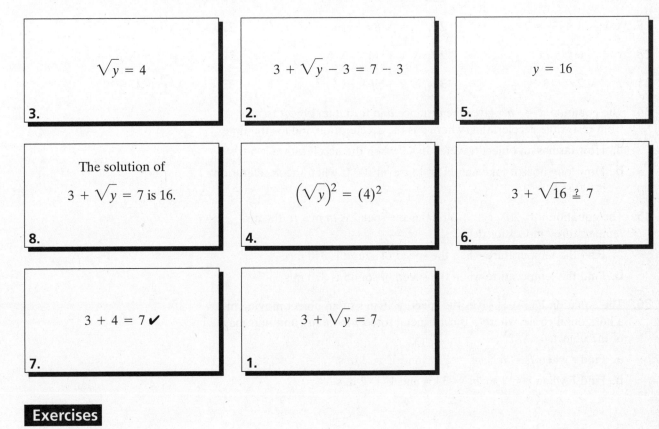

Solve each radical equation.

1. $\sqrt{3a} - 9 = 0$
2. $\sqrt{n - 2} = 3$
3. $c = \sqrt{3c - 8}$
4. $\sqrt{b} - 6 = -2\sqrt{b}$
5. $s = \sqrt{24 - 10s}$
6. $\sqrt{5x - 1} = \sqrt{3x + 9}$
7. $\sqrt{3y + 1} = 6$
8. $\sqrt{5x} - 3 = 2$
9. $\sqrt{2x + 1} = 5$

Name ______________________ Class ______________ Date ______________

Practice 11-5

Solving Radical Equations

Solve each radical equation. Check your solutions. If there is no solution, write *no solution*.

1. $\sqrt{x} + 3 = 11$

2. $\sqrt{x + 2} = \sqrt{3x - 6}$

3. $x = \sqrt{24 - 10x}$

4. $\sqrt{4x} - 7 = 1$

5. $\sqrt{x} = \sqrt{4x - 12}$

6. $x = \sqrt{11x - 28}$

7. $\sqrt{x} = 12$

8. $x = \sqrt{12x - 32}$

9. $x = \sqrt{13x - 40}$

10. $\sqrt{3x + 5} = \sqrt{x + 1}$

11. $\sqrt{x + 3} = 5$

12. $\sqrt{6x - 4} = \sqrt{4x + 6}$

13. $2 = \sqrt{x + 6}$

14. $x = \sqrt{2 - x}$

15. $\sqrt{4x + 2} = \sqrt{x + 14}$

16. $\sqrt{x + 8} = 9$

17. $x = \sqrt{7x + 8}$

18. $\sqrt{3x + 8} = \sqrt{2x + 12}$

19. $\sqrt{2x + 3} = 5$

20. $\sqrt{3x + 13} = \sqrt{7x - 3}$

21. $x = \sqrt{6 + 5x}$

22. $\sqrt{3x} - 5 = 4$

23. $\sqrt{3x + 4} = \sqrt{5x}$

24. $x = \sqrt{x - 12}$

25. $\sqrt{x - 4} + 3 = 9$

26. $x = \sqrt{8x + 20}$

27. $12 = \sqrt{6x}$

28. $x = \sqrt{60 - 7x}$

29. $\sqrt{x + 14} = \sqrt{6x - 1}$

30. $\sqrt{5x - 7} = \sqrt{6x + 11}$

31. $7 + \sqrt{2x} = 3$

32. $\sqrt{x + 56} = x$

33. $5 + \sqrt{x + 4} = 12$

34. The equation $d = \frac{1}{2}at^2$ gives the distance d in ft that an object travels from rest while accelerating, where a is the acceleration and t is the time.

a. How far has an object traveled in 4 s when the acceleration is 5 ft/s^2?

b. How long does it take an object to travel 100 ft when the acceleration is 8 ft/s^2?

35. The equation $v = 20\sqrt{t + 273}$ relates the speed v, in m/s, to the air temperature t in Celsius degrees.

a. Find the temperature when the speed of sound is 340 m/s.

b. Find the temperature when the speed of sound is 320 m/s.

36. The equation $V = \sqrt{\frac{Fr}{m}}$ gives the speed V in m/s of an object moving in a horizontal circle, where F is centripetal force, r is radius, and m is mass of the object.

a. Find r when $F = 6$ N, $m = 2$ kg, and $V = 3$ m/s.

b. Find F when $r = 1$ m, $m = 3$ kg, and $V = 2$ m/s.

Name ____________________ Class ____________ Date ____________

Reteaching 11-6

Graphing Square Root Functions

OBJECTIVE: Graphing and exploring square root functions	**MATERIALS:** Graph paper

Make a table of the values for x and y. These values can be plotted as ordered pairs.

Example

Make a table and then graph the function $y = \sqrt{6 + x}$.

Step 1 Select a domain that makes the expression under the radical greater than or equal to zero.

$6 + x \geq 0$

$x \geq -6$

Domain $= -6, -5, -2, 3, \ldots$

Step 2 Make a table like the one below. Replace x with each member of the domain to find y.

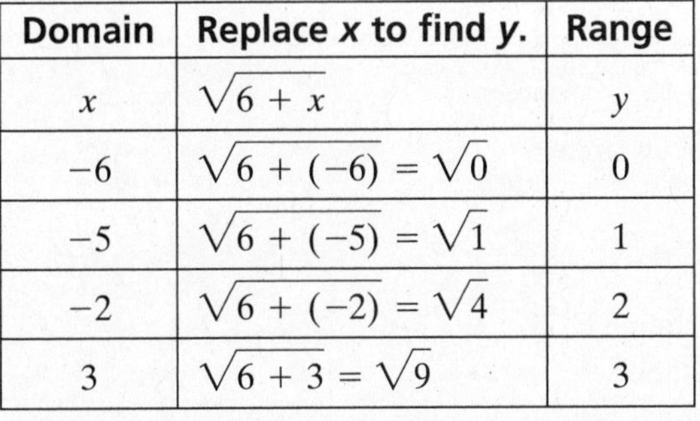

Domain	Replace x to find y.	Range
x	$\sqrt{6 + x}$	y
-6	$\sqrt{6 + (-6)} = \sqrt{0}$	0
-5	$\sqrt{6 + (-5)} = \sqrt{1}$	1
-2	$\sqrt{6 + (-2)} = \sqrt{4}$	2
3	$\sqrt{6 + 3} = \sqrt{9}$	3

Step 3 Use the values for x and y from the table to graph the function.

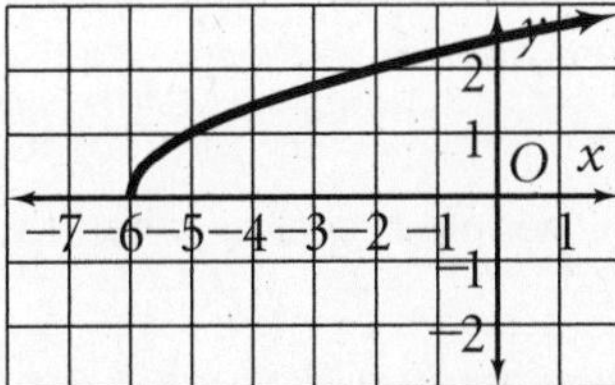

What do all of the y-values have in common? They are all positive.

Exercises

Graph each function using Steps 1–3.

1. $y = \sqrt{4 + x}$ **2.** $f(x) = \sqrt{x - 2}$ **3.** $y = \sqrt{x - 3}$

Graph each function.

4. $y = \sqrt{x - 1} + 2$ **5.** $f(x) = \sqrt{x} - 4$ **6.** $f(x) = \sqrt{5 - x} + 1$

7. $f(x) = \sqrt{x - 1} - 2$ **8.** $f(x) = \sqrt{x} + 3$ **9.** $f(x) = \sqrt{1 - x} + 3$

10. $f(x) = \sqrt{x + 5} - 1$ **11.** $f(x) = \sqrt{3x + 1} + 2$ **12.** $f(x) = \sqrt{3 - 2x} + 2$

Name ____________ Class ____________ Date ____________

Practice 11-6

Graphing Square Root Functions

Find the domain of each function.

1. $f(x) = \sqrt{x - 7}$
2. $f(x) = \sqrt{3x - 12}$
3. $y = \sqrt{4x + 11}$
4. $y = \sqrt{x - 12}$
5. $f(x) = \sqrt{x + 14}$
6. $y = \sqrt{x + 8}$
7. $y = \sqrt{5x + 13}$
8. $y = \sqrt{2x}$
9. $y = \sqrt{6x}$

Use a table of values to graph each function.

10. $y = \sqrt{x} - 12$
11. $y = 3\sqrt{x}$
12. $y = \sqrt{x + 8}$
13. $y = \sqrt{x + 7} - 6$
14. $y = \sqrt{x - 6} - 8$
15. $y = \sqrt{x - 10}$
16. $y = 2\sqrt{x - 2}$
17. $y = \sqrt{x - 8} + 6$
18. $y = \sqrt{x} + 7$

Using expressions such as "shift up," "shift down," "shift left," and "shift right," describe how each of the graphs compare to the graph of $y = \sqrt{x}$.

19. $y = \sqrt{x} - 9$
20. $y = \sqrt{x} - 8$
21. $y = \sqrt{x + 20}$
22. $y = \sqrt{x - 19}$
23. $y = \sqrt{x + 18}$
24. $y = \sqrt{x - 32}$
25. $y = \sqrt{x} + 11$
26. $y = \sqrt{x + 14}$
27. $y = \sqrt{x - 4} - 7$

28. The number of people involved in recycling in a community is modeled by the function $n = 90\sqrt{3t} + 400$, where t is the number of months the recycling plant has been open.
    a. Graph the function.
    b. Find the number of people recycling when the plant has been open for 6 mo.
    c. Find the month when about 670 people were recycling.

29. The time t, in seconds, that it takes for an object to drop a distance d, in feet, is modeled by the function $t = \sqrt{\frac{d}{16}}$. Assume no air resistance.
    a. Graph the function.
    b. Find the time it takes for an object to fall 1000 ft.
    c. How far does an object fall in 10 s?

Name ______________________ Class ______________ Date ______________

Reteaching 11-7

Trigonometric Ratios

OBJECTIVE: Exploring and calculating trigonometric ratios

MATERIALS: None

To make sure you are applying a trigonometric formula correctly, you should label the triangle's adjacent leg, opposite leg, and hypotenuse before you get started. Remember these key points:

- The *hypotenuse* is *opposite* the right angle.
- *Adjacent* means *next to.*
- Use a pencil when labeling sides so that your marks can be erased when the problem is for a different angle.

Example

For ΔABC find the sine, cosine, and tangent of $\angle$A and $\angle$B.

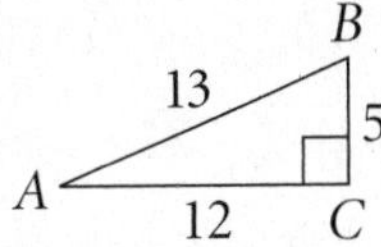

For $\angle A$

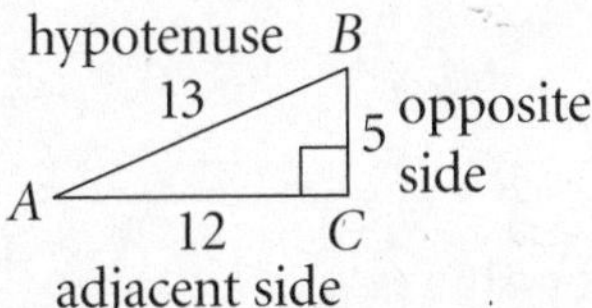

Redraw and label the sides of ΔABC for sine, cosine, and tangent of $\angle A$ and $\angle B$.

For $\angle B$

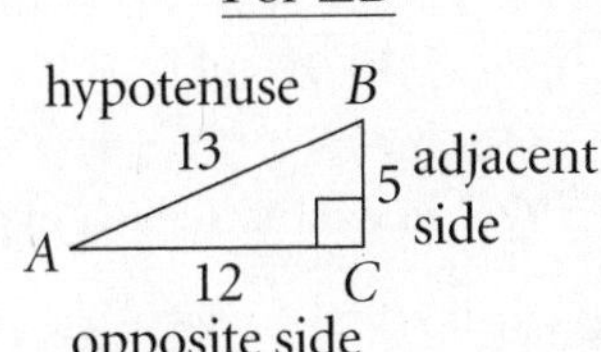

For $\angle A$	Trigonometric Ratios	For $\angle B$
$\sin A = \frac{5}{13}$	sine $= \frac{\text{length of opposite leg}}{\text{length of hypotenuse}}$	$\sin B = \frac{12}{13}$
$\cos A = \frac{12}{13}$	cosine $= \frac{\text{length of adjacent leg}}{\text{length of hypotenuse}}$	$\cos B = \frac{5}{13}$
$\tan A = \frac{5}{12}$	tangent $= \frac{\text{length of opposite leg}}{\text{length of hypotenuse}}$	$\tan B = \frac{12}{5}$

Exercises

Use ΔABC to evaluate each expression.

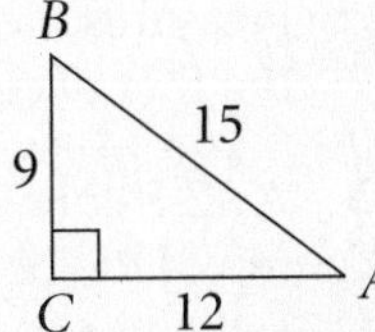

1. $\sin A$ **2.** $\cos A$ **3.** $\tan A$

4. $\sin B$ **5.** $\tan B$ **6.** $\cos B$

Name ______________________ Class ______________ Date ______________

Practice 11-7

Trigonometric Ratios

Use $\triangle ABC$ to evaluate each expression.

1. $\sin A$ **2.** $\cos A$ **3.** $\tan A$

4. $\sin B$ **5.** $\cos B$ **6.** $\tan B$

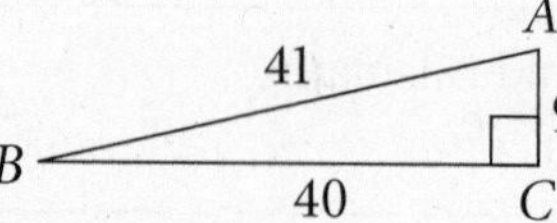

Evaluate each expression. Round to the nearest ten-thousandth.

7. $\tan 59°$ **8.** $\sin 75°$ **9.** $\sin 8°$ **10.** $\cos 13°$ **11.** $\sin 32°$

12. $\tan 67°$ **13.** $\cos 17°$ **14.** $\cos 36°$ **15.** $\tan 19°$ **16.** $\cos 58°$

Find the value of x to the nearest tenth.

17.

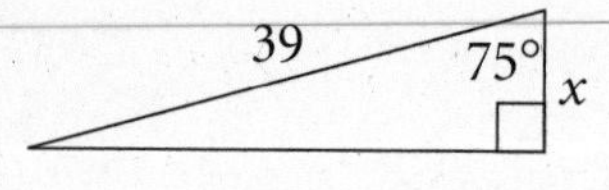

18.

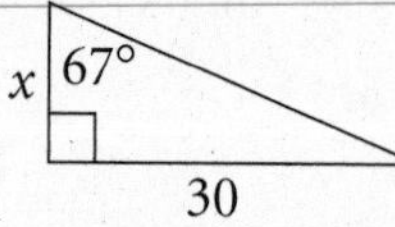

19.

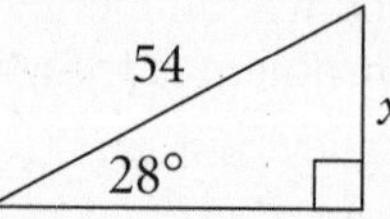

20.

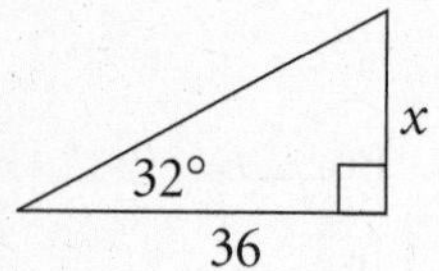

21.

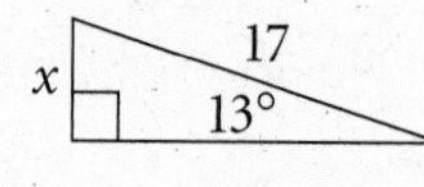

22.

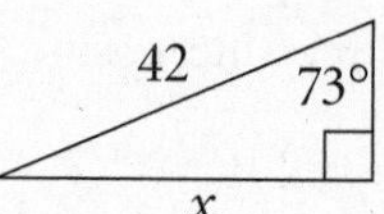

Use $\triangle PQR$ to evaluate each expression.

23. $\sin P$ **24.** $\cos P$ **25.** $\tan P$

26. $\sin R$ **27.** $\cos R$ **28.** $\tan R$

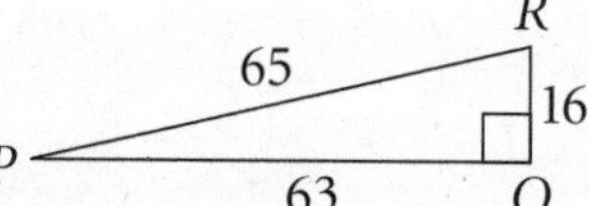

29. A tree casts a shadow that is 20 ft long. The angle of elevation of the sun is 29°. How tall is the tree?

30. Suppose your angle of elevation to the top of a water tower is 78°. If the water tower is 145 ft tall, how far are you standing from the water tower?

31. The angle of elevation from the control tower to an airplane is 49°. The airplane is flying at 5000 ft. How far away from the control tower is the plane?

32. A Boy Scout on top of a 1700-ft-tall mountain spots a campsite. If he measures the angle of depression at 35°, how far is the campsite from the foot of the mountain?

33. A 12-ft-long guy wire is attached to a telephone pole 10.5 ft from the top of the pole. If the wire forms a 52° angle with the ground, how high is the telephone pole?

Name ______________________ Class ______________ Date ______________

Reteaching 12-1

Inverse Variation

OBJECTIVE: Solving inverse variations

MATERIALS: None

- The relationship shown by the equation $xy = k$, where $k \neq 0$, is called an inverse variation.
- The two quantities x and y multiplied together result in a constant k. As one quantity increases, the other decreases.

Example

Two young graduates from the business school of the University of Texas decided to open a music store. On the first day of business, they charged $12.00 for a CD. They sold 138 CDs. On the basis of their research, they believe there is an inverse variation between sales and price. If they are correct and the price of the CDs is lowered, the number sold should increase. They decide to lower the price of the CDs to $11.50. How many CDs can they expect to sell?

Price	No. Sold
$12.00	138
$11.50	x

← **Put the data into a table.**

← **Let x represent the missing quantity.**

(Price 1)(No. sold at price 1) = (Price 2)(No. sold at price 2) ← **Write an equation showing the relationship of the variables.**

($12.00)(138) = ($11.50)(x) ← **Substitute the values.**

$1656 = 11.5x$

$x = 144$ ← **Solve for x.**

Dropping the price by $.50 will result in selling 144 CDs. This is an increase of 6 CDs.

Exercises

Refer to the example to answer each question.

1. How many CDs can the owners expect to sell if they drop the price to $11.00? What if they raise the price to $12.50? (Round your answers to the nearest whole number.)
2. If the owners want to sell 162 CDs, what price should they charge for each?
3. Make a table with the data from Exercises 1 and 2.

Name ______________________ Class ______________ Date ______________

Practice 12-1

Inverse Variation

Suppose y varies inversely with x. Write an equation for each inverse variation.

1. $x = 9$ when $y = 6$
2. $x = 3.6$ when $y = 5$
3. $x = \frac{3}{4}$ when $y = \frac{2}{9}$
4. $x = 7$ when $y = 13$
5. $x = 8$ when $y = 9$
6. $x = 4.9$ when $y = 0.8$
7. $x = 11$ when $y = 44$
8. $y = 8$ when $x = 9.5$
9. $y = 12$ when $x = \frac{5}{6}$

Each pair of points is on the graph of an inverse variation. Find the missing value.

10. $(5, 8)$ and $(4, m)$
11. $(16, 5)$ and $(10, h)$
12. $(14, 8)$ and $(c, 7)$
13. $(3, 18)$ and $(a, 27)$
14. $(4, 28)$ and $(3, p)$
15. $(100, 25)$ and $(4, a)$
16. $(x, 7)$ and $(2, 14)$
17. $\left(\frac{2}{5}, \frac{3}{2}\right)$ and $\left(k, \frac{5}{2}\right)$
18. $(16, 3)$ and $(g, 24)$
19. $(2.4, 19.8)$ and $(h, 13.2)$
20. $(12.4, 6.6)$ and $(f, 8.8)$
21. $(3.2, k)$ and $(9.2, 0.8)$
22. $(18, 24)$ and $(72, v)$
23. $(17, 0.9)$ and $(5.1, x)$
24. $\left(\frac{3}{4}, y\right)$ and $\left(\frac{2}{3}, 18\right)$

Explain whether each situation represents a direct variation or an inverse variation.

25. The cost of a \$50 birthday gift is split among some friends.
26. You purchase some peaches at \$1.29/lb.

Tell whether the data in each table is a *direct variation*, or an *inverse variation*. Write an equation to model the data.

27.

x	2	7	10
y	35	10	7

28.

x	3	6	24
y	16	8	2

29.

x	5	6	8
y	55	66	88

30.

x	2	8	16
y	9	36	72

31.

x	2	3	9
y	18	12	4

32

x	2	6	10
y	4.2	12.6	21

33.

x	2	5	12
y	12.8	32	76.8

34.

x	1.2	1.5	2.4
y	5	4	2.5

35.

x	6	9	36
y	3	2	0.5

36. The volume V of a gas in a closed container varies inversely with the pressure p, in atmospheres, that is applied to that gas.
    a. If $V = 20\ \text{m}^3$ when $p = 1$ atm, find V when $p = 4$ atm.
    b. If $V = 24\ \text{m}^3$ when $p = 3$ atm, find p when $V = 36\ \text{m}^3$.
    c. If $V = 48\ \text{m}^3$ when $p = 2$ atm, find V when $p = 5$ atm.
37. The time t to travel a fixed distance varies inversely with the rate r of travel.
    a. If $t = 3$ h and $r = 25$ mi/h, find t when $r = 50$ mi/h.
    b. If $t = 120$ s and $r = 40$ ft/s, find r when $t = 25$ s.

Name ______________________ Class ____________ Date ____________

Reteaching 12-2

Graphing Rational Functions

OBJECTIVE: Graphing rational functions **MATERIALS:** None

A vertical asymptote occurs at a value for which the function is not defined. The function $y = \frac{2}{x + 1}$ is undefined at $x = -1$. Therefore, the vertical asymptote is $x = -1$.

Example

Graph the rational function $y = \frac{4}{x + 2} - 1$.

Step 1 Find the vertical asymptotes.

$x + 2 = 0$ ⟵ **Set the denominator equal to zero.**

$x = -2$ ⟵ **Solve for x.**

Step 2 Find the horizontal asymptotes.

From the form of the function ($y = \frac{a}{x - b} + c$) we know there is a horizontal asymptote at $y = -1$.

Step 3 Make a table of values using values of x near -2.

x	−6	−4	−3	−1	1	2	0
y	−2	−3	−5	3	$\frac{1}{3}$	0	1

Step 4 Graph the data.

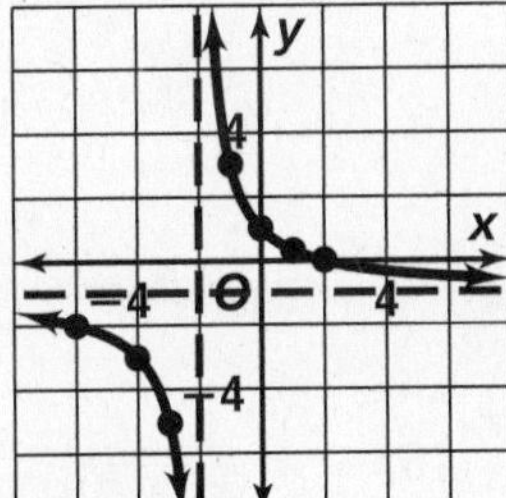

Exercises

Graph each rational function.

1. $y = \frac{4}{x + 2}$
2. $y = \frac{2}{x - 3} + 2$
3. $y = \frac{2}{x} + 5$
4. $y = \frac{1}{x} - 5$
5. $y = \frac{3}{x} + 2$
6. $y = \frac{2}{x + 2} + 1$

Name ____________ Class ____________ Date ____________

Practice 12-2

Graphing Rational Functions

Describe the graph of each function.

1. $f(x) = x^2 - 4$
2. $y = \frac{5}{x} - 1$
3. $y = \frac{3}{x}$
4. $g(x) = \sqrt{x + 2} - 1$
5. $y = -8x + 2$
6. $h(x) = 3x^2 - 4x + 1$
7. $h(x) = |2x + 7|$
8. $y = 0.2^x$
9. $y = \frac{x}{4}$

10. In an electric circuit the resistance R, in ohms, increases when the current I, in amps, in the circuit decreases. The function $R = \frac{1000}{I^2}$ relates the resistance to the current.
    a. What is the resistance when the current is 4 amps?
    b. What is the resistance when the current is 20 amps?
    c. What is the resistance when the current is 10 amps?

11. Light intensity decreases as you move farther away from the source of light. The function $I = \frac{12{,}000}{d^2}$ relates the light intensity I, in lumens, to the distance d, in feet, from the light source.
    a. What is the light intensity 2 ft away from the light source?
    b. What is the light intensity 8 ft away from the light source?
    c. What is the light intensity 25 ft away from the light source?

12. In a cylinder of constant volume, the height increases as the radius decreases. The function $h = \frac{360}{r^2}$ relates the height of the cylinder to the radius of the cylinder.
    a. What is the height of the cylinder when the radius is 5 m?
    b. What is the height of the cylinder when the radius is 12 m?

What value of x makes the denominator of each function equal to zero?

13. $y = \frac{5}{2x - 8}$
14. $y = \frac{12}{x}$
15. $y = \frac{5}{x + 7}$
16. $y = \frac{5x}{4x - 10}$
17. $y = \frac{7x}{x + 3}$
18. $y = \frac{3}{x - 8}$
19. $y = \frac{6}{5x - 6}$
20. $y = \frac{9x}{3x + 5}$

Graph each function. Include a dashed line for each asymptote.

21. $y = \frac{2}{x}$
22. $y = \frac{2}{x - 1}$
23. $y = \frac{1}{x + 4}$
24. $y = \frac{2}{x} + 3$
25. $y = \frac{-2}{x + 6}$
26. $y = \frac{2x}{x - 6}$
27. $y = \frac{x + 3}{x - 2}$
28. $y = \frac{3}{x - 1} - 3$

Name _______________ Class _______________ Date _______________

Reteaching 12-3

Simplifying Rational Expressions

OBJECTIVE: Simplifying rational expressions **MATERIALS:** None

Example

Simplify $\frac{3x + 6}{2x + 4}$.

$3x + 6 = 3(x + 2)$ ← **Factor the numerator.**

$2x + 4 = 2(x + 2)$ ← **Factor the denominator.**

$= \frac{3(x + 2)}{2(x + 2)}$ ← **Rewrite the expression in terms of the factors.**

$= \frac{3\cancel{(x + 2)}}{2\cancel{(x + 2)}}$ ← **Mark through common factors in the numerator and denominator. These two factors cancel because any number divided by itself equals 1.**

$= \frac{3}{2}$ ← **Simplify.**

Example

Simplify $\frac{4x - 24}{x^2 - 9x + 18}$.

$4x - 24 = 4(x - 6)$ ← **Factor the numerator.**

$x^2 - 9x + 18 = (x - 6)(x - 3)$ ← **Factor the denominator.**

$= \frac{4(x - 6)}{(x - 6)(x - 3)}$ ← **Rewrite the expression in terms of the factors.**

$= \frac{4\cancel{(x - 6)}}{\cancel{(x - 6)}(x - 3)}$ ← **Mark through common factors in the numerator and denominator. These two factors cancel because any number divided by itself is 1.**

$= \frac{4}{x - 3}$ ← **Simplify.**

Exercises

Simplify each expression.

1. $\frac{5x - 15}{3x - 9}$

2. $\frac{x + 7}{2x + 14}$

3. $\frac{2x - 2}{x - 1}$

4. $\frac{5x - 20}{x^2 - 16}$

5. $\frac{x^2 - 6x - 16}{x^2 - x - 6}$

6. $\frac{6x^2 + 3x}{2x^2 + 11x + 5}$

Name ______________________ Class ______________ Date ______________

Practice 12-3

Simplifying Rational Expressions

Simplify each expression.

1. $\frac{6x^4}{18x^2}$
2. $\frac{15a^2}{25a^4}$
3. $\frac{32h^3}{48h^2}$
4. $\frac{12n^4}{21n^6}$
5. $\frac{3x - 6}{6}$
6. $\frac{x^2 - 2x}{x}$
7. $\frac{4t^2 - 2t}{2t}$
8. $\frac{a^3 - 2a^2}{2a^2 - 4a}$
9. $\frac{21x^2y}{14xy^2}$
10. $\frac{32x^3y^2}{24xy^4}$
11. $\frac{x^2 + 3x}{3x + 9}$
12. $\frac{x^2 - 5x}{5x - 25}$
13. $\frac{x^2 + 13x + 12}{x^2 - 144}$
14. $\frac{x^2 - 9}{x^3 - 3x^2}$
15. $\frac{x^3 + x^2}{x + 1}$
16. $\frac{3x - 2y}{2y - 3x}$
17. $\frac{x^2 + x - 6}{x^2 - x - 2}$
18. $\frac{x^2 + 3x + 2}{x^3 + x^2}$
19. $\frac{2x^2 - 8}{x^2 - 3x + 2}$
20. $\frac{2x^2 - 5x + 3}{x^2 - 1}$
21. $\frac{3x + 3y}{x^2 + xy}$
22. $\frac{10 + 3x - x^2}{x^2 - 4x - 5}$
23. $\frac{9 - x^2}{x^2 + x - 12}$
24. $\frac{x^2 + 2x - 15}{x^2 - 7x + 12}$
25. $\frac{x^2 + 7x - 8}{x^2 + 6x - 7}$
26. $\frac{x^2 + 3x - 10}{25 - x^2}$
27. Write and simplify the ratio $\frac{\text{perimeter of rectangle}}{\text{area of rectangle}}$. The perimeter of the rectangle is $10w$ and the area of the rectangle is $4w^2$.
28. The ratio $\frac{3 \cdot \text{volume of cone}}{\text{area of base}}$ determines the height of a cone. Find the height when the volume is $4r^3 + 2r^2$ and the area of the base is $6r^2$.
29. The ratio $\frac{2 \cdot \text{area of triangle}}{\text{height of triangle}}$ determines the length of the base of a triangle. Find the length of the base when the area is $3n^2 + 6n$ and the height is $2n + 4$.
30. The ratio $\frac{\text{volume of rectangular solid}}{\text{area of rectangular base}}$ determines the height of a rectangular solid. Find the height when the volume is $5s^3 + 10s^2$ and the area is $5s^2$.

Name ______________________ Class ______________ Date ______________

Reteaching 12-4

Multiplying and Dividing Rational Expressions

OBJECTIVE: Multiplying and dividing rational expressions

MATERIALS: None

When multiplying rational expressions, look for common factors.

Example

Multiply $\frac{3x-6}{5x-20} \cdot \frac{10x-40}{27x-54}$.

$$\frac{3x-6}{5x-20} \cdot \frac{10x-40}{27x-54} = \frac{3(x-2)}{5(x-4)} \cdot \frac{10(x-4)}{27(x-2)}$$ ← **Factor each expression.**

$$= \frac{\cancel{3}\cancel{(x-2)}}{\cancel{5}\cancel{(x-4)}} \cdot \frac{\cancel{10}^{2}\cancel{(x-4)}}{\cancel{27}_{9}\cancel{(x-2)}}$$ ← **Divide out common factors and reduce fractions.**

$$= \frac{2}{9}$$ ← **Simplify.**

When dividing rational expressions, multiply by the reciprocal. The reciprocal of a fraction is the fraction with the numerator and denominator interchanged.

Example

Divide $\frac{x^2+x}{3x-15} \div \frac{x^2+2x+1}{6x-30}$.

$$\frac{x^2+x}{3x-15} \div \frac{x^2+2x+1}{6x-30} = \frac{x^2+x}{3x-15} \cdot \frac{6x-30}{x^2+2x+1}$$ ← **Multiply by the reciprocal.**

$$= \frac{x(x+1)}{3(x-5)} \cdot \frac{6(x-5)}{(x+1)(x+1)}$$ ← **Factor the numerators and denominators.**

$$= \frac{x\cancel{(x+1)}}{\cancel{3}\cancel{(x-5)}} \cdot \frac{\cancel{6}^{2}\cancel{(x-5)}}{\cancel{(x+1)}(x+1)}$$ ← **Divide out common factors.**

$$= \frac{2x}{x+1}$$ ← **Simplify.**

Exercises

Simplify.

1. $\frac{x^2-x}{2x+4} \cdot \frac{x+2}{x}$
2. $\frac{x^2+x}{x^2+8x+7} \cdot (x+7)$
3. $\frac{x^2-1}{x^2+4x+3} \div \frac{x-1}{x^2+2x-3}$
4. $\frac{x^2-9}{5x+15} \div \frac{x-3}{x+3}$
5. $\frac{x^2-x-30}{6x-36} \div \frac{5x+25}{x}$
6. $\frac{x^2-9}{x^2+4x-12} \div \frac{x^2+2x-3}{x^2+5x-6}$

Name ______________________ Class ______________ Date ______________

Practice 12-4

Multiplying and Dividing Rational Expressions

Find each product or quotient.

1. $\frac{5}{9} \cdot \frac{6}{15}$

2. $\frac{8}{3} \div \frac{16}{27}$

3. $\left(-\frac{3}{4}\right) \div \frac{16}{21}$

4. $\frac{2}{9} \div \left(-\frac{10}{3}\right)$

5. $\frac{18m}{4m^2} \div \frac{9m}{8}$

6. $\frac{8x}{12} \cdot \frac{4x}{6}$

7. $\frac{9}{15x} \cdot \frac{25x}{27}$

8. $\frac{12x^3}{25} \div \frac{16x}{5}$

9. $\frac{6x^3}{18x} \div \frac{9x^2}{10x^4}$

10. $\frac{4r^3}{10} \cdot \frac{25}{16r^2}$

11. $\frac{8n^2}{3} \div \frac{20n}{9}$

12. $\frac{14x^2}{5} \div 7x^4$

13. $\frac{4n^3}{11} \cdot \frac{33n}{36n^2}$

14. $\frac{24r^3}{35r^2} \div \frac{12r}{14r^3}$

15. $\frac{a^2 - 4}{3} \cdot \frac{9}{a + 2}$

16. $\frac{4b - 12}{5b^2} \cdot \frac{6b}{b - 3}$

17. $\frac{2b}{5} \cdot \frac{10}{b^2}$

18. $\frac{2b}{b + 3} \div \frac{b}{b + 3}$

19. $\frac{5y^3}{7} \cdot \frac{14y}{30y^2}$

20. $\frac{4p + 16}{5p} \div \frac{p + 4}{15p^3}$

21. $\frac{3(h + 2)}{h + 3} \div \frac{h + 2}{h + 3}$

22. $\frac{a^3 - a^2}{a^3} \cdot \frac{a^2}{a - 1}$

23. $\frac{h^2 + 6h}{h + 3} \cdot \frac{4h + 12}{h + 6}$

24. $\frac{n^2 - 1}{n + 2} \cdot \frac{n^2 - 4}{n + 1}$

25. $\frac{x^2 - x}{x} \cdot \frac{3x - 6}{3x - 3}$

26. $\frac{5x - 10}{x + 2} \cdot \frac{3}{3x - 6}$

27. $\frac{x^2 - 16}{x - 4} \div \frac{3x + 12}{x}$

28. $\frac{x^2 - 1}{3x - 3} \div \frac{x + 1}{3}$

29. $\frac{x^2 - 2x - 24}{x^2 - 5x - 6} \cdot \frac{x^2 + 5x + 6}{x^2 + 6x + 8}$

30. $\frac{x^2 + 2x - 35}{x^2 + 4x - 21} \cdot \frac{x^2 + 3x - 18}{x^2 + 9x + 18}$

31. $\frac{3x^2 + 14x + 8}{2x^2 + 7x - 4} \cdot \frac{2x^2 + 9x - 5}{3x^2 + 16x + 5}$

32. $\frac{8 + 2x - x^2}{x^2 + 7x + 10} \div \frac{x^2 - 11x + 28}{x^2 - x - 42}$

33. $\frac{x^2 - x - 6}{3x - 9} \cdot \frac{x^2 - 9}{x^2 + 6x + 9}$

34. $\frac{6x^2 + 13x + 6}{4x^2 - 9} \div \frac{6x^2 + x - 2}{4x^2 - 1}$

35. $\frac{x^2 - 2x - 35}{3x^2 + 27x} \div \frac{x^2 + 7x + 10}{6x^2 + 12x}$

36. $\frac{x^2 - x - 6}{2x^2 + 9x + 10} \div \frac{x^2 - 25}{2x^2 + 15x + 25}$

37. $\frac{15 - 14x - 8x^2}{4x^2 + 4x - 15} \div \frac{4x^2 + 13x - 12}{3x^2 + 13x + 4}$

38. $\frac{x^2 - 4x - 32}{x^2 - 8x - 48} \cdot \frac{3x^2 + 17x + 10}{3x^2 - 22x - 16}$

39. $\frac{9x^2 - 16}{6x^2 - 11x + 4} \div \frac{6x^2 + 11x + 4}{8x^2 + 10x + 3}$

40. Two darts are thrown at random onto the large rectangular region shown. Find the probability that both darts will land in the shaded region.

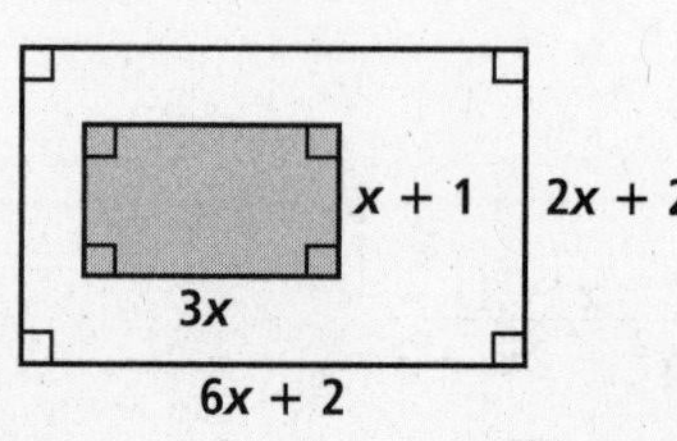

Name ______________________ Class ______________ Date ______________

Reteaching 12-5

Dividing Polynomials

OBJECTIVE: Dividing polynomials

MATERIALS: None

The procedure for dividing two polynomials is similar to the one for dividing whole numbers.

If the dividend or the divisor has missing terms, remember to insert these terms with zero coefficients.

Example

$(x^2 - 5x + 8) \div (x - 3)$

$$\begin{array}{r} x \phantom{{}-5x+8} \\ x - 3\overline{)x^2 - 5x + 8} \\ \underline{x^2 - 3x} \phantom{{}+8} \\ -2x + 8 \end{array}$$

← **Think** $x\overline{)x^2} = \frac{x^2}{x} = x$.

← **Multiply** $x(x - 3) = x^2 - 3x$.

← **Subtract** $(x^2 - 5x) - (x^2 - 3x) = -2x$**, and bring down the 8.**

Repeat the process.

$$\begin{array}{r} x - 2 \\ x - 3\overline{)x^2 - 5x + 8} \\ \underline{x^2 - 3x} \phantom{{}+8} \\ -2x + 8 \\ \underline{-2x + 6} \\ 2 \end{array}$$

← **Think** $x\overline{)-2x} = \frac{-2x}{x} = -2$.

← **Multiply** $-2(x - 3) = -2x + 6$.

← **Subtract** $(-2x + 8) - (-2x + 6) = 2$**. The remainder is 2.**

The answer is $x - 2 + \frac{2}{x - 3}$.

Exercises

Divide.

1. $(x^2 + 5x + 6) \div (x + 3)$
2. $(2x^2 + 5x - 1) \div (2x - 1)$
3. $(x^3 - 8) \div (x + 2)$
4. $(x^3 - 2x + 1) \div (x - 1)$
5. $(x^2 - 8x + 16) \div (x - 4)$
6. $(6x^2 + 42x + 60) \div (x + 4)$
7. $(2x^2 - 2x - 24) \div (x + 3)$
8. $(2x^3 + 17x^2 + 38x + 15) \div (x + 5)$
9. $(x^3 + 7x^2 + 8x - 16) \div (x - 2)$
10. $(4x^3 + 22x^2 + 36x + 18) \div (x + 3)$

Name ______________________ Class ______________ Date ______________

Practice 12-5

Dividing Polynomials

Divide.

1. $\frac{10x - 25}{5}$
2. $\frac{4x^3 - 3x}{x}$
3. $(3x^2 - 6x) \div 3x$
4. $(10x^2 - 6x) \div 2x$
5. $(-8x^5 + 16x^4 - 24x^3 + 32x^2) \div 8x^2$
6. $(15x^2 - 30x) \div 5x$
7. $(x^2 - 14x + 49) \div (x - 7)$
8. $(2x^2 - 13x + 21) \div (x - 3)$
9. $(4x^2 - 16) \div (2x + 4)$
10. $(x^2 + 4x - 12) \div (x - 2)$
11. $(x^2 + 10x + 16) \div (x + 2)$
12. $(12x^2 - 5x - 2) \div (3x - 2)$
13. $(x^2 + 5x + 10) \div (x + 2)$
14. $(x^2 - 8x - 9) \div (x - 3)$
15. $(3x^2 - 2x - 13) \div (x - 2)$
16. $(x^3 + 3x^2 + 5x + 3) \div (x + 1)$
17. $(5 - 23x + 12x^2) \div (4x - 1)$
18. $(24 + 6x^2 + 25x) \div (3x - 1)$
19. $(2x^2 + 11x - 5) \div (x + 6)$
20. $(x^2 + 5x - 10) \div (x + 2)$
21. $(8x + 3 + 4x^2) \div (2x - 1)$
22. $(3x^2 + 11x - 4) \div (3x - 1)$
23. $(x^3 + x - x^2 - 1) \div (x - 1)$
24. $(10 + 21x + 10x^2) \div (2x + 3)$
25. $(6x^2 - 35x + 36) \div (3x - 4)$
26. $(-2x^2 - 33x + x^3 - 7) \div (x - 7)$
27. The volume of a rectangular prism is $15x^3 + 38x^2 - 23x - 6$. The height of the prism is $5x + 1$, and the width of the prism is $x + 3$. Find the length of the prism.
28. The width of a rectangle is $x + 1$, and the area is $x^3 + 2x^2 - 5x - 6$ cm. What is the length of the rectangle?

Name ______________________ Class ______________ Date ______________

Reteaching 12-6

Adding and Subtracting Rational Expressions

OBJECTIVE: Adding and subtracting rational expressions

MATERIALS: None

Use the flowchart to add and subtract rational expressions.

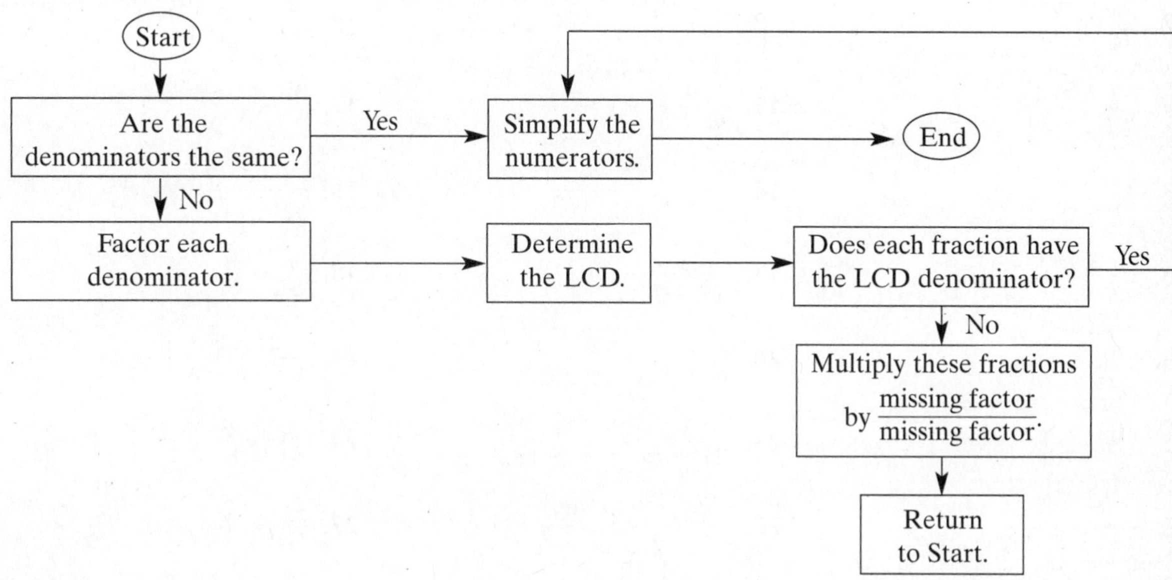

Example

Simplify $\frac{2x}{x^2 - 1} + \frac{3}{x - 1}$ by following the flowchart.

$x^2 - 1 = (x - 1)(x + 1)$ ⟵ **Factor each denominator. If a denominator is already simplified, rewrite it in a set of parentheses.**

$x - 1 = (x - 1)$

$(x - 1)(x + 1)$ ⟵ **Determine the LCD.**

$\frac{3}{x - 1} \cdot \frac{(x + 1)}{(x + 1)} = \frac{3x + 3}{x^2 - 1}$ ⟵ **The first fraction already has the LCD for a denominator, but the second one does not. Multiply the second fraction by the factor it is missing.**

$\frac{2x}{x^2 - 1} + \frac{3x + 3}{x^2 - 1} = \frac{2x + 3x + 3}{x^2 - 1}$ ⟵ **Simplify the numerators.**

$= \frac{5x + 3}{x^2 - 1}$

Exercises

Simplify the following using the flowchart.

1. $\frac{x + 1}{x^2 - 4} + 3$
2. $\frac{2x - 5}{x^2 + 3x + 2} + \frac{4}{x + 2}$
3. $\frac{3z + 2}{16 - z^2} + \frac{3}{z - 4}$
4. $\frac{x + 1}{x + 5} - \frac{5}{x^2 + 6x + 5}$
5. $\frac{1}{x^2 - 9} + \frac{4}{x + 3}$
6. $\frac{x + 1}{x + 3x + 2} + \frac{2}{x + 2}$

Name ______________________ Class ______________ Date ______________

Practice 12-6

Adding and Subtracting Rational Expressions

Simplify.

1. $\frac{3x}{4} - \frac{x}{4}$
2. $\frac{3}{x} + \frac{5}{x}$
3. $\frac{5x}{6} - \frac{2x}{3}$
4. $\frac{x}{3} + \frac{x}{5}$
5. $\frac{3m}{4} + \frac{5m}{12}$
6. $\frac{4x}{7} - \frac{3x}{14}$
7. $\frac{6}{7t} - \frac{3}{7t}$
8. $\frac{d}{3} + \frac{4d}{3}$
9. $\frac{7}{2d} - \frac{3}{2d}$
10. $\frac{3}{2d^2} + \frac{4}{3d}$
11. $\frac{9}{m+1} - \frac{6}{m-1}$
12. $\frac{3}{x} - \frac{7}{x}$
13. $\frac{7a}{6} + \frac{a}{6}$
14. $\frac{4}{k+3} - \frac{8}{k+3}$
15. $\frac{3}{4z^2} + \frac{7}{4z^2}$
16. $\frac{6}{x^2-1} + \frac{7}{x-1}$
17. $\frac{2x}{x^2-1} - \frac{3}{x+1}$
18. $\frac{3t}{8} + \frac{3t}{8}$
19. $\frac{4}{3a^2} - \frac{1}{2a^3}$
20. $\frac{4}{a+4} + \frac{6}{a+4}$
21. $\frac{4}{x+3} + \frac{6}{x-2}$
22. $\frac{6}{7t^3} - \frac{8}{3t}$
23. $\frac{3}{2x+6} + \frac{4}{6x+18}$
24. $\frac{5}{8a} - \frac{3}{8a}$
25. $\frac{5}{r^2-4} + \frac{7}{r+2}$
26. $\frac{6}{a^2-2} + \frac{9}{a^2-2}$
27. $\frac{5x}{4} - \frac{x}{4}$
28. $\frac{4}{3x+6} - \frac{3}{2x+4}$
29. $\frac{4}{c^2+4c+3} + \frac{1}{c+3}$
30. $\frac{6}{x^2-3x+2} - \frac{4}{x-2}$

31. Brian rode his bike 2 mi to his friend's house. Brian's bike had a flat tire, so he had to walk home. His walking rate is 25% of his biking rate.

   a. Write an expression for the amounts of time Brian spent walking and riding his bike.

   b. If Brian's biking rate is 12 mi/h, how much time did he spend walking and riding his bike?

32. Trudi and Sean are on a river canoeing. Because of the current of the river, their downstream rate is 250% of their upstream rate. They canoe 3 mi upstream and then return to their starting point.

   a. Write an expression for the amount of time Trudi and Sean spend canoeing.

   b. If their upstream rate is 2 mi/h, how much time do Trudi and Sean spend canoeing?

   c. If their upstream rate is 3 mi/h, how much time do Trudi and Sean spend canoeing?

Reteaching 12-7

Solving Rational Equations

OBJECTIVE: Solving equations involving rational expressions

MATERIALS: None

Example

Solve the equation $\frac{4}{3x} + \frac{3}{4x} = \frac{5}{2x^2}$.

Step 1 Find the LCD.

$3x = (3) \cdot x$

$4x = (2 \cdot 2) \cdot x$

$2x^2 = 2 \cdot (x \cdot x)$

← **Factor the denominators. Find where each factor appears the most times and circle it.**

$3 \cdot 2 \cdot 2 \cdot x \cdot x = 12x^2$ ← **Multiply the circled terms to find the LCD.**

Step 2 Solve the equation.

$12x^2\left(\frac{4}{3x}\right) + 12x^2\left(\frac{3}{4x}\right) = 12x^2\left(\frac{5}{2x^2}\right)$ ← **Multiply each term by the LCD.**

$16x + 9 = 30$ ← **Simplify.**

$25x = 30$ ← **Solve.**

$x = \frac{6}{5}$

Exercises

Solve each equation.

1. $\frac{3}{2x} + \frac{5}{6x} = \frac{4}{5x^2}$
2. $\frac{2}{3x} + \frac{4}{5} = \frac{3}{2x}$
3. $\frac{6x}{5} - \frac{1}{2} = \frac{2x}{3}$
4. $\frac{2}{5x} - \frac{5}{2x} = \frac{3}{5x^2}$
5. $\frac{3}{y-3} = \frac{3}{y^2-9}$
6. $\frac{5}{2x-2} = \frac{15}{x^2-1}$
7. $\frac{1}{m-1} = \frac{3}{m^2-1}$
8. $\frac{x}{x-2} = \frac{3x}{x+2}$
9. $\frac{4}{x} + 1 = \frac{6}{x}$
10. $\frac{x+2}{3} = x - 2$
11. $\frac{5}{x} - \frac{4}{x} = 8 + \frac{1}{x}$
12. $\frac{11}{x} + \frac{13}{x} = 12$
13. $\frac{x}{2x} + \frac{2}{4x} = \frac{5x}{x}$
14. $\frac{9}{x} + \frac{6}{5x} = \frac{6}{2x^2}$
15. $\frac{5}{3x} - \frac{x}{x^2} = \frac{1}{6x^2}$
16. $\frac{x}{x+1} + 2 = 5$
17. $\frac{2}{x-5} + 1 = \frac{5}{x-5}$
18. $\frac{21}{x^2} - \frac{10}{x} = \frac{15}{x^2}$
19. $\frac{3}{2x} - \frac{2}{x^2} = \frac{2}{x}$
20. $\frac{3}{x^2-9} = \frac{2}{x-3}$
21. $\frac{5}{x^2-4} + \frac{2}{x-2} = \frac{3}{x+2}$

Name ____________ Class ____________ Date ____________

Practice 12-7

Solving Rational Equations

Solve each equation. Check your solution.

1. $\frac{1}{x} + \frac{1}{2x} = \frac{1}{6}$

2. $\frac{x}{x+2} + \frac{4}{x-2} = 1$

3. $\frac{1}{3s} = \frac{s}{2} - \frac{1}{6s}$

4. $\frac{x+2}{x+8} = \frac{x-2}{x+4}$

5. $1 - \frac{3}{x} = \frac{4}{x^2}$

6. $\frac{7}{3(a-2)} - \frac{1}{a-2} = \frac{2}{3}$

7. $\frac{n}{n-4} = \frac{2n}{n+4}$

8. $x + \frac{6}{x} = -7$

9. $\frac{2}{r^2 - r} - 1 = \frac{2}{r-1}$

10. $\frac{y}{y+3} = \frac{6}{y+9}$

11. $\frac{d}{3} + \frac{1}{2} = \frac{1}{3d}$

12. $\frac{2m}{m-5} = \frac{2m+16}{m+3}$

13. $\frac{1}{m-4} + \frac{1}{m+4} = \frac{8}{m^2 - 16}$

14. $\frac{5}{x-2} = \frac{5x+10}{x^2}$

15. $\frac{k^2}{k+3} = \frac{9}{k+3}$

16. $\frac{h-3}{h+6} = \frac{2h+3}{h+6}$

17. $\frac{h}{6} - \frac{3}{2h} = \frac{8}{3h}$

18. $4 - \frac{3}{y} = \frac{5}{y}$

19. $\frac{1}{b-3} = \frac{b}{4}$

20. $\frac{1}{t^2} - \frac{2}{t} = \frac{3}{t^2}$

21. $\frac{2}{3n} + \frac{3}{4} = \frac{2}{3}$

22. David and Fiona have a house painting business. It takes Fiona 3 days to paint a certain house. David could paint the same house in 4 days. How long would it take them to paint the house if David and Fiona worked together?

23. Suppose the Williams Spring Water Company has two machines that bottle the spring water. Machine X fills the bottles twice as fast as Machine Y. Working together, it takes them 20 min to fill 450 bottles. How long would it take each machine working alone to fill the 450 bottles?

24. Chao, who is an experienced architect, can draw a certain set of plans in 6 h. It takes Carl, who is a new architect, 10 h to draw the same set of plans. How long would it take them working together to draw the set of plans?

25. For exercise, Joseph likes to walk and Vincent likes to ride his bike. Vincent rides his bike 12 km/h faster than Joseph walks. Joseph walks 20 km in the same amount of time that Vincent rides 44 km. Find the rate that each of them travels.

26. The Ryan Publishing Company has two printing presses. It takes the new printing press 45 min to print 10,000 fliers. Together the two presses can print the 10,000 fliers in 30 min. How long does it take the older printing press by itself to print the 10,000 fliers?

Name ______________________ Class ____________ Date ____________

Reteaching 12-8

Counting Methods and Permutations

OBJECTIVE: Using permutations to count outcomes

MATERIALS: Calculator

Think of the Multiplication Counting Principle as choices · choices · choices . . .

Example

You are hosting a New Year's party at which a total of seven people are present. You decide to distribute gag gifts in the following way: Guests will pick a number from a jar and will open a gift in order of their numbers. In how many possible ways can the gifts be distributed?

Person	No. of Choices
1	7
2	6
3	5
4	4
5	3
6	2
7	1

The number of possible ways in which the gifts can be distributed is $7 \cdot 6 \cdot 5 \cdot 4 \cdot 3 \cdot 2 \cdot 1 = 7! = 5040$

The next year, you decide to make your party more interesting. Now, Person 1 will open a present. Person 2 will choose between opening a new present or taking the present that person 1 opened. If Person 2 takes Person 1's gift, Person 1 gets to open another. Person 3 can open a new present or can take an already opened gift. In how many ways can the gifts be distributed now?

Person	No. of Choices
1	7
2	7
3	7
4	7
5	7
6	7
7	7

Now each person will have seven gifts to choose from, counting both opened and unopened gifts. The number of possible distributions of gifts is now

$7 \cdot 7 \cdot 7 \cdot 7 \cdot 7 \cdot 7 \cdot 7 = 7^7 = 823{,}543.$

Exercises

For each situation, make a table and calculate the number of possible gift distributions.

1. There are 11 guests. Each chooses in turn from the unopened gifts.
2. There are 11 guests. Each chooses any gift, opened or unopened.
3. There are 14 guests. Each chooses in turn from the unopened gifts.
4. There are 14 guests. Each chooses any gift, opened or unopened.

Name ______________________ Class ______________ Date ______________

Practice 12-8

Counting Methods and Permutations

Simplify each expression.

1. ${}_7P_2$	**2.** ${}_{12}P_6$	**3.** ${}_{11}P_3$	**4.** ${}_{10}P_3$	**5.** ${}_9P_8$	**6.** ${}_{12}P_7$
7. ${}_{20}P_7$	**8.** ${}_{15}P_3$	**9.** ${}_{16}P_4$	**10.** ${}_{25}P_3$	**11.** ${}_{17}P_2$	**12.** ${}_{15}P_2$

13. Suppose a license plate consists of five different letters.

- **a.** How many five-letter license plates are possible?
- **b.** In how many ways can a five-letter license plate be made with the letters from APRIL if none of the letters are repeated?
- **c.** Suppose a license plate is assigned randomly. What is the probability that it will contain the letters from APRIL?

14. In how many ways can nine mopeds be parked in a row?

15. Suppose there are three different ways in which you could go from your house to a friend's house. From your friend's house, there are four different ways in which you could go to the library. In how many different ways can you go from your house to the library after meeting your friend?

16. A sports card collection contains 20 baseball players, 15 basketball players, and 25 football players. In how many ways can you select one of each?

17. Suppose you are electing student council officers. The student council contains 24 students. In how many ways can a president, a vice-president, and a secretary be elected?

18. Suppose the code to a lock consists of three different numbers from the numbers 1 to 20, inclusive.

- **a.** How many three-number codes are possible?
- **b.** How many of the codes contain the numbers 6, 13, and 17?

19. A car dealer sells four different models of cars. Each of the cars can come in six different colors. For each of the cars, there are two different option packages available. In how many different ways can you select a car?

20. Teams in a math competition consist of six students. In how many ways can the six students be selected to work a problem on the board?

Name ______________________ Class ______________ Date ______________

Reteaching 12-9

Combinations

OBJECTIVE: Finding combinations

MATERIALS: Calculator

The expression $_nC_r$ represents the number of combinations of n objects arranged r at a time. Your calculator allows you to calculate $_nC_r$ quickly.

Example

You have 12 CDs in your collection. You select 4 CDs at random to take to a party. How many different sets of CDs could you select?

$_{12}C_4$ ← **Write the expression.**

= 12 MATH ◄ ▼ ▼ ENTER 4 ENTER ← **Use these calculator keystrokes to find $_{12}C_4$.**

= 495 ← **Write the answer.**

There are 495 different combinations possible.

Exercises

Use a calculator to solve each combination problem.

1. You are hosting a dinner party. You are making a salad for each guest from lettuce and three other ingredients. The other ingredients that the guests may choose from are tomatoes, cucumbers, mushrooms, croutons, and bacon bits. How many different salads can be made?

2. You have 12 players on your volleyball team. How many different combinations of 6 players can the coach choose?

3. There are 11 girls and 9 boys trying out for the cheerleading squad at the high school. The squad will contain 5 boys and 5 girls.

a. How many different combinations of girls are possible?

b. How many different combinations of boys are possible?

4. You have a list of 20 errands to do by the end of the day. By 8:00 P.M., you have completed 6 of the 20 errands. How many different combinations of errands could you have completed?

5. Five students are running for student council. Only three students can be elected. How many different combinations of students are possible?

Name ______________________ Class ______________ Date ______________

Practice 12-9

Combinations

Simplify each expression.

1. ${}_{9}C_{4}$
2. ${}_{12}C_{8}$
3. ${}_{9}C_{6}$
4. ${}_{15}C_{9}$
5. ${}_{10}C_{8}$
6. ${}_{13}C_{6}$
7. ${}_{18}C_{5}$
8. ${}_{16}C_{3}$
9. ${}_{17}C_{7}$
10. ${}_{9}C_{5}$
11. ${}_{17}C_{13}$
12. ${}_{14}C_{7}$

13. A group of six tourists arrive at the airport 15 min before flight time. At the gate, they learn that only three seats are left on the airplane. How many different groups of three could get on the airplane?

14. In how many ways can you select 5 greeting cards from a choice of 12 cards at a store?

15. A committee of 4 students is to be formed from members of the student council. The student council contains 13 girls and 12 boys.
    a. How many different committees of four students are possible?
    b. How many committees will contain only boys?
    c. What is the probability that the committee will contain only boys?

16. Suppose your math class consists of 24 students. In how many ways can a group of 5 students be selected to form a math team?

17. A jar of marbles contains 6 yellow and 8 red marbles. Three marbles are selected at random.
    a. How many different groups of three marbles are possible?
    b. How many groups of three marbles will contain only red ones?
    c. What is the probability that the group of marbles will contain only red ones?

18. Suppose two members of your class need to be selected as members of the student council. Your class has 26 students in it. How many groups of two students can be selected?

19. The letters of the alphabet are written on slips of paper and placed in a hat. Three letters are selected at random.
    a. How many different combinations of three letters are possible?
    b. How many combinations consist only of the letters A, C, H, I, K, or Y?
    c. What is the probability that the letters selected consist only of the letters A, C, H, I, K, or Y?

20. Three boys and four girls are running for president and vice-president of the student council. What is the probability that a boy will be elected president and a girl will be elected vice-president?

21. A lottery requires that you match three numbers in order. The three numbers are chosen from the numbers 1–20. What is the probability that you will win this lottery if numbers can be chosen only once?